Look Who's
Watching

Look Who's Watching

Surveillance_Treachery_and Trust_Online

Fen Osler Hampson_and_Eric Jardine

CIGI

ISBN 978-1-928096-19-1 (hardcover)

ISBN 978-1-928096-20-7 (e-book)

Published by the Centre for International Governance Innovation.

Centre for International Governance Innovation
67 Erb Street West
Waterloo, ON Canada N2L 6C2

www.cigionline.org

Contents

Foreword

Trust as the Currency of Cyberspace

Trust *no one* is a well-worn adage in Internet security. But the phrase may not apply to contemporary cyberspace any more than it applies to the real world. Societies function on the basis of trust. Driving down a highway requires confidence that other travellers will follow basic safety conventions. Depositing a monthly paycheque requires faith in financial institutions and systems of government-backed insurance. Everyday functioning in society requires confidence in surgeons, spouses, babysitters, the food supply, energy systems and much more. The simple act of flying to Paris requires certitude in an entire ecosystem of trust — in mechanics, materials and rivets, security screening personnel, pilots and air traffic control systems. So much of life is already predicated upon trust in systems that are unseen, behind the scenes and sometimes unknowable. So too it is with cyberspace. Trust has always been the scaffolding enabling Internet usage and investment, but its systems, like Internet infrastructure itself, have largely been running behind the scenes, assumed and unexamined by most users, until relatively recently. In *Look Who's Watching*, Fen Osler Hampson and Eric Jardine consider the many elements of trust enmeshed in the Internet "ecosystem," how their erosion impacts ordinary people's use and experience of the Internet the world over, and why we should all be concerned.

The world is now in the midst of contentious policy debates over the very nature of cyberspace. What are the implications of the increasing societal dependencies and risks in digital systems? What types of rights should be afforded to citizens online, and who decides? Several phenomena at the intersection of digital technologies and society highlight how trust issues are at the very heart of these questions. Citizens are increasingly concerned about expansive government surveillance. Even democracies might not allow for the possibility of private communication between people or will all reside in the constant shadow of invasive and indiscriminate state surveillance? Rising awareness of surveillance is accompanied by rising understanding that this level of invasive scrutiny is only possible because of ubiquitous privatized surveillance. Companies providing free social media services, email, Internet search functions and countless apps collect and aggregate data about users to support business models based on highly targeted online advertising. What should be the limits on these practices?

The problem of the Dark Web also looms large for society. This part of the Internet is not locatable via standard search engines and relies upon strong encryption and nearly impenetrable anonymizing tools such as The Onion Router (Tor) browser. These privacy-enhancing techniques are not intrinsically problematic, and indeed are advantageous in some contexts — such as the employment of strong encryption for financial transactions or the use of anonymizing technologies to protect activist communication in repressive political environments. But as technologies shaping the Dark Web, they also mask some of the most nefarious types of social transactions imaginable, such as illegal markets in assassins, arms, drugs and child pornography. The media focus on the former Silk Road marketplace has attracted the attention and concern of Internet users around the world to the Dark Web.

At more visible layers of the Internet, a number of high-profile consumer data breaches have contributed to a loss of trust in digital infrastructure. These breaches, such as the hack of consumer data from large retail companies, affect people who don't even use the Internet but simply use credit cards to make retail transactions. Digital attacks bleed into areas such as personnel records, government data, retail transactions and, of course, financial records. Off-line and online worlds are no longer distinct, if they ever were. Internet outages, too, affect off-line worlds. The Internet is the infrastructure upon which all other infrastructures operate, so disruptions to its functioning create interruptions in the functioning of all businesses — from the transportation sector to health care systems — just as a power outage would. The recent spate of ransomware attacks crippling health systems illustrates these heightened dependencies and risks. The issue of trust online profoundly affects the material realities of everyday life.

More routinely, trust underpins the ability to make an everyday online commercial transaction or even to deliver data from point A to point B. Is a website actually what it appears to be, and who certifies this and how? How does a system authenticate a user? How does one network trust the Internet routes advertised as reachable through another network? The Internet began as a shared network among trusted users, but has been marked by constant change and increasing global complexity. Thus, protocols, systems of public key cryptography and security platforms have often trailed the heterogeneity of systems and the constant creative destruction of new technologies.

The seriousness of trust challenges will intensify as the Internet continues to transform from a communication and knowledge network linking people to a control network in which exponentially more objects than people — cars, appliances, industrial sensors, medical devices — will be connected. How much more important will trust in the Internet be when tens of billions of objects are online and real-world infrastructure is even more dependent upon the security and reliability of digital infrastructure? This question will become still more complicated as new forms of warfare bleed into online systems. The domains of warfare have already expanded from sea, air, land and space to cyberspace. In this environment, trust and the need for cooperation among nations will complicate questions of trust between Internet users; among citizens, the state and the private sector; and between Internet users and digitally connected objects.

If the Internet is the infrastructure supporting all social and economic infrastructures, then the question of how to promote trust in cyberspace is one of the great public policy problems of our time. Half the world's population is still not online, but the next billion will primarily come online in emerging markets with users primarily accessing the Internet via mobile phones. The Internet is expected to continue growing, contributing to the already massive digital economy and providing the benefits of access to knowledge around the world. But, as Hampson and Jardine point out, this future is predicated upon creating a reliable and accountable trust infrastructure.

Given what is at stake for social and economic life, the issue of ensuring trust in cyberspace is paramount. Yet there is empirical evidence that a constellation of issues — including government surveillance, data breaches, economic and social risks online, and concerns about the Dark Web — have measurably diminished trust in the Internet. In this regard, this new book by Fen Osler Hampson and Eric Jardine is a well-timed, groundbreaking and prescient examination of digital trust infrastructures. Drawing on the findings of two recent public surveys of nearly 24,000 Internet users in 24 countries and territories (conducted first in 2014 and again in 2016), the authors examine the shifting state of online trust and its manifold implications.

Previously distinct topic areas such as the digital economy, the digital public sphere and national security now share a common dependency in that they all require a secure and reliable digital trust infrastructure. The freedom to speak and the freedom to transact everyday life now require the freedom to be protected from invasive privacy breaches and the right to a secure and reliable Internet. Will policy choices and technical design promote trust in cyberspace or lead to greater economic and social vulnerabilities? The authors are correct to say that the Internet is at a "tipping point" and that the direction society takes is up to all of us.

Laura DeNardis

Laura DeNardis is a professor and associate dean in the School of Communication at American University and an affiliated fellow at Yale Law School's Information Society Project. She has written numerous books, including The Global War for Internet Governance *(Yale University Press, 2014).*

Preface

The world is losing faith in the Internet. That is the central argument of this book, which has been written in support of the work of the Global Commission on Internet Governance (GCIG) chaired by Carl Bildt, Sweden's former foreign minister and prime minister. In advancing this argument, we have drawn on a series of major global public opinion surveys that were carried out over two years by Ipsos for the Global Security & Politics Program at the Centre for International Governance Innovation (CIGI), as well as other supporting data from a variety of sources.

This loss of confidence and trust does not necessarily result in people using the Internet less — though some clearly are — but it is making people alter their online behaviour in ways that could erode the Internet's full economic, social and political potential. And if that erosion occurs, new users — and there are billions of them still coming online — may well find themselves using an Internet that is not only less trustworthy but also stunted, without the full array of content and services that propelled economic growth and innovation among early adopters of the Internet.

If efforts to restore user trust are not effectively undertaken, some of these changes could become permanent and we could lose out on the benefits of this digital wonder.

This book does not only identify the causes and dimensions of eroding user trust — it also proposes solutions. Some of these address technical matters, others consider behavioural issues, and all of them involve changes in norms and systems of governance at the national and international levels. Unless citizens — netizens — take steps to stem this erosion of trust soon, we will find ourselves living in an Orwellian cyber world of epic proportions, as more and more of the ordinary objects of daily life — cars, houses, even clothing — become connected to the Internet. The so-called Internet of Things or Internet of Everything is already lapping at our feet. Our message about the future is neither Pollyannaish nor entirely pessimistic. But it is intended to be something of a sober wake-up call for policy makers, private sector leaders and above all ordinary citizens, all of whom need to understand the various dimensions of the problem we now face and the potential ways forward.

We have written this book for the general reader, as well as for those in the Internet technology field who have a deep appreciation of these issues. With the hopes of engaging as wide an audience as possible, we have done our best to avoid jargon in discussing how user trust is so central to the entire operation and architecture of the Internet.

In the course of writing *Look Who's Watching*, we have benefited enormously from the work of the GCIG and its global research advisory network, the latter of which has been so ably led by Professor Laura DeNardis of American University in Washington, DC.

Although we accept full responsibility for any errors or omissions of fact or interpretation in this book, we would like to thank the following individuals who carefully read and commented on the manuscript. Joseph Nye Jr. read the entire manuscript twice and provided many useful comments and suggestions for revision.

In addition, Michael Chertoff, Laura DeNardis, Eileen Donahoe, Dame Wendy Hall, Rohinton Medhora, Mathias Müller von Blumencron, Sir David Omand and Gordon Smith also read the manuscript and provided many useful suggestions. Samantha Bradshaw, Derek Burney, Kevin Dias, Bill Graham, Philip Hampson, Jeremy Frydman, Leanna Ireland, Fred Kuntz, David Jardine, Mark Madsen, Gail McNicol Jardine, Simon Palamar and Mark Raymond deserve special thanks for their comments on earlier chapters or various iterations of the arguments that appear both in this book and elsewhere. Jacqueline Lopour provided superb research assistance in assembling some of the stories that appear in chapters three, four, five and seven, and the box of cyber espionage attacks in chapter seven, for which we are grateful.

The McKinsey Global Institute provided invaluable data and graphics that help us paint the landscape of the Internet's sweeping effects. Paul Twomey provided some crucial facts that helped us to better understand why inclusive governance matters for user trust. We would especially like to thank our colleagues Darrell Bricker and Sean Simpson at Ipsos who worked closely with us in drafting the survey questions and analyzing the survey data that appear in this book.

The surveys, and by implication the whole book, were only possible due to the generous financial support of a number of foundations, agencies and corporations. In particular, The John D. and Catherine T. MacArthur Foundation and the International Development Research Centre (IDRC) helped to fund the 2014 survey. Microsoft Corporation provided generous support for the 2016 survey. Eric Sears at MacArthur, Laurent Elder and Fernando Perini at IDRC and Carolyn Nguyen at Microsoft have been extraordinarily supportive of this project from start to finish.

Carol Bonnett, publisher at CIGI, has been a strong supporter and stabilizer of this project from its inception to its conclusion. Along with Carol Bonnett, Lynn Schellenberg gave us superb editorial guidance. Melodie Wakefield and Sara Moore worked tirelessly on the book's jacket, interior design and layout. Nicole Langlois lent fresh eyes to proofreading the index. Brenda Woods deserves special thanks for keeping us pointed in the right direction.

Finally, we thank CIGI President Rohinton Medhora and all of our CIGI colleagues for their generous support for this project, making CIGI the very special organization that it is.

Fen Osler Hampson and Eric Jardine
June 2016

Acronyms & Initialisms

3D	three-dimensional
APIs	application programming interfaces
CAPTCHA	Completely Automated Public Turing Test To Tell Computers and Humans Apart
CATI	computer assisted telephone interviewing
CEO	chief executive officer
CIGI	Centre for International Governance Innovation
DARPA	Defense Advanced Research Project Agency
DDoS	distributed denial of service
DHS	Department of Homeland Security (United States)
DNS	Domain Name System
DNSSEC	Domain Name System Security Extensions
E3	Electronic Entertainment Expo
ECJ	European Court of Justice
FBI	Federal Bureau of Investigation
FINRA	Financial Industry Regulatory Authority
FISA	Foreign Intelligence Surveillance Act
G20	Group of Twenty
GCIG	Global Commission on Internet Governance
GGE	group of government experts
GPS	Global Positioning System
HTTPS	Hypertext Transfer Protocol
IAB	Internet Architecture Board

ICANN	Internet Corporation for Assigned Names and Numbers
ICT	information and communications technology
IDNs	internationalized domain names
IETF	International Engineering Task Force
IoE	Internet of Everything
IoT	Internet of Things
IP	Internet Protocol
IPR	intellectual property rights
IPv4	IP version four
ISIS	Islamic State of Iraq and al-Sham
ISOC	Internet Society
ISPs	Internet service providers
IT	information technology
ITU	International Telecommunications Union (UN)
MAD	mutual assured destruction
MIT	Massachusetts Institute of Technology
MLATs	mutual legal assistance treaties
MTBS3D	Meant To Be Seen 3D forum
NASA	National Aeronautics and Space Administration
NATO	North Atlantic Treaty Organization
NGOs	non-governmental organizations
NSA	National Security Agency (United States)
OECD	Organisation for Economic Co-operation and Development
PCs	personal computers
PLA	People's Liberation Army
RTBF	right to be forgotten
SMEs	small and medium-sized enterprises
SOPA	Stop Online Piracy Act
SSL	Secure Sockets Layer
TCP/IP	Transmission Control Protocol/Internet Protocol
TLS	Transport Layer Security
Tor	The Onion Router
USB	Universal Serial Bus
USTR	United States Trade Representative
VPNs	virtual private networks
VR	virtual reality
WTO	World Trade Organization

One

Sex, Spies and the Internet

"Life is short. Have an affair." That is the slogan of the online infidelity site Ashley Madison. Users of Ashley Madison's services place an inordinate amount of trust in the online matchmaker and purveyor of adulterous sex. Users sign up for an account by providing their names, addresses and credit card information. Frequently, they also lay out in juicy detail the boundaries of their sexual fantasies. If someone's conscience should get the better of them, Ashley Madison offers an extra service of a "full delete" of a user's account, providing a veneer of security. From 2001, when the company first opened its digital doors, to early 2015, the trust users placed in the company seemed well founded.

All of that changed in July of 2015 when Ashley Madison got hacked. The records of 37 million users were stolen. The supposed culprits — hackers calling themselves the "Impact Team" — initially threatened to post all the stolen user details online if the site did not shut down. To hear the hackers tell it, they executed the breach to demonstrate that the "full delete" service that Ashley Madison delivered was nothing close to what the company promised. User data continued to reside on the corporate servers, even as the business owners raked in a revenue of $1.7 million in 2014 alone from the service.[1]

The motive for the cyber attacks does not diminish the anxiety that users must have felt knowing that the dagger of their infidelity hung by a thread above their heads, waiting to be severed at the whim of the Impact Team. It took a month, but eventually the thread snapped and the Impact Team dumped the files from the Ashley Madison hack onto the anonymized underbelly of the Internet, known colloquially as the Dark Web. From there, the list was propagated across the Internet and sites were soon available where people could enter a name or email address into a search box and instantly go through the entire database.[2] Some high-profile names, such as Jason Doré, the head of the Louisiana Republican party, appeared on the list.[3]

The immediate marital, financial and professional consequences aside, one thing is certain: users of Ashley Madison will never trust the website to the same extent again, if at all. Many users might even trust the whole ecosystem of cyberspace just a little bit less, recognizing that personal data stored online can be stolen. As we will see again and again in this book, when users lose trust in the Internet ecosystem, they change their behaviour. In the case of Ashley Madison, web traffic to the site fell by a stunning 82 percent between the time of the breach in the summer of 2015 and December that year.[4]

The Ashley Madison breach is certainly not an isolated incident. Companies get hacked all the time, with serious implications for the trust people place in the online ecosystem. In 2013, for example, the US retail giant Target had its network broken into through stolen log-in credentials. The thieves installed malware that could steal credit card data, and as a result, 110 million credit card records were compromised. In early 2014, all 145 million eBay users had their personal information stolen. Later that year, Home Depot's credit card processing system was hacked and 53 million records were breached. The list goes on and on.

While people might trust some private companies with some of their personal information, they are likely to trust their governments with almost everything. Private companies might get a customer's address and the details of a credit card, but governments hold some of their citizens' most sensitive personal information: health care records, social insurance numbers and tax records. Governments are supposed to keep this information safe and secure, but lately they have not been able to do that.

Governments have been shifting more and more personal data online in efforts to provide services more efficiently. Unfortunately, this move also makes data vulnerable to theft. There are numerous examples of highly sensitive data that has been compromised while held in the trusted hands of government. In 2015, for instance, hackers attacking the US Office of Personnel Management got away with over 21 million records of everyone who had undergone a government background check during the previous 15 years. These forms contained a great deal of sensitive information, including addresses, family members' names, references, any criminal records, disclosures of medical conditions and mental health treatments, and self-reported instances of drug and alcohol use. The thieves also stole social security numbers and some fingerprints, the latter particularly valuable for foreign governments, which could use the unique biometric identifiers to keep US operatives out of their countries.[5] In 2014, multiple computer servers at the US Postal Service were hacked. The intrusion likely happened months before its discovery, with the US Postal Service unaware of the problem until law enforcement agencies identified the breach and told them. The hackers made off with social security numbers, birthdates, names and other identifying information for 800,000 employees and almost 3 million customers.[6] In 2012, the Utah Department of Health was hacked into and 280,000 social security numbers were stolen by online bandits, along with personal information (names, addresses and medical billing codes) of another 500,000 patients.[7] The point should be clear. We trust our governments to keep that information safe and secure — the trouble is that they don't.

These private and public data breaches are extremely disconcerting for Internet users. In a series of surveys in 2014 and again in late 2015 and early 2016, people were asked about their online behaviour and the level of trust they place in the Internet. For each survey question, people were polled from 23 countries and Hong Kong, and the results of each round capture the opinions and perceptions of almost 24,000 Internet users.[*]

Much of this book is based on our analysis of their responses. Of course, there is a perennial problem with making too much hay from survey results. People are notorious for saying that they believe one thing and then acting differently. Such a limitation requires that we be modest in the inferences we draw. To help bolster our case, we also draw upon other sources of data, much of which actually trace people's behaviour rather than just their declared preferences. Together, this combination of evidence paints a clear picture about a growing trust deficit in cyberspace.

The 2014 survey, for example, vividly illustrates how cybercrime and data theft are eroding people's trust of the Internet. For instance, 77 percent of those surveyed expressed concern about the risk of hackers stealing personal information such as photos and messages. Another 78 percent were concerned that hackers might steal their personal financial information. Overall, only 36 percent of respondents thought that private information stored online was "very secure."

Government censorship and snooping into citizens' private communications and transactions online are also major worries. Sixty-four percent of those polled were concerned about governments censoring the Internet; 62 percent were concerned about government agencies from *other countries* secretly monitoring their online activities;

---

[*] Please see the Appendix for more about the CIGI-Ipsos Global Surveys on Internet Security and Trust, or visit www.cigionline.org/internet-survey. The individual surveys are hereafter cited as "the CIGI-Ipsos [2014 or 2016] Global Survey."

61 percent were concerned with the police or other government agencies from their *own country* secretly monitoring their online activities. Such fears are greater in the developing world and so-called emerging market countries than they are in the world's advanced industrial democracies.

Both surveys also show that concerns about privacy and the security of data stored online are evidently growing each year. The 2014 survey found that 64 percent of respondents were more concerned with their online privacy compared to the previous year. As we explain in later chapters, Edward Snowden's disclosure of National Security Agency (NSA) surveillance and large-scale breaches of personal data have contributed to this concern. When respondents were asked the same question in the 2016 survey, the figure was also high, 57 percent.

Internet users are also worried that the network is becoming a military battlefield to attack critical infrastructure (such as nuclear power plants, electricity grids and airport traffic control systems) and the key governmental institutions of a country. Almost three-quarters of those surveyed worry about such cyber attacks.

The vital issue of public trust also extends to the mundane, day-to-day management and governance of the Internet. When it comes to questions of who should ultimately be responsible for running the Internet, users prefer the broadest form of inclusive governance. The 2014 survey shows that most people feel that governments on their own are not up to the job. Among the surveyed Internet users from 23 countries and Hong Kong, only 47 percent believe their government does a very good job of making sure the Internet in their country is safe and secure. In contrast, 57 percent would better trust a joint body to run the Internet — the stakeholders to include, besides government, technology companies, engineers, non-governmental organizations (NGOs) and institutions representing the interests and will of ordinary citizens. That figure is also higher than the level of trust users would place in the United Nations or private corporations fulfilling the role of competent stewards of the Internet.

A Looming Trust Deficit and the Erosion of the Internet's Digital Social Capital

This book looks at why the general public the world over is losing faith in the Internet. When the trust of Internet users is lost, the consequences will be huge. We will truly lose out on one of the real marvels of the modern age. Without trust, the Internet cannot be used as a driver of prosperity and innovation. Without trust, the network will cease to be a vital instrument for communications and social engagement. Without trust, the Internet will end up a broken, useless tool.

Another way of thinking about the problem is that the trust that people place in the Internet ecosystem is a bit like the stock market. Investors use it, more join over time, and everyone keeps investing and trading, but no one really thinks that they have it all figured out. No one can be dead sure that there won't be, at some point, a market run, leading to financial loss or, in the worst-case scenario, another major crash. A loss of trust in the Internet can do the same. People's trust is always conditional. People will move away from using particular online services and websites if their faith in those sites or services is shaken. And, they might even stop using the Internet altogether if there was a major, catastrophic attack on the Internet that had dire consequences for its users. The analogy goes further. Just as regulators make it illegal to trade on insider information and require true and plain disclosure of financial results and other material news to preserve the integrity of the market and investors confidence in it, the same principles apply to the governance of the Internet, explained later in this book.

That being said, people use the Internet because it is generally reliable, provides them with the content they want to view and is secure, private, efficient, safe to use and inclusive. In other words, more and more people are using the Internet because they trust it to do what they want it to do. User trust is the bedrock of the ways in which the Internet gets used. User trust also connects to the well-established and broader concept of social capital.

Social capital is generally defined as the "the network of social connections that exist between people, and their shared values and norms of behaviour, which enable and encourage mutually advantageous social cooperation."* These connections are based on trust and allow cooperation to grow and flourish. The concept has a long pedigree. As early as 1835, Alexis de Tocqueville, in his telling analysis *Democracy in America*, referred to the "habits of the heart," which constitute not only the social mores that guide human interactions in a civilized society, but also "the whole moral and intellectual state of a people" that supports political institutions "and the very lifeblood of democracy itself."[9]

Unlike other forms of capital, such as labour or money, social capital — as trusted connections or relationships between people — is intangible. Nevertheless, it produces real value in human interactions. Accordingly, we argue that there is a strong analogy between the real world and the virtual one when it comes to the importance of social capital and trust to the functioning of the Internet. We define digital social capital as the intangible networks that form between people and devices on the Internet. Such networks are informal or "virtual," but, as in the real world, based upon trust and the principle of reciprocity. As a result, these networks are tenuous and often hard to observe directly, but their effects are large and widespread. In short, just as social capital is crucially important in the generation of wealth in the global economy,[10] we argue that digital social capital is the all-important foundation of the Internet's value-generation capability and that it is continuously produced by the different kinds of trust that users place in the system (Figure 1.1).

---

* Collins, Online Dictionary, www.collinsdictionary.com/dictionary/english/ social-capital. As noted by Robert D. Putnam, the term was coined by the writer L. F. Hanifan at the beginning of the twentieth century, and defined as "those tangible substances that count for most in the daily lives of people: namely good will, fellowship, sympathy, and social intercourse among the individuals and families who make up a social unit."[8]

Figure 1.1: The Internet's Social Foundations — Trust, Digital Social Capital and the Generation of Wealth

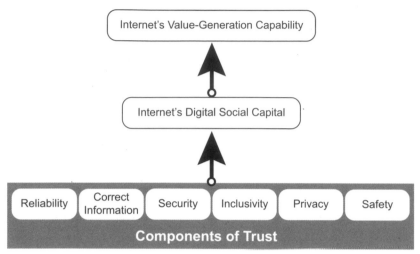

Source: Authors.

Our argument is a simple one. We show in this book that the social, political and even the economic value that the Internet creates is, in large measure, contingent upon the quality and quantity of digital social capital — always based upon trust — that is present in the system. The reasoning behind this intuition is simple. In high-trust environments where social capital is robust, people act in ways that are open, generous, mutually beneficial and reciprocal. In low-trust environments where social capital is thin or practically non-existent, people are cut off from each other, isolated, and the prospects for human interchange and the generation of wealth are limited.

In the first scenario, innovation, knowledge and prosperity come from people interacting with each other through their devices that operate across the cables and wireless signals of the Internet. In the second scenario, the network begins to resemble something of a Wild West, where anarchy and lawlessness reign supreme. Viewed this way, digital social capital is actually the intangible wellspring of the economic, social and political value that is generated by the Internet. The different sources of trust that contribute to the Internet's digital social capital are depicted in Figure 1.1.

The implication of this relationship is that when the actions of governments, companies, hackers, criminals and others undermine the core elements of trust that users place in the Internet, people will use the network less, or so restrictively that they are unable to harness the Internet's full complete potential. In fact, people are already changing their behaviour as their anxiety about the Internet grows. More than one-quarter of those surveyed in the 2014 CIGI-Ipsos poll self-censored what they did online. Over 40 percent avoided certain websites, which is also a sign of growing consumer wariness. Eighteen percent limited who they communicated with. And most starkly, a full 10 percent of those surveyed actually used the Internet less often compared to a year earlier, which is the most worrying statistic of all, because it demonstrates that some people are actually beginning to turn away from the Internet.

The results of the 2016 survey are even more worrisome. Thirty-three percent of Internet users now self-censor online, up from 28 percent the previous year. More users closed social media accounts; more users avoided certain websites; more users changed who they communicated with online. A slightly larger number (13 percent) also reported that they now use the network less often (Table 1.1).

The trend in these data shows two things. On the one hand, people are more savvy about what they do and how they conduct themselves

Table 1.1: Shifts in Users' Behaviour Online

	2014	2016
Change your password regularly	39%	41%
Avoid certain websites	43%	46%
Self-censor	28%	33%
Change who you communicate with	18%	25%
Close social media accounts	11%	15%
Use the Internet less often	10%	13%

Source: Data from the CIGI-Ipsos 2014 and 1016 Global Surveys.

online. This is generally a good thing. For example, more people are exercising good Internet hygiene such as changing their passwords regularly and avoiding certain websites.

On the other hand, a growing number are using the Internet less often, self-censoring what they say and do, or simply going off-line altogether. If people use the Internet in more restrictive ways, infrequently or not at all, the Internet's digital social capital and its potential to promote economic growth and foster human development will be compromised. Like all tools, the Internet can be either a sharp or a dull instrument of human creativity and expression.

Different Birds of Prey: The Actors Eroding User Trust

Waning trust has many different sources. One way to think about the issue is to give a more definite shape to the shadowy actors whose quiet surveillance preys on our trust (and our fears). For this exercise, imagine a setting where the inhabitants' activities are disguised by its murkiness — a dark forest populated by nocturnal creatures remarkable for their keen vision in low light. These creatures — owls — come in many different shapes and sizes. And, they are very smart.

So, how far can this metaphor take us? First, consider a particularly stealthy species of watcher, the Horned Owls of the electronic eavesdropping agencies of governments, which are engaged in the business of espionage, intelligence collection and spying. In liberal democracies, the Horned Owls aim to catch terrorists and criminals. In more repressive states, these owls target terrorists and political dissidents in nearly equal measure. These Horned Owls fly great distances and across borders in search of their quarry.

The hunting habits of these Horned Owls are of much concern to the smaller creatures living on the forest floors, namely you and me. As the 2016 CIGI-Ipsos survey reveals, 60 percent of people around the world link the actions of their government to their worsening view of online privacy.

There are other owls in this forest. The Long-eared Owls of the private sector, tech giants such as Google and Facebook, scrutinize every communication and action of the forest creatures using their freely provided platforms and services. Their intentions are different from those of the Horned Owls. Not only do these owls want to serve us better by figuring out our basic wants, needs, interests and concerns, they also want to make us all better consumers by marketing their analysis of our collective online behaviour to other corporations and purveyors of goods and services. These owls see themselves as being in the business of making us all happy.

However, these Long-eared Owls of the private sector have gotten the formula slightly wrong. Consumers may love their services, but they also strongly feel that these companies' behind-the-scenes activity is threatening online privacy. According to CIGI-Ipsos's 2016 survey, fully 72 percent of respondents indicated that private companies are a major source of their growing anxiety about their online privacy.

Next are the small Burrowing Owls of the criminal underworld, many of whom inhabit the recesses of what is often referred to as the Dark Web, those parts of the electronic forest that never see the light of day and where everyone is literally invisible. Some of these owls are in the business of stealing our online identities so that they can rob us with abandon or cause other kinds of mischief. Others are in the business of exploitation, of minors for sexual purposes, or of other vulnerable groups, such as the elderly, who might fall for some new, online Ponzi scheme. And then there are those Burrowing Owls who simply want to wreak havoc and create mayhem because they can — often just for the fun of it.

Public concern about online privacy and security are mounting with the population explosion of the Burrowing Owls species. Fifty-five percent of those surveyed said that criminals contributed "a great deal" to their worsening perceptions of online privacy. Another 24 percent indicated that criminals contributed "somewhat" to their worsening privacy perceptions. In other words, fully 79 percent of people feel that their online privacy is threatened by cybercrime.

Finally, this forest is also home to unassuming Barn Owls. Members of this widely distributed species are simply ordinary Internet users, but they take an exceptional interest in the Internet habits and lives of their fellow citizens. These owls hunt for tantalizing tidbits of sensational information that can easily be found online via web searches and social media sites. These Barn Owls are curious about the smallest facts of our existence — such as where we work, who we know or where we live — which, when put together, paint an alarmingly detailed picture of our existence. Internet users worry a great deal about these Barn Owls and their ability to peer — jealously, sympathetically, idly or maliciously — into our lives. In fact, 66 percent of those polled by CIGI-Ipsos in 2016 said regular Internet users contributed to their eroding sense of online privacy. Oddly, and not for the last time, we see how people's attitudes about privacy and other issues somewhat contradictory. People want their online lives to be viewed only by those that they trust, but they still post personal details about themselves on public forums all the time.

This book is an exploration of the impact that these owls of the Internet are having on us all, on our daily lives and on a world where, increasingly, everything we do when we communicate and reach out to others happens online. It will explore the effect that the erosion of different elements of trust has on the overall stock of digital social capital that is so essential to the operation and effectiveness of the Internet. It is also a study of what we should do to deal with those owls breaking our trust, so that we can have greater peace of mind as we explore that growing ecosystem we call the Internet.

One-third of the world's citizens — over three billion and growing — are now on the Internet. It is a network intimately linked to our physical survival and livelihood. The water we drink is managed by it, as is the food we eat, the clothes we wear and the energy we use to light and heat our homes. When we drive our cars or hop aboard a train, ship or airplane, our movements are tracked and managed electronically.

And when we go to work, we depend on the Internet for many of the things we do.

But, as our dependence on the Internet grows, many of us increasingly feel vulnerable to the predators that inhabit it. Our fears and perceptions of the dangers lurking online are conditioned by our own circumstance and history. Some of those fears, as we demonstrate in this book, are misunderstood or exaggerated (the danger of cybercrime being one). But, in a world where perception is often reality, many of our fellow citizens are losing faith in what the Internet has to offer.

It is undeniable that the risks we are exposed to when we go online will mount steadily as the everyday objects of ordinary life — our cars, our homes and even our appliances — become linked to the Internet too. Ordinary objects "talking" to each other through the Internet is a reality that is coming soon. These changes imply that human users will be constantly monitored, with burgeoning databases recording everything from our driving habits or the time we wake up in the morning to the time we leave our homes or go to bed at night. Soon — and in many ways, it's happening already — our virtual tracks will bear an even closer resemblance to our physical ones, to the point where they are indistinguishable. The basic right to privacy, something we all cherish, may become a thing of the past if everything we do, say, or even feel leaves an electronic signature that can be retrieved and read by others, whether we like it or not.

In this new world, known as the Internet of Things (IoT) or the Internet of Everything (IoE), the risk of our online identities being compromised may grow unless the data management and retrieval systems that link those objects are made watertight and properly secured.

What Makes the Internet Work?

The Internet is built on trust, but it is a trust between strangers — a blind trust. We don't actually have many ways of seeing or verifying who is sitting behind the other screen when we go to a particular website, send emails or chat online. Increasingly, as artificial intelligence becomes more common and more sophisticated, the "person" with whom we are interacting may not even be real. Some technologies do exist that substitute trust for verification, such as Domain Name System Security Extensions (DNSSEC), certificate authorities and blockchain distributed ledgers (which we will talk about more later). In the complex edifice that is the Internet, the basic rules of interaction assume a high level of trust among billions of users. In fact, the Internet could not operate if its operators and users did not share a basic faith that the hardware and software underpinning the system was generally secure, stable, reliable and free of unwarranted interference and intrusion. Digital social capital, in this sense, is both technical and social.

Think of it this way. When you send an email to someone, you assume that the email will be delivered to its addressee. That addressee may be someone you know, but it may also be someone you don't know. Even if you have an unreliable or unstable Internet connection — a common frustration in many parts of the world — you are still reasonably confident that, once you actually get online, the Internet will allow you to send emails and function normally, anywhere in the world, the same way it does at home.

Trust is also implicit when you conduct commercial activities online. Purchasing a book from Amazon or an article of clothing online requires that we trust the vendor selling us the product. We need to trust that they will send us the product we have paid for, and that their online payment system is secure and our valuable financial information will not be compromised. If trust breaks down (as we will show it sometimes does), users will shy away from the system, and the Internet's ability to connect people and reduce transaction costs will be lost.

That same kind of trust applies to our online activities when we access content on the Internet. We are reasonably confident that the websites we go to are legitimate and that the content we are downloading or the services we are accessing are accurate and reliable. When we make an airline booking to travel to London or

Los Angeles, purchase the ticket by giving our credit card information over the Internet and check in online, we are quite certain that when we show up at the airport we will be able to board the aircraft and take our pre-assigned seat.

Fortunately, when we go to a particular website to do business, we do not have to take it on faith that the site is legitimate and trustworthy. Firms and other vendors on the Internet have been able to develop sophisticated online feedback systems that help to build reputations, ensure reliability and give us greater assurance in the security and stability of our online activities and commercial transactions. These systems are the virtual equivalent of "getting to know" someone in our daily lives, where trust is built incrementally as we become better acquainted with people by interacting with them directly and testing relationships by sharing information, and where reputations and trust are also based on the feedback we get from others.

The online retail hub eBay provides an early example, as Paul Resnick and his colleagues have described. [11] eBay offers no guarantees to its users to mitigate the risks associated with making purchases from strangers. Still, fraudulent transactions are kept to a minimum. The ingenious trust-building mechanism at work is a simple one. The ability to rate sellers and buyers reduces abuses and produces trust in the online marketplace. So long as people want to continue using the site to sell things, there will be an incentive to deal fairly with buyers.

That simple system has been widely adopted. Amazon allows buyers to rate book sellers and to provide comments describing the services rendered. These activities improve customer service and keep merchants honest. The ride sharing application Uber takes it a step further and allows both the driver and the passenger to rate their shared experience. Poor ratings for a driver will cost them money, so they have an incentive to act well, maintain their car and go where they are directed. Poor ratings for a passenger will really stymie their ability to catch a lift, forcing them to return to taxis or public transportation.

With trust being the foundation of so many of the ways in which the Internet functions, its loss can change fundamentally, and perhaps irrevocably, the way in which the network works. As we show throughout this book, a loss of trust can result in tremendous economic, social and political costs.

What Is to Be Done?

Any study of our growing existential online fears would be seriously remiss if it did not also discuss practical policy solutions to the dilemmas we face as we find ourselves online every minute of every day.

In dealing with the "owls" of the Internet, and in trying to restore user trust in the system, one of the problems we face is the multi-faceted and interconnected nature of trust.[12] Sometimes policies that are designed to restore trust by manipulating one aspect of the issue (say, calling for data localization — which will be discussed in detail later — to increase user privacy) can actually undermine other elements of user trust (for instance, security, reliable access and the ability to access correct content). This interconnection precludes simplistic policy solutions or quick technical fixes, making restoring the trust people place in the Internet ecosystem no simple matter.

The revelations and political fallout of Edward Snowden's disclosures of NSA surveillance have had a major impact on global public trust in attitudes about the Internet. But, as we are also learning, all governments are actively involved in the business of electronic eavesdropping. Other countries besides the United States are snooping too, spying on their enemies but also on their friends and their own citizens. One of this book's key messages is that governments and regulatory authorities must exercise greater self-restraint in their use of new technologies to scour and comb the Internet. Just because they can snoop doesn't mean that they should.

Rather than just relying upon the good will of governments, citizens must also hold their governments and elected officials to a much higher level of transparency and accountability than they do now when it comes to privacy and surveillance, even when electronic eavesdropping is being carried out in the name of national security, self-defence or law enforcement. Doing so may require the development of a new social compact on digital privacy and security to help secure the rights of citizens, as advanced by the GCIG.[13] As we stand on the edge of the IoT revolution, a status quo, steady-as-she-goes public policy approach to these issues is simply not adequate.

Private corporations, also in the business of providing online services and collecting data from consumers and their users, have to come out of the shadows. They need to come clean about the information they are gathering from us when we use their products and services. Citizens should also be able to opt out of their services or, if they opt in, to at least have a say in how their personal information is being gathered, used and shared. As we enter the age of the IoT, citizens must have the choice to take themselves off-line. The fundamental right to privacy and freedom of choice must remain, as ordinary objects used in our daily existence become part of the virtual world and go online.

Private corporations must also do a better job of storing and protecting their data and ensuring that criminals and thieves do not gain access to their treasure troves of data and personal information stored in the Cloud. They will have to make substantial investments to secure the continued trust of their consumers so that they will continue to do business with them. Big companies have the resources to do this and their insurers will also demand it to reduce liabilities. However, small and medium-sized enterprises (SMEs), which populate the economy and provide the bulk of jobs in the private sector, may not have the resources to mount an effective defence against the predators of the Internet. Creative regulatory and financing solutions may be required to ensure that SMEs erect the right kinds of firewalls and engage appropriate preventive measures to protect their data.

As with the association between social capital and democratic governance, there is a reciprocal relationship between the quality of digital social capital and the institutional arrangements that govern the Internet.[14] Higher levels of social capital tend to produce better institutional arrangements as students of democracy and democratic processes argue. Likewise, better, more trustworthy institutional arrangements can also help to also produce more digital social capital. Right now, many good Internet governance institutions exist, but most are in need of reform so that they can become more functionally inclusive of the growing diversity of people and opinions online. Movements in this direction will build better institutions and help restore trust in the system.

Individuals must also be more prudent about what they put online and share with others, including the content of text messages and personal photos sent from cellphones to family, friends, lovers and colleagues — as more than one celebrity and politician have learned to their deep chagrin and personal embarrassment. No one is immune to hackers and we are all potential lunch to those pesky owls. That doesn't mean that our personal data and communications will inevitably be compromised or that we should all be paranoid as we move about in cyberspace. But the risks are real, and we need to be vigilant in protecting our personal information, security and online identities.

At the end of the day, however, it is an educated and Internet-savvy citizenry that will ultimately help secure and reduce the vulnerabilities of the Internet. Nico Sell, the chief executive officer (CEO) of the encrypted messaging application Wickr, has adopted a highly imaginative, educational approach to this problem. She frequently attends a conference of hackers in Las Vegas, Nevada, called DEF CON (self-described as one of the oldest continuously running hacker conventions around), to teach young people just how vulnerable the networks of the Internet — and the systems that rely upon them — really are. She does so by showing them how to hack. Her favourite example is showing teenaged kids how to take down a power grid with an iPhone. Her thinking is that with knowledge comes temperance. Knowing the damage that can be done spurs people to behave better, which in turn generally makes things more secure.[15]

In the Internet age, a lot comes back to the individual user. Harmful computer viruses gain toeholds and multiply in personal computers because unsuspecting users have unwittingly revealed their computer passwords to someone else, failed to use or update their antivirus software, clicked a seemingly harmless link in an email or gone to a website where they have downloaded pirated music or movie software that contains malware and computer viruses. As we will see in later chapters, the idea of digital hygiene is central to the security of the Internet. Everyone has to practise better digital hygiene when they go on online. That is the only way to secure cyberspace over the longer term. Individual users also need to stand up to companies that use their personal data as the coin of the realm, and they need to tell governments that overreaching with online surveillance cannot be tolerated.

Staring down those dangerous owls of the Internet requires a steady focus — and devising effective strategies of protection and prevention begins with us.

What Is to Come?

In the next chapter, we talk more about what the Internet is and how it operates. We go on to show how this amazing system of networked people and devices has grown from a few computers networked in research universities to a system with a global reach. We highlight, too, how trust is composed of six dimensions — reliability, correct information, security, inclusivity, privacy and safety — and how the actions of governments, private companies or malicious online actors can undermine it.

In the third chapter, we shift our attention to the positive bounty that the Internet is creating in addition to the spread of ideas and the proliferation of personal connections between people. The chapter aims to provide a sense of what we stand to lose if the erosion of trust continues unabated.

The next several chapters consider how the actions of governments, companies and others are affecting the trust of users, causing them to change their online behaviours, and how the cumulative effect of these changes could break the Internet.

In the fourth chapter, we turn to government surveillance and censorship. We show the extent of Big Brother's activities and their repercussions. We look at how individuals, companies and even nations have responded in maladaptive ways to the loss of trust, generating unnecessary costs and hampering the potential of the Internet.

In the fifth chapter, the theme of Internet fragmentation — the increasing disassembly of the Internet through the discrete actions of governments and regulatory authorities, sometimes undertaken in an effort to restore trust, but also for reasons of self-interest or in search of commercial advantage and gain — is explored.

In chapter six, we discuss how the nefarious work of online hackers, criminals and trolls has eroded people's trust in the Internet, and the consequences for business, governance and the economy. We point to how the improvement of everyone's basic digital hygiene can help to limit or deter the occurrence of Internet-based crime.

In chapter seven, we zoom in on the high politics of the Internet. We haven't yet seen a full-scale cyberwar break out, but politically motivated cyber attacks abound. We unpack the how and the why of this subject, including how people are deeply concerned about attacks against their national institutions, which can have consequences for how the Internet is used in areas as far-ranging as aerospace to critical infrastructure.

In chapter eight, we move on to what is known as the "digital divide." While access to the Internet is expanding rapidly, there are still large segments of the population — often people who are poor, disabled, marginalized or living in rural or developing countries — that still cannot access the network. How they come online impacts the trust that they place in the system and affects how they will come to use the system over the long term. Since the Internet is set to be crucial to economic development, political expression and communication in the coming years (indeed, it is in many ways already crucial now), the first experience of new users can have a reinforcing effect on user behaviour toward either greater levels of engagement and prosperity or continued levels of disenfranchisement and an even large gap between the Internet haves and the have-nots.

Finally, in chapter nine, we gather all the threads together and try to weave a whole cloth to strengthen user trust in the Internet ecosystem, involving a combination of institution building, behavioural change, technological innovation and new "rules of the road."

Two

An Ecosystem Based on Trust

Every day millions, indeed billions, of people use the Internet to view the news, communicate with friends and loved ones, or look at funny pictures of cats and dogs. For millions of us, the Internet is becoming integral to our daily lives, as foundational as electricity. And yet, just as most of us cannot explain exactly how our cars' intricate systems work, or take apart the motherboard of our computers, we hardly know how the technology of the Internet works, let alone what the various parts of the system actually are.

To wrap our heads around the technical complexity of the Internet, we often turn to metaphors — for example, the popular concept of the network as the "the information superhighway," or our own description of the array of predatory Internet players as owls. Metaphors can help make the technical complexity of the Internet more easily understandable. One of the most common analogies used in describing the Internet is that of the ecosystem — a system, or a group of interconnected elements, formed by the interaction of a community of organisms with their environment.

In this chapter, we will use the notion of the ecosystem to map some of the basic building blocks of the Internet, and then continue our discussion of why trust matters for this ecosystem's survival.

To begin, imagine one of the most complex ecosystems on the planet: a tropical rainforest. The upper canopy, the jungle denizens, the tree-top homes and the lower, darker flora and fauna — we'll use all to represent different parts of the Internet.

A Network of Networks

Viewed from above, a tropical rainforest looks like a single mass of green. It is hard to discern from this view that it is composed of single trees that have grown into an intermeshed whole. Similarly, gazing at the computer screen, you would never know that the Internet is not a single, coherent network. The ability to access webpages all over the world with a few keystrokes further solidifies this notion that the Internet is one big thing. But that notion, as much as it might seem correct, is actually wrong. The Internet is a massive network of functionally separate networks, just as the rainforest canopy is a single thing encompassing numerous trees.

As of 2011, the Internet was composed of 5,039 individual networks that were all interconnected, thereby joining millions of computers (hosts) globally.[1] Since then, as Internet access has expanded further into rural areas and developing countries, it is likely that the number of distinct networks that are connected to form the Internet has grown.

Squawking Toucans and Web Traffic

Returning to our ecosystem analogy, both the rainforest and the Internet are teeming with life's activity. Creatures fly and swing from branch to branch and from tree to tree in the canopy of the rainforest. On the Internet, small so-called packets of data move across the fibre optic wires and wireless signals of the Internet, often flowing from one network to another as bits of information circumnavigate the globe. Essentially, every email you send, every website you view, every tweet you tweet, every video you watch and every song you download involves the flow of packets of data. The vibrancy of a rainforest is truly remarkable. And the amount of energetic activity among the trees of the Internet rainforest is simply staggering.

The numbers are so large as to be almost incomprehensible to anyone without advanced training in computer science. Yet the numbers can be put into fairly concrete (and understandable) terms. In 2010, the technology company Cisco Systems predicted that Internet traffic would grow to 63,904 petabytes of data *per month* by 2014.[2] A single petabyte is 10^{15} bytes, which works out to a million gigabytes. That figure's enormity is still pretty hard to grasp conceptually unless you love math, but a few examples give a sense of the real-world size we are talking about here. For instance, one petabyte of stored music on an MP3 player would take about 2,000 years to play.[3] Humans really don't have that kind of processing time. Thank goodness for computers.

Jungle Homes and Websites

The upper canopy of the rainforest suggests another point of comparison. Many jungle creatures live throughout this top layer of the ecosystem. Think of their individual home spaces as websites. Each space exists in one part of the interconnected ecosystem but is accessible from the other parts (and sometimes needs to be defended from predators). Much of what the typical user views as "the Internet" is hosted in this bright upper canopy of the cyberspace ecosystem. This layer hosts all the content that can be found with a Google, Bing or Yahoo! web search.

The spaces in this upper canopy are the Internet's "normal" websites, hosted on the so-called World Wide Web — an information-sharing model that rides on top of the infrastructure of the Internet and gives rise to the "www." before a website address. As of 2014, there were some 968,882,453 websites, up from an already whopping 172,338,726 in 2008.[4] The online ecosystem of websites is big — and getting bigger every day.

The Jungle Floor and the Deep Dark Web

Far below the airy top layer of the tropical rainforest lies a dark forest floor. Light rarely penetrates its depths or recesses. Here inhabitants scurry in the shadows seeking food, shelter and other tidbits. The Internet has a parallel layer. Beneath the normally accessible sites hosted in the upper canopy of the Internet is its shadowy underworld, known colloquially as the Dark Web or the Dark Net.[5] Unlike the regular Internet, the Dark Net is not accessible through standard search engines. Instead, travelling there requires special tools, such as "The Onion Router," commonly known as the Tor Browser or the Tor anonymity network.

The "Dark Web" certainly has some ominous connotations, conjuring up images of illegal activity and illicit and socially unacceptable behaviours. Indeed, the content of the Dark Web is far different from the usual content of the Internet's top level. The Dark Web is populated by websites providing a range of services — some good, many bad. For example, Facebook is available on the Dark Web, so that individuals in repressive regimes can access it freely. The online illegal marketplace Silk Road, where people could buy anything from drugs to weapons and munitions, was also hosted on the Dark Web, before being shut down in 2013. Fraud sites, illegal download sites, gambling sites, whistle-blower sites, chat rooms on all manner of subjects, hacking sites, child abuse sites and sites selling assassination services are all part and parcel of the Dark Web.

And people definitely use these sites — they are not just set up by a few social malcontents and then left fallow. Two computer scientists from Portsmouth University recently conducted a study to look at the flow of traffic on the Tor hidden services, which are websites hosted on the Tor anonymity network within the Dark Web. These sites are only accessible through the Tor Browser. To go about tracking traffic on the otherwise anonymous network, these computer scientists volunteered a series of computers for use in the

Tor network to act as relays routing traffic to Dark Web websites (in fact, the entire Tor network is based upon people who volunteer their computers for use by others). Over the course of their study, these researchers were able to catalogue all of the sites that users of their relays connected to, and found the range of sites listed above. Sadly, they also found that more than 80 percent of traffic on the Tor services went to child abuse sites, with other traffic going to porn, marketplaces, drug, wiki (collaborative content), news and directory sites.[6]

The general reaction to such findings (as we shall see in chapter six) is that we need to shut the Dark Web down, because it is harming society. But the trouble is that the anonymity of the Dark Web is also used by good guys — political activists, to avoid detection in repressive regimes, and by whistle-blowers who are too scared for themselves and their loved ones to "out" the secrets of governments and large, shadowy corporations through the usual channels.[7] The Dark Web has its name for a reason, but not everything that happens on the Dark Web is bad for society.

This brings us to one final and truly fantastical similarity between the ecosystem of the tropical rainforest and the ecosystem of the Internet: no one is in charge.

Nature, Red in Tooth and Claw

The rainforest has its predators and its prey, and the plant life of its canopy, understory and forest floor, but no one element of the ecosystem controls who gets "what, when, how."[8] Nature, as the old Tennyson poem goes, is "red in tooth and claw" and its constant rebalancing works as if "led by some invisible hand," to use Adam Smith's classic phrase describing the functioning of markets.[9] One unfortunate reality of this ecosystem is that sometimes the rainforest of the Internet has its wildfires that can burn the forest down.

The Internet is much the same. No one "controls" the Internet and no one can dictate who gets what, or when and how they get it. Governments, private corporations, civil society and the technical community are the four primary stakeholders of the Internet community, pushing and pulling. Different stakeholders write the collective set of rules, regulations, ideas and codes that govern the Internet.[10]

To this list of stakeholders, we would add a fifth — and more amorphous — category: normal Internet users. The cumulative force of consumer preference is often one of the most powerful drivers of how the Internet functions and what is available online. For example, when consumers wanted encryption in the wake of Edward Snowden's disclosures about NSA surveillance of private online correspondences, companies responded and provided it.[11] In 2016, the debate about encryption came to a head when Apple, acting in support of the idea that its customers want their data to be private, refused to open for the FBI an iPhone owned by one of the terrorists who killed 14 people in the San Bernardino, California, shooting in December 2015. Apple refused to obey a court order to unlock the iPhone, but the issue became moot when the FBI was able to get a third party to unlock the device.[12]

An Ecosystem Based on Trust

Clearly, the Internet is a complex ecosystem with many moving parts and players that often conflict. So what keeps this system functioning? What has allowed the Internet to scale to a global system generating trillions of dollars in economic windfalls (as we'll show in chapter three)? In a word, trust. Trust is the glue that holds the whole system together, determining both how and how much the Internet is used. But it is not always clear what trust means when it comes to the Internet, or whether everyone is using the term the same way.

Much of this confusion occurs because trust itself is a multidimensional concept. An early examination of why people place trust in a networked system noted that trust has five components: correctness, reliability, security, privacy and safety.* To these five, we add the notion that trusted networks are ones where the governance of the system includes its different stakeholders. Users trust the Internet for different reasons and similarly lose trust for a variety of reasons. Users, in this case, can include individual citizens, private companies and states.

Before we unpack these six components, the obvious question is "So what?" Why does the erosion of trust in the Internet matter?

The answer is simple. When trust is lost, there tends to be a negative adjustment to how people use the Internet that undermines the wealth and benefits that the system can provide. The Internet's digital social capital — that intangible but all-important fabric of the network, woven of the six core elements of trust — becomes threadbare. These key threads are described in the next sections.

Correctness

Correctness is the first core element of trust. People trust when they go online that the Internet will provide them with the correct content. Sitting at work or at home or travelling on vacation, you fire up the Internet, type in a web address and trust that you will be sent to the right webpage. If you are not given the right information, your trust that the system is working as it is supposed to will decline, and you will likely change your behaviour to rely on the network less.

Imagine yourself in this real-world situation from June 2014. You are a small business owner who has set up a "virtual machine" on Microsoft's Azure Cloud services. A virtual machine is a lot like a normal computer, except your data, operating system and applications

---

* Fred B. Schneider's framework for trusted networked technologies[13] originally included a sixth component, survivability. Since the networks of the Internet were explicitly designed with survival in mind, we have elected to exclude this component from our application of the trust framework, adding instead a political dimension of inclusiveness.

are stored on distant Microsoft servers housed in climate-controlled rooms around the world. You use this service because it allows you to access your computer system away from the office, which is great for your productivity. You also use a virtual machine because it puts generous computing power at your fingertips but does not require that you spend buckets of money on costly servers for your office. Overall, your business has benefited greatly from your use of a virtual machine and Microsoft's Azure Cloud.

Now, imagine that one day you sign in to your virtual machine (as you have hundreds of times before) and go to check the news. You begin surfing, but something weird happens. Instead of getting a list of English websites in response to your web search, you get a bunch of sites in Portuguese. Confused, you cut your losses and close the window. Momentarily discouraged, you decide to take a short break from work and sign into your Netflix account, to watch a bit of *House of Cards*. Again, something weird happens. You log in and are taken to Brazil's version of Netflix. You are at a loss. You are not getting the correct content you are looking for. The network is failing you.

To understand what went wrong, we need to detour briefly to describe some of the technology of the Internet. Each device connected to the Internet is given a unique Internet Protocol (IP) address. These digital addresses are like street addresses — in the bricks and mortar world, every house has an address, and on the Internet, every device connected to it has one IP address. The current IP address version is called IP version four (IPv4). Each IPv4 address has 32 digits combined in a unique order. This system gives rise to many potential addresses — over four billion in fact.

The problem is that every device connected to the Internet needs a *unique* address or else conflicts emerge and the whole system doesn't work. Given that there are over three billion Internet users and even more devices online,[14] the number of available addresses is increasingly becoming too small to accommodate the number of people who want to use the Internet. This scarcity causes problems.

So, what happened in June 2014? When you tried to use your virtual machine in the Azure Cloud, why did you receive the wrong content and end up at the wrong Netflix site? As Dan York of the Internet Society put it, Microsoft ran out of North American IPv4 addresses.[15] To make up the shortfall, Microsoft started borrowing addresses from Latin America. Because you were given an IP address, you could still get online. But, because the IP address that you were given was a part of the pool of IP addresses assigned to Latin America, to the rest of the Internet it looked like your virtual machine was in Brazil — hence, the Portuguese news and Brazilian Netflix.

In this case, the correctness of the information you were trying to access was undermined by current technical limitations to the network (there is a solution in place, called IP version six, but it is not yet widely adopted). As long as this problem remained an isolated incident, many users would chalk it up to chance and continue using the Azure Cloud service. But what if the problem recurred? Many people would, at the very least, migrate their business to another Cloud company. That move would have economic ramifications for Microsoft and be time-consuming, not to mention annoying, for individuals and businesses using their services. And what if the problem became widespread and you could never be sure what IP address you would be assigned and what content you would be able to access on any given day? Individuals, businesses and governments would trust the network less to satisfy their basic content needs and would turn to other sources of content. In short, if people cannot trust that the network will provide them with the correct information, they will use it less — which in turn will hinder the bounty that the network of networks can provide.

Reliability

Let's look at another component of trust: *reliability*. Why reliability matters is fairly straightforward. Users will trust the Internet more for work and play if the system is dependable — if they are able to routinely and consistently use it. Unreliable services lead to significant losses of trust.

Even highly developed countries can have unreliable Internet services, with some clear ramifications for how much trust people place in the Internet. Take this example from Canada. At 6:40 p.m. Eastern Standard Time on Wednesday, October 9, 2013, the telecommunications company Rogers experienced a massive wireless network outage. At the time, Rogers had around 10 million wireless users across Canada. The outage was originally reported in the provinces of Ontario and Quebec, but it quickly affected wireless services across the country. The problem persisted until 11:45 p.m., when the company announced wireless services were fully restored.[16] The problem was relatively short-lived and reportedly caused by a software problem.

It turns out that Canadian Internet users are fairly prickly about the issue of reliable access. During and shortly after the outage, many Rogers customers turned to social media to express their dissatisfaction (something that is a bit ironic in the context of a network outage!). Enter poor Glenn Rogers of Brooklyn, New York.

Glenn Rogers innocently used the handle @rogers for his Twitter account. During the outage, thousands of Canadians sent him irate tweets — "@rogers is down again? No surprise there! I think a carrier pigeon is more reliable than they are" and "@ rogers U suck!" being typical — because they thought @rogers was the telecom company's handle.[17]

Shortly after the barrage, the public learned that @rogers was not in any way associated with the Canadian telecom giant and was instead the personal account of a young Australian living in New York City. Glenn Rogers was then flooded by another wave of tweets from the Great White North, this time apologizing for the misunderstanding. In response to the outpouring, Glenn Rogers — who has since moved on to a different Twitter handle — tweeted back, "Thanks for all the kind tweets Canada. May they never take your phone or Internet from you again."[18]

This event involved a few hours of Internet outage, followed by a wrathful storm from Internet users provoked by the unreliability of the Rogers network. Imagine if the network outage had lasted longer, or if several had occurred in a burst one after another. It's probable that people would have voted with their feet and moved to other Internet service providers (ISPs). And imagine what could happen if an outage was not confined to one network but affected all of Canada's major wireless providers. If people could not trust the Internet to function reliably, they would opt for other communications systems and use the Internet less often or for less important tasks. Once again, the Internet's potential to facilitate communication, enhance cultural expression and generate economic growth would have been stunted through the loss of trust.

Security

So, a loss of correct information and reliable access is bad. Let's now turn to the third component of trust: *security*. Security of the Internet captures the idea that people want to use the Internet without undue risk that their personal and financial information will be compromised. Secure systems have layers of authentication that protect our most precious information, while insecure systems are typically accessible to everyone. If people don't think a system is secure, they will refrain from using it, which can have large economic ramifications, as the following example illustrates.

The year 2014 was a bad year for online retail services. In May, the computer servers of eBay, one of the biggest online retail giants, were hacked. At the end of the first quarter of 2014, eBay had 145 million active accounts.[19] With most hacks compromising the personal data of users, there is some cover to be had among the masses. It is not totally unreasonable to think that, yes, maybe the company has been hacked, but there are 145 million other people who could be affected instead of you, right? True sometimes, yes — but definitely not in this case. In May 2014, eBay confirmed that each and every one of its 145 million account holders had their personal email addresses stolen in the cyber attack. It was a vivid demonstration that e-commerce platforms hosted on the Internet are not that secure.[20]

In late May and early June 2014, *USA Today* commissioned a poll of 790 Internet users in the United States to get a sense of how major violations of security, such as the one that happened to eBay, affected how people use the Internet.[21] They found that as people grew to distrust the network because of a perceived lack of online security, online commerce declined. The major headline finding of this *USA Today* poll was that fully 24 percent of those surveyed had stopped online shopping because of concern over the security of personal information held by online retailers. Another 56 percent indicated that they had changed their behaviour to be more selective in the websites that they frequented, using fewer sites overall.

So, how does security affect trust in the Internet and why does it matter? Without security, people begin to distrust the Internet. They stop online shopping, and growth, consumption and the vibrancy of consumer-driven economies like those in most Western countries could stall.

Privacy

Now, let's consider the fourth component of trusted network systems: *privacy*. We all have secrets that only we know. Next on the scale are things we would only tell immediate family. Then there are the personal facts and stories we might tell our inner circle — our closest friends and associates. Finally, there is the stuff we don't care who knows. The precise boundaries of privacy are different for each person, but a desire and need for privacy at some level is just a part of being human.

Increasingly, we use the Internet to convey personal information at all, or almost all, of these levels in one way or another. While we might not expect our posts on a public forum to be private, we do expect other things, such as the content of private messages sent to a loved one, to be safe from prying eyes. When this expectation is violated, the perceived privacy of the Internet is compromised and people lose trust in the system. As we have seen with the other components, a loss of trust is quickly followed by behavioural changes and even less use of the Internet, all to the detriment of the abundant potential of the system. One example, more than any other, drives home the importance of this component.

In the spring of 2013, a 29-year-old contractor with the defence and security company Booz Allen Hamilton blew the whistle on a massive NSA surveillance program.[22] That contractor was Edward Snowden, and he would quickly become a household name. Some would damn him as a traitor who wanted to jeopardize national security. Others would applaud his actions as those of a conscientious citizen concerned with the preservation of freedom and privacy in the Internet age.

The clear lesson that emerged from Snowden's revelations about NSA surveillance is that what is said and done online is not as private as many people had thought. Before word broke, there was some expectation both nationally and globally that private messages sent online would remain more or less private, potentially being stored on an ISP's server for a while before being eventually deleted. Snowden changed all that.

Snowden's disclosures have had many repercussions (as we'll discuss in detail in chapter four). For now, let's think about what they meant for the level of trust ordinary people placed in the network. What Snowden revealed rocked their understanding of how the Internet worked. Their trust eroded rapidly, and they started taking steps, often time-consuming and costly, to safeguard their privacy online, all of which undermined the efficiency of the system as a whole.

The 2014 CIGI-Ipsos Global Survey shows the magnitude of the effect of Snowden's revelations on people's behaviour. In Canada, for example, 62 percent of those surveyed had heard of Snowden. Among those Canadians, 30 percent had taken concrete steps to protect their online privacy. Interestingly, in India, among those in the population who had heard of Snowden (also 62 percent), 69 percent subsequently changed their behaviour.

So, how many people across all the countries in the sample actually changed their behaviour in response to a loss of trust in the privacy of the Internet? Well, we know the percentage of respondents from the 2014 CIGI-Ipsos Global Survey who had heard of Snowden. We also know, courtesy of the World Bank, how many Internet users there are in each of these 23 countries and Hong Kong. Finally, we know from the CIGI-Ipsos survey the percentage of people who actually changed their behaviour. With these three bits of information, we can estimate how many Internet users spent time and money in response to Edward Snowden's disclosures that the Internet is less private than we all thought. When the numbers are crunched, the result is pretty staggering: more than 739 million people changed their behaviour because they lost faith in the idea that the Internet facilitated private communication (Figure 2.1). That's well over double the entire population of the United States! At the end of the day, the condition of privacy tends to enhance the trust that people place in the Internet, while online surveillance tends to deter widespread Internet usage.

Figure 2.1: Estimate of Users Changing Online Behaviour Following Edward Snowden's Disclosures

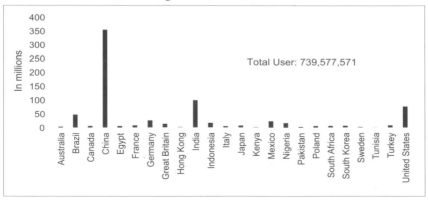

Source: Data from the CIGI-Ipsos 2014 Global Survey and World Bank, n.d., "Data — Indicators," http://data.worldbank.org/indicator.

Safety

Safety is the fifth component of a trustworthy Internet. It makes sense that users will trust the Internet more if they think it is not going to cause harm to people or property. As a simple proposition, everything else being equal, safe systems will be used generously, while unsafe systems will be used less frequently or with strict caveats.

This proposition is illustrated well by the example of nuclear power generation. Preceding the construction of a new nuclear power plant, there will be much discussion about whether the technology is safe. No one doubts the potential of nuclear power to provide electricity, but people rightly want to know whether they can use the technology without unduly risking the safety of communities and the environment. One nuclear meltdown and the balance shifts abruptly. People don't believe in the safety of the technology any longer, and their distrust sends the power plant "off-line."[23] Similarly, people don't doubt the power of the Internet — but that doesn't mean they want to be exposed to danger online. People need to trust that technologies are safe in order to use them.

Take flying in an airplane as a case of why people need to trust that the Internet, and networked systems generally, won't cause physical harm. No one likes long, tedious flights. On-board entertainment systems with the TV embedded in the seat in front of you are okay, but your selection is limited and neither the screen nor the sound quality is particularly good. Airlines know this and are gradually (very gradually) evolving in an effort to make flights more bearable for customers. The most recent innovation: inflight Wi-Fi.

The idea sounds great. No longer would we need to power down our devices during long flights across the country. We could remain connected to friends and colleague. Those who like to work on board wouldn't have to take a several-hours-long hiatus from email. Those who wished to zone out to Netflix on a long flight could do so. Inflight Wi-Fi seems to have a lot to recommend it.

Consumers clearly do want inflight Wi-Fi. A survey conducted in 2014 by Honeywell Aerospace shows that 66 percent of those surveyed factored Wi-Fi connectivity into their choice of a flight, and 22 percent were willing to pay an additional fee on board in order to get it. Most telling is that a full 17 percent of those polled reported switching from their "preferred" airline to an airline with inflight Wi-Fi.[24] As it stands, consumers are responding to the possibility of free inflight Wi-Fi with an emphatic "yes, please."

But safety concerns creep in here. Most people like the idea of inflight Wi-Fi because they view it as beneficial, but this view is predicated on their implicit trust that using on-board Wi-Fi is safe. However, some evidence suggests that on-board Wi-Fi is not safe at all. In early 2015, the Government Accountability Office in the United States issued a report pointing to how, as they put it, "[I]nternet connectivity in the cabin should be considered a direct link between the aircraft and the outside world, which includes potential malicious actors."[25] Hackers could target the airplane from laptops on board the plane, but also from computers ensconced safely on the ground. The dangers these hackers could unleash include disrupting the airplane's navigation systems, putting a virus on its computer control systems and even taking control of the airplane's flight controls.[26] All the potential problems conjure up images of planes crashing into runways or buildings or simply falling from the sky — in a word, disaster.

Right now, airline travellers are clamouring for on-board Wi-Fi because they recognize its value for inflight work and entertainment, but also, crucially, because they think it is safe. It will take just one hacked and hijacked plane to make people reconsider using the Internet on airplanes. If that airplane crashed, people would no longer trust having the Internet integrated into a sensitive system such as an aircraft. In short, the safety component of trust matters for how the Internet gets used and where.

Inclusive Governance

The final component of user trust is more political and less technical than many of the others. Certainly, people trust systems that are technically correct, reliable, safe, secure and private, but these design choices are also laden with political meaning. Sometimes, for some people, that meaning runs against the way that they would like things to be organized. The Internet will be more trustworthy, and thereby better able to bolster the digital social capital of the network, when the processes that lead to decisions affecting users are open and inclusive — that is, when users can, if they want, have a say in how things run.

Lawrence Lessig once famously wrote that, online, "[computer] code is law."[27] His meaning is that coding design choices come to affect who can use the network, how they can use it and under what conditions that use can unfold. Dictating how the network gets used in all of its manifestations is not, however, limited to code alone, as Lessig himself notes. Instead, regulatory policies, evolving codes of conduct and hard-nosed economics are paired with technical code to determine the use of the network. Each of these can be shaped, in turn, by various actors in the ecosystem — the Internet's stakeholders (private companies, technologists, civil society).

Inclusion is the final dimension of trust. This dimension really boils down to how much room exists for people of all stripes to participate in the governance of the Internet ecosystem. Albert Hirschman once pointed out that when faced with a declining organization, members of that system have three options: to *exit*, to give *voice*, or to maintain *loyalty*.[28] A networked governance system produces the same set of options for its users. People are most likely to exit when they perceive the organization as exclusive, without room for their input. They are most likely to be loyal when they perceive the organization as running well and inclusively. Giving voice — openly expressing one's views or protesting — is most likely when the system is open (as in the current Internet sytem) and in need of change. Exiting could break the system, fragmenting the network into a bunch of separate networks (we talk more about "the Fragnet" in chapter five). Loyalty is a peaceful option, but loyalty can mask troubles when the nature of technology and the user base of the system are shifting in radical ways (both conditions apply, again, in the current system). Giving voice is healthy when the network is changing because it means people want the system to adapt to better meet the evolving needs of users. Yet giving voice is only possible when the system is inclusive.

Already, we see the three options playing out on the world stage, as we will detail in various parts of this book. Take China as an example. In December 2015, it hosted the World Internet Conference in Wuzhen. China's view of how the Internet ought to be governed is different from that of Western countries. They have expelled most major Western Internet companies from the mainland, heavily censor the content that Chinese Internet users are able to access online and, as Chinese President Xi put it during his remarks at the conference, maintain that no one should ever "seek network hegemony, interfere in other nations' internal affairs and never engage, indulge or support cyber activities that harm other countries' national security."[29] In a pithy phrase, China is calling for a norm of "Internet sovereignty," meaning it wants how the Internet operates within a country's borders to ultimately be determined by that country's government.

China's move to advance Internet sovereignty as an alternative to the current governance model, where the voice of governments is thrown into the mix with private companies, technologists, civil society and ordinary Internet users, is long in the making. As early as 2012, during the World Conference on Information Technologies, China was pushing for more state-based governance arrangements for the Internet. China is not alone in this endeavour. Russia, India and many other countries supported (or at least did not oppose) the effort to shift some of the core governance arrangements of the Internet into a United Nations-based body.

These efforts are, at least in part, a response to both real and perceived Western — and particularly American — dominance of the Internet governance system. Many of the core non-governmental Internet governance actors are based in the United States. Most major Internet companies are American.

China's move is, for now at least, a combination of strongly uttered *voice*, with some inklings of *exit*. It also shows that voice options can fall along a continuum, from constructive to destructive. China oscillates between the two. Other nations, such as Iran and Russia, have already taken steps toward *exit*, by developing plans to hive off their portion of the Internet from the rest of the system in case of emergency. Again, their reason is the perceived dominance of the West, particularly of the United States. To put it plainly, there are many nations that simply don't trust the current system to operate in their interest and that feel as though the decisions affecting them are not inclusive of their points of view. The digital social capital of the network cannot withstand moves to break apart the network, as we discuss in later chapters.

How Public Policies, Trust and Digital Social Capital Interact

Because trust is a multi-dimensional concept, it can be eroded in a number of ways. In the aggregate, lost trust weakens the social bonds that hold the Internet together and that let it act as a social and technological platform for growth, innovation and free expression. The nebulous and multi-dimensional nature of trust means that policies aimed to achieve or enhance one form of trust can have the opposite effect on another crucial element of the social capital of the network. It is like one of Rube Goldberg's complex contraptions. Pulling one lever of policy can set off a chain reaction with unexpected consequences. Figure 2.2 illustrates this logic.

Let's take as an example the effects of NSA surveillance on trust and digital social capital. One cycle of the process unfolds over the course of six steps:

Figure 2.2: Trust, Social Capital and Fragmentation

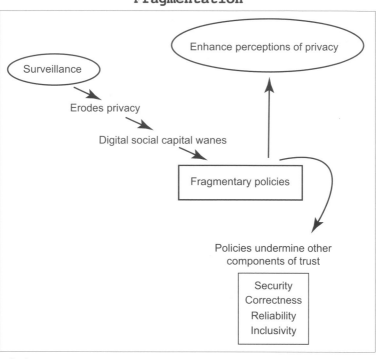

Source: Authors.

- In the first step, government surveillance programs impinge upon the privacy of Internet users.

- In the second step, a lack of privacy erodes the trustworthiness of the system.

- In the third step, reduced trust comes to undermine the digital social capital of the network, prompting a policy response from governments and companies.

- In the fourth step, in an effort to restore the trust that users place in the system and to bolster the social capital of the network, policy makers implement a series of fragmentary policies to provide more privacy to network users, such as ensuring that data is stored on secure local servers away from the prying eyes of the NSA.

- In the fifth step, these policies, if well conceived, bolster the amount of privacy in the system, raising the level of trust people place in the system.

- However, in the sixth step (one that would actually be concurrent with step five), those same policies designed to increase user privacy, such as data localization or data routing requirements, can, when taken to the extreme, also affect trust in a negative way through impacts on the security, reliability, correctness of content and inclusivity of the network. As these elements of trust erode, so do the trustworthiness and health of the overall system, cueing another drop in the Internet's stock of social capital and perhaps more calls for disruptive policies. (Of course, there is also the potential for virtuous cycles to form if policies are properly calibrated, as we'll see later.)

To recap, the Internet's ecosystem is complex and adaptive, its elements intricately connected and entwined. Myopic, single-lever policies simply won't work.

Conclusion

The analogy of a tropical rainforest can explain many of the core components of the Internet. The digital social capital of the Internet is comprised of the correctness, reliability, security, privacy, safety and inclusivity of the system and a decline in any of these elements of trust results in people adjusting how they use the Internet. These negative changes in behaviour can be as drastic as simply stopping using the network. Trust matters. If individuals, companies and states do not trust the Internet, the network won't be able to provide us with the full benefit of its potential. Our collective online future is jeopardized when trust in the network declines.

Three

A World Online —
Economics, Innovation and
the Internet of Things

I t is sometimes difficult to grasp just how important the Internet is to communications, innovation, productivity and global commerce in today's world. Without any exaggeration, the Internet has become vital to the world and its economic future and prosperity. The next major revolution of the Internet — the era of big data and the IoT (or the IoE)   is on our doorstep. Our dependence on the Internet for our livelihood and prosperity is only going to grow in coming years, assuming the Internet continues to function and operate the way it does now — mostly free, open and unfettered by technological or regulatory restrictions or barriers.

However, that assumption is a big if, because trust in the Internet is eroding. The public policy response to the erosion of trust, combined with more sinister efforts by criminals and authoritarian regimes to disrupt operations on the Internet or erect barriers and controls, might well lead to its fragmentation, if not its destruction — thereby creating what some now refer to as a "Fragnet" or "Splinternet," an ecosystem that has been ravaged or clear-cut, leaving vast tracts demolished and exposed, where little of direct value remains.

In this chapter, we show how the Internet is supporting myriad innovations the world over. We also point to how the system is generating literally trillions of dollars in economic growth per year. Lastly, we consider how the rapidly emerging IoT presents new ways in which trust can be eroded.

Taylor Wilson: Child Prodigy-Turned-Inventor

Some years ago, I* found myself seated next to a young man at the opening session of the Halifax Security Forum, an annual gathering of defence officials and other experts hosted by the Canadian government and sometimes referred to as the "Davos" of international security. Because it was still a few minutes before the session began, we struck up a lively conversation. He was amiable, outgoing and exceedingly bright. I was curious why someone so young — who was at most a third of the age of the other Forum participants — was there.

It did not take long to find out why. He was no ordinary teenager. He was Taylor Wilson, the American child prodigy-turned-inventor and science advocate, who had built a nuclear fusion reactor in his parents' garage in Reno, Nevada, at the age of 14 — an age when most of us are still struggling to master basic algebra, geometry and high school chemistry.

Though not the first person to achieve the remarkable feat of fusing atoms together, Taylor Wilson is likely the youngest to do so. In the years since this achievement, he has turned his mind to novel applications of his mini-nuclear reactor design to treat cancer, defeat nuclear terrorists and promote sustainable energy. Among his inventions is a portable reactor that could bombard shipping containers coming into North American ports with neutrons, thus detecting the presence of a hidden nuclear bomb or any other explosive device.

---

* As told by Fen Hampson.

When I asked Taylor what was the secret to his success, with characteristic modesty he stated that most of the ideas behind his inventions were already out there. However, he said that he was able to connect different scientific ideas and concepts in new ways to solve scientific and engineering problems that had confounded others. He also mentioned that the Internet had been an invaluable tool in his research. It had allowed him to read up on the scientific and engineering literature in different fields — a veritable treasure trove of information at his fingertips — while reaching out to other scientists and researchers along the way.

Taylor's use of the Internet demonstrates its obvious power to enable the investigations of a brilliant young scientist. But his experience is not all that different from our own. How often have we turned to the Internet and Googled our way around it to hunt down a piece of information, learn more about a subject or someone, find a recipe or a book, or simply track the latest breaking news story?

Although few of us are likely to put the Internet to the creative and imaginative uses of a Taylor Wilson, we can all identify with his story and recognize the importance of the World Wide Web to the process of learning, scientific inquiry and innovation. Indeed, the 2014 CIGI-Ipsos poll shows this recognition in stark relief. Across those surveyed in the sample from 23 countries and Hong Kong, 81 percent felt that the Internet was important for their economic livelihood, and 91 percent thought it was crucially important to their ability to access the latest scientific knowledge.

Palmer Luckey: How an Online Forum Turned His Virtual Reality Prototype into a $2 Billion Company

Like Taylor Wilson, Palmer Luckey is a home-schooled electronics prodigy who started tinkering in his parents' garage at the age of 11. At age 15, he became obsessed with online gaming and decided he needed a more immersive experience.[1] From 2009 to 2011, Luckey started playing around with virtual reality (VR) headsets and purchased dozens of outdated models at government liquidation auctions to see if he could modify them and make them better.[2] Meanwhile, Luckey fixed iPhones and other video game consoles to fund his VR and gaming hobby.[3]

Luckey was convinced he could make a better VR headset and set about doing so. During the process of building different prototypes, he frequently posted details about his experiments on the online 3D gaming forum, *Meant To Be Seen* (MTBS3D). It seems that his posts to this forum are what allowed his invention to take off.* He seemed genuinely surprised when people thought it could be commercialized.

In April 2012, Luckey posted to MTBS3D that he was planning to use a Kickstarter crowd-funding campaign to fuel the development of approximately 100 units of his most recent prototype, Oculus Rift.[4] In his post, he explained, "I won't make a penny of profit off this project, the goal is to pay for the cost of parts, manufacturing, shipping, and credit card/Kickstarter fees with about $10 left over for a celebratory pizza and beer."[5] Luckey said in an interview in 2013, "I wasn't actually aiming all that big," and went on to explain that he simply wanted to share his VR headsets with a "vanishingly small" community of VR enthusiasts.[6]

Meanwhile, John Carmack, one of the industry's most prominent video game programmers (of *Doom* fame), had stumbled across Luckey's posts on MTBS3D. Carmack offered to buy one of the prototypes; Luckey sent it to him for free.[7] Carmack then used Luckey's prototype to demo the video game *Doom 3* at the June 2012 Electronic Entertainment Expo (known as E3), the video game industry's annual trade fair. Interest in Luckey's prototype grew from a few dozen enthusiasts on MTBS3D to thousands of industry specialists.[8]

---

* If you have time, check out Luckey's posts at www.mtbs3d.com/phpBB, which convey his boyish enthusiasm and innocent passion for the project.

Luckey's Kickstarter campaign began in June 2012 and ran for a month. His goal was to raise an ambitious US$250,000 and "jumpstart a bigger VR community."[9] By the end, he had raised $2.4 million and joined with technology veterans Brendan Iribe, Nate Mitchell and Michael Antonov to found Oculus VR.[10]

Luckey and his partners sold Oculus to Facebook in March 2014 for approximately US$2 billion.[11] While Luckey initially envisioned a more immersive video game experience, the applications of his technology are endless. Mark Zuckerberg, the founder of Facebook, announced the acquisition with a Facebook post that observed, "Imagine enjoying a courtside seat at a game, studying in a classroom of students and teachers all over the world, or consulting with a doctor face-to-face — just by putting on goggles in your home."[12]

"I've seen five or six computer demos that made me think the world was about to change: Apple II, Netscape, Google, iPhone... then Oculus," said Chris Dixon, a general partner at one of the largest technology venture capital firms.[13] The technology has the possibility to revolutionize education, engineering, big data, emergency response, military simulations, mental therapy and environmental responsibility, among other categories. But these possibilities depend upon the Internet remaining an open vehicle for the transmission of data. If the Internet breaks into parts due to a loss of trust, then the potential of Oculus will be lost. At this point, we cannot begin to predict the sort of groundbreaking innovations that we would miss out on in the future if the Internet were to be torn asunder.

TaskRabbit: Online Marketplace for Odd Jobs

Leah Busque picked an interesting time to quit her job as an IBM software engineer and start her own company. She made the leap in 2008, mere months before the financial crisis hit, and created an online marketplace that connects workers with people needing help with small jobs or skilled tasks.[14]

Busque is the founder of TaskRabbit, a company *Wired Magazine* described as "eBay for real-world labor." The process starts when users post to the online marketplace, describe the task they need done and list the maximum amount they will pay. Workers, dubbed "taskers," bid on the task and indicate the minimum amount they will accept. Users then hire the tasker of their choice based on price and the individual's reviews from previous users. TaskRabbit ensures that all of its taskers are fully vetted, including a criminal background check.[15]

Some of the tasks are downright strange. One tasker was hired to dress up as a hot dog for a surprise birthday party.[16] Another acted as a human alarm clock and physically visited a woman's house to wake her up each morning.[17] Other jobs are more ordinary — buying groceries, putting together IKEA furniture and helping with moving and packing.

In 2014, Busque described the taskers as "micro-entrepreneurs" and explained that the company's "vision is huge: to revolutionize the way people work…It's about offering people more choice on how they work, what their schedules are like, how much they get paid, [and the choice of] being their own bosses."[18] Approximately 10 percent of the taskers use the marketplace as a full-time job and spend considerable energy on marketing and building up their reputations.[19]

More importantly, the service has provided many taskers with an opportunity to earn an income during the economic downturn. Michael Powell, a former medical scientist, became a tasker when he was between jobs, and said TaskRabbit helped by "giving unemployed people something to do and keeping them attuned to the work place. If you're unemployed for a long time, you lose that workplace edge."[20]

TaskRabbit is really an example of the positive side of society-wide change brought on by the Internet. The interconnection potential of the network has generated a situation where, more than at any other time in human history, the gap between having the ambition to do something and the ability to realize it is bridged. But, as we will see in later chapters, bridging the gap between ambition and execution also has its dark side.

A program like TaskRabbit relies upon the Internet and is a boon for both would-be employees and employers. Without an open, accessible and secure Internet, TaskRabbit could not function.

Captricity: Using the Internet to Help Low-Resource Organizations and Communities Digitize Their Information

Expanding access to the Internet is critical — but so is the ability to make the most of being online. Many places, once connected, still have huge obstacles to actually using the network well.

Captricity is the brainchild of Kuang Chen. The company uses a combination of machine learning and human brainpower (crowdsourcing) to cheaply digitize information on paper forms.[21] Chen's idea sprang from his Ph.D. thesis, for which he performed fieldwork on health in rural areas and explored the information systems available to related low-resource organizations.[22] Often, converting paper data into structured, searchable digital information can be very expensive, labour intensive and slow — a huge obstacle for these organizations.[23]

The Internet is central to how Chen devised Captricity, the solution to this problem. Chen's process starts when a small set of the information that needs to be digitized or structured is sent to an online crowdsourcing marketplace comprised of an enormous community of workers.[24] This marketplace, the Amazon Mechanical Turk, has claimed that it draws from an online, global community of 500,000 workers from more than 190 countries (as of 2011).[25] Privacy is ensured by breaking up the information into distinct fields, so that each person sees only a non-identifiable part of the information.[26] Then this verified sample of information is put into a machine-learning engine that predicts the value for the rest of the data set.[27]

Initial pilots focused on the government and charity organizations in Africa and India.[28] For example, Chen brought the service to Mali in 2011, where Captricity successfully processed a 37,000-page survey on government perceptions. It would have taken clerks eight months to do it by hand. Chen's combination of software and crowdsourcing reduced the process to a week.[29]

The success of his venture in an African village has now transferred to use by government agencies, health clinics, global health practitioners and major research organizations. According to the *MIT Technology Review*, Captricity funds its free or low-cost services in poor countries partly with revenue from paying customers such as Dell, Harvard Law School and the US government.[30]

The Internet is crucial to Captricity's ability to exist at all. The Internet enabled the advances in machine learning. The Internet facilitates the company's use of a global online community of workers (Amazon Mechanical Turk) and provides these workers with a flexible means of earning an income. And by using the Internet, Captricity helps underdeveloped countries move beyond hard copy records into a more streamlined, modern and globally connected way of optimizing business and using their data.

From Trickle to Raging Torrent

Despite these success stories, it remains clear that good ideas still die on the Internet vine because of a lack of financial support, poor marketing, or simply because there are not enough takers.

Euphoric claims about the Internet and its ability to transform lives and the way we do business have been around since its beginnings in the late 1980s and early 1990s. But so too have been its naysayers, especially after the dot-com bubble — which sent publicly traded Silicon Valley stocks into the stratosphere and created millionaires overnight — burst in 2002. As the Nasdaq market went into a tailspin, losing roughly 60 percent of its peak value, many of the same starry-eyed investors who had built a fortune lost their shirts.

However, the reason why many start-ups that looked to leverage the Internet failed in those early years has less to do with what they were trying to sell (or the unrealistic expectations of pumped-up investors), and is more about the fact that many North Americans were not online. The basic hardware and technical infrastructure were not available, so most people had not yet had a chance to discover the hidden fruits of this new Garden of Eden.

Remember those tiresome dial-up modems that many of us had to use to access the Internet — the slow tone-pulse of the telephone number we were dialling, followed by those grating squeaks and squeals of the modem handshake? And then — if we were lucky enough to get a proper connection on the first try — the waiting — sometimes endlessly — for a webpage to appear on our screens like a phantom emerging from the fog. Email was a novelty, but surfing the net with ease was still beyond the reach of most users.

At the beginning of this century, more than half of North America's population wasn't even connected to the Internet. Even fewer had high-speed broadband — a paltry 4.5 percent.[31] Web browsers and dedicated search engines such as Google were still in their infancy. When we went online, it was generally to get our email, but we could do little else. You could forget about downloading a movie, a song, an e-book or even a short video clip. The system simply couldn't handle the speeds that were required to make it practical.

As Robert D. Atkinson and his colleagues explain,

Because the underlying Internet infrastructure had not been sufficiently diffused or adopted, subscribers lacked technologies, especially the Internet connectivity speeds, to fully access the Web services and functionalities envisioned by the Internet pioneers. Consider the case of Boo.com, a poster child for "dot-bomb" failures. As a start-up showered with $100 million of venture capital in 1999, its goal was to sell designer clothes across 18 European countries. But since unmetered dial-up access was only then being introduced in Europe, few customers who looked at the Web site ever managed to make it as far as the checkout stage. Boo.com spent $188 million in just six months in its effort to create a global online fashion store before going bankrupt in May 2000. If slow Internet speeds and relatively few Internet users made it difficult for shopping sites to thrive, it made it virtually impossible for early Web players, such as Broadcast.com, who were trying to offer video and multimedia services, to succeed. As *Wired* elegantly wrote about Broadcast.com's failed business model, "Internet video before broadband was like pouring tar through a garden hose."[32]

Today, that once-plugged garden hose has become a gushing firehose. Wait times have been reduced, even though users who have access to fibre optic broadband through their regular telephone lines sometimes have to wait longer than they want to download a movie or their favourite song. But technological innovation will eventually take care of those waiting times too.

Suffice to say, in the short span of a decade, the Internet has become an integral part of our daily existence and an essential instrument of communication and business.[33]

We can now read magazines and books online and download music or our favourite movies onto our iPads or mobile phones. There are also literally hundreds of thousands of apps — many free — that allow us to talk to our friends, share pictures, monitor our heart rates and the number of steps we walk daily, prepare our taxes, order a taxi, book a hotel or flight, or whatever else happens to catch our fancy. And while all of this may be making life easier and perhaps even happier, it is proving a real boon to the economy and also making some people who have been lucky to come up with a great idea — like Facebook's Mark Zuckerberg — incredibly rich.

No small wonder that the majority of the world's people see the Internet as a key instrument for communication and personal expression and vital to their daily existence. In the 2016 CIGI-Ipsos survey, 83 percent of respondents believe that *affordable* access to the Internet should be a basic human right, and 81 percent said

Figure 3.1: Access to the Internet — An Important Right and Tool for Making a Living

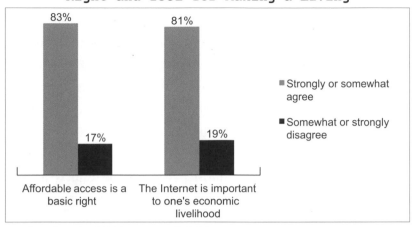

Source: Data from the CIGI-Ipsos 2016 Global Survey.

that the Internet is important to their own economic future and livelihood (Figure 3.1) — in fact, almost half (45 percent) said "very important."

The Hidden Wiring of Globalization

The Internet is one of the major drivers of globalization in the twenty-first century; it is putting producers and consumers in much closer reach and, in the process, upsetting traditional ways of doing business.

The global flow of data stands poised to cue off another wave of globalization. Digital flows are cutting costs, improving productivity and positively affecting countries' growth rates around the world. Without these cross-border flows, economic growth could falter.[34]

Data flows across the Internet are increasing exponentially. The McKinsey Global Institute predicts that cross-border Internet traffic, which has grown by a factor of 500 since the beginning of this century, could expand another eight-fold by 2025.[35] Several factors are coalescing to drive up data flows. More and more people purchase everything from books to songs in digital format, avoiding cumbersome physical copies.

These goods are made up of digital bits and bytes, and travel around the world at almost no cost. Many industries, from textiles to heavy manufacturing, are likely to be radically transformed in the next few years by new technologies such as three-dimensional (3D) printing, which takes blueprints in the form of data and prints the final product onsite. Moreover, as goods and services become more deeply integrated into the Internet-based economy, corruption and loss are minimized as real-time data is generated by Global Positioning System (GPS) and radio frequency identification technologies that allow merchants to carefully track their goods in transit.[36] Already, the result of a greater reliance upon the Internet as a platform for commerce has been the veritable explosion of cross-border data flows.

Undergirding these increased data flows is a large and growing information and communications technology (ICT) sector. According to the Organisation for Economic Co-operation and Development (OECD), some 14 million people are employed in ICT in the 34 countries of the OECD block. This figure amounts to fully three percent of all jobs across the organization's membership.[37]

Entrepreneurs have seized on the myriad possibilities afforded by the Internet to create digital platforms that bridge the manufacturing-services divide, as in the case of 3D printing or crowd-sourced innovations that bring individuals together through a common platform to solve design problems such as ironing out the bugs in a piece of software, raising money for a charitable cause (for example, helping the victims of a major humanitarian disaster), providing a loan to people in other countries who want to start a new business or simply marketing a great idea through a new app.

While enabling to many, these possibilities are also challenging many traditional businesses, which is why some now refer to the Internet as a "disruptive enabling technology."[38]

As Nathan Blecharczyk, the founder of Airbnb — a website that allows individuals across the globe to rent their homes to each other — explained to a captive audience at the 2014 World Economic Forum in Tianjin, the Internet has eliminated the need for the middleman by putting consumers and service providers in direct contact with each other. That is the story of Airbnb, which is giving the hotel business a run for its money. It is also the story of Uber, the online taxi service that allows private individuals to rent their own car-and-driver services on a mobile app. Uber has been strongly opposed by established taxi service companies, which are highly regulated in most cities and are rapidly losing customers and market share to Uber.

Another economically disruptive enabling innovation, and one already having a profound impact on business, is the crypto-currency bitcoin. Bitcoin and other potential digital currencies use something called a blockchain ledger to allow online transactions. Think of the blockchain as a kind of online ledger or virtual record where every transaction that occurs using a bitcoin is recorded, decoded and validated by a whole series of computers forming part of a global network. One day, physical paper and metal money might be completely replaced by digital bits and bytes.

The great advantage of digital currencies such as bitcoin is that they reduce transaction costs. There is no intermediary, such as a bank, collecting processing fees, and any transaction can be processed instantaneously, easily and safely. For smaller companies, the arrival of digital currencies, which are still in their infancy, will allow them to enter new markets and potentially operate on a global scale.

According to a major study from the Chartered Accountants of Australia & New Zealand and PricewaterhouseCoopers, bitcoin, which was created in 2008, has quickly gained global acceptance.[39] This study says that at "the start of February 2015 the Bitcoin market capitalisation exceeded $US3 billion and will continue to grow as more Bitcoins are created digitally." Furthermore, "tens of thousands of retailers have started using Bitcoin in order to save money on payment and processing fees." Consequently, "nearly $US300 million has been invested in Bitcoin-related businesses such as clearing houses and processing businesses."[40]

For example, people have purchased everything from "sandwiches to fine art" to Tesla Model S cars with the digital currency.[41] In Canada, British Columbia's Simon Fraser University accepts bitcoins in its campus bookstore, making it easier for students and parents to shop for course material.[42]

However, digital currencies also have their downside, as we will explain in more detail in chapter six. Online anonymity allows bitcoins to be used for money laundering and other criminal purposes. Banks and public regulators are struggling with the bitcoin's broader implications for financial and banking services. They currently treat these "currencies" as commodities or digital assets, but not as a form of legal tender. Some jurisdictions have banned their use outright. But the digital currency revolution, which is only just underway, will be hard to stop because of the fraction of the time and cost it takes to transfer money from one jurisdiction to another. Think of it. No bank fees. No extra charges that come from a regular wire transfer. The Australian study noted above also highlights that most accountants (more than two-thirds of those surveyed) believe that digital currencies will be widely used in 10 years' time.

Measuring the Internet's Economic Impact

Placing an actual dollar figure on the contribution of the Internet to the global economy is exceedingly difficult. As megabytes, gigabytes and terabytes of data fly across cyberspace, it's a bit like the magician's handkerchief trick — now you see it, now you don't. That hasn't stopped economists and others from trying to measure the direct economic contribution of the Internet to global growth. However, it is important to draw a clear distinction between those aspects of the global virtual storefront — the goods and services purchased or traded online, which are visible and measurable — and the hidden rivers of the global economy — the communication flows and surging torrents of data, which support everything we do online, but cannot easily be quantified or priced.

On June 23, 2014, Fadi Chehadi, the CEO of ICANN — the Internet Corporation for Assigned Names and Numbers, the organization that manages and regulates the handing out of top-level domain names on the Internet (such as .com, .org, .ca) — stepped onto the stage at the ICANN 50 meeting in London, England, to discuss, among other things, the importance of the Internet to the world's economic future. "Think of it," he told his audience, a large gathering of technical experts and representatives of civil society, business and government,"$4.2 *trillion* — that will be the contribution of the Internet to the G20 economies alone in 2016."[43]

The figure comes from a Boston Consulting Group study on the Internet economy.* The study goes on to paint a stunning portrait of the Internet's contribution to national and economic growth. In the United Kingdom, the Internet-based economy added more to the nation's GDP in 2010 than construction and education combined. The Internet economy in the United States is greater than the government's spending as a share of GDP. The Internet economy is set to grow at around eight percent per year in G20 countries and will expand potentially at a rate of 18 percent in developing nations.[45]

The study also points out that many consumers now use the Internet to research products online that they subsequently go to purchase in stores directly. This too is proving a boon to economic growth. In 2010, the value of such off-line purchases in G20 countries was US$1.3 trillion or 7.8 percent of total consumer expenditures.[46]

---

* The BCG study reports that the "Internet economy will reach $4.2 trillion in the G-20 economies. If it were a national economy, the Internet economy would rank in the world's top five, behind only the U.S., China, Japan, and India, and ahead of Germany."[44] Like all estimates, the number is imprecise and not an accurate measure of the Internet's contribution to global growth, because it appears to be referring only to the volume of goods and services traded online.

McKinsey has also studied the affect of the net on the economic performance of specific economies. As Table 3.1 highlights, the Internet has had a positive effect on 22 countries' overall GDP, ranging from a high of 6.3 percent in Sweden to a low of 0.1 percent

Table 3.1: The Internet Landscape and Its Economic Effects

	Internet Users (in Millions)	Internet Penetration (%)	Online Retail Share of Total Retail (%)	Internet Contribution to GDP (% of GDP)	Internet Contribution to GDP Growth (as % of GDP Growth)
Argentina	26	64	1.1	2.2	2.7
Brazil	79	41	3.1	1.4	2.4
Canada	28	81	0.9	2.7	10.2
China	486	36	1.1	2.6	3.4
France	50	78	3.8	3.2	17.6
Germany	67	82	3.8	3.2	24.3
Hungary	7	68	1.1	3.9	11.4
India	98	8	0.3	3.2	5.2
Italy	33	54	0.9	1.7	12.2
Japan	101	79	3.2	4.0	–
Malaysia	16	55	4.4	4.1	2.3
Mexico	39	34	0.5	1.0	2.2
Morocco	16	49	0.5	0.9	1.2
Nigeria	52	33	0.1	0.5	0.9
Russia	61	43	2.1	0.8	0.9
South Korea	40	83	12.3	4.6	16.0
Sweden	8	90	3.8	6.3	32.9
Taiwan	16	72	3.0	5.4	12.7
Turkey	36	49	0.8	0.9	1.5
United Kingdom	53	85	7.7	5.4	22.7
United States	250	81	4.0	3.8	14.9
Vietnam	27	31	–	0.9	1.6

Source: Adapted with permission from Exhibit E3, Chandra Gnanasambandam et al., 2012, *Online and upcoming: The Internet's impact on India*, McKinsey & Company, 7.

in Nigeria. It also shows that the Internet is becoming a driver of growth itself, with the network adding a high of 32.9 perecnt to the GDP growth rate in Sweden and a minimum of 0.9 percent in both Nigeria and Russia.

The Internet is also changing systems of production and distribution, notably expanding the global reach of SMEs, which, in many countries, are the key drivers of economic growth and contributors to job creation. As noted in a 2013 study by the International Labor Organization, SMEs account for "two thirds of all formal jobs in developing countries and up to 80 percent in low income countries."[47]

With the Internet, online SMEs can now market their goods and services to producers and consumers anywhere with relative ease and, importantly, at low marginal cost — an advantage previously available only to large multinational corporations. SMEs can tailor their goods and services to specific local markets via the Internet. Social media and other Internet-based customer interactions, such as online surveys, can be used to identify — as well as shape — the needs of consumers. SMEs with a web-based presence can also recruit employees and manage their finances more easily.

Again, the figures are astonishing. SMEs — the backbone of most economies — grew far more quickly if they employed web technologies. In sectors ranging from commerce to services and manufacturing, high users of web technologies grew 2.1 times faster than those companies that did not rely upon the Internet as a platform

Table 3.2: SMEs, Web-based Technologies, Growth and Revenue

Web-intensity	Annual Growth over Three-year Period (%)	Revenues Due to Exports (% of Total)
Low (Web index <20%)	6.2	2.5
Medium (Web index 20–40%)	7.4	2.7
High (Web index >40%)	13.0	5.3

Source: Adapted with permission from Exhibit 6, Jacques Bughin and James Manyika, 2012, *Internet Matters: Essays in Digital Transformation,* McKinsey & Company, 15.

for business. They also had around 2.1 times as much revenue due to exports, underscoring the extremely positive role that the Internet can play in allowing small firms to reach across borders and, in effect, become global players like large transnational corporations.

By dramatically reducing the marginal costs of production and distribution, the Internet has thus transformed the global economy in three crucial ways: "through the creation of purely digital goods and services that are either transformations of physical flows or entirely new products, through 'digital wrappers' that enhance the value of physical flows, and through digital platforms that facilitate cross-border production and exchange."[48]

The OECD also estimates that the value of the ICT sector as a whole accounts for an average of 5.5 percent of the value added to a country's products. Spread across the 34 OECD countries, that percentage amounts to an economic boon of US$2.4 trillion in 2013 alone.[49] Some nations gain a lot more than the average (for example, Korea, at 10.7 percent), while others gain less (for instance, Ireland and Mexico). Global exports of ICT-manufactured goods have also been on the rise, increasing by six percent per year between 2001 and 2013. They now measure over US$1.6 trillion.[50] There is money to be had in allowing the ICT sector to boost the value added to an economy's products.

Big Data and the Internet of Things

The Internet revolution is now entering a new phase: the era of big data and the IoT — or the IoE, as it is sometimes called — where the ordinary physical objects of daily life (your car, your clothes, your refrigerator, your furnace and air conditioner, and even your toothbrush) are connected to the Internet.

Why is it called the IoT or IoE? The reason is simple. It is because in the world today there are more physical objects than people hooked up to the Internet. According to experts at Cisco Systems, the IoT was launched in 2010 when the "[e]xplosive growth of smart phones and tablet PCs [personal computers] brought the number of devices connected to the Internet to 12.5 billion…, while the world's human population increased to 6.8 billion, making the number of connected devices per person more than 1 (1.84 to be exact) for the first time in history."[51] Cisco estimates that there might have been as many as 15 billion devices connected to the Internet in 2015 and could potentially grow to 50 billion by 2020.[52] These relatively conservative estimates do not take into account innovations in new technology or the ways such innovations might be used.

In the IoT, even cows will be connected to the Internet via earpiece sensors that monitor their eating habits, health and daily movements. Some day, a day that is coming very soon, tiny, remotely controlled micro-sensors will be available to place inside human bodies where they will stay forever, monitoring a person's health 24/7, with the capability to warn of an impending heart attack or other major illness. The potential uses of the connectivity that comes from integrated "networks of networks" of the IoT are vast, but they extend well beyond the particular benefits they offer to individuals.

The public sector, for example, stands to be a major beneficiary of the IoT in terms of the vastly more efficient delivery of services and government operations. One study suggests that the IoT may eventually "generate $4.6 trillion in Value at Stake for the public sector over the next decade (compared with $14.4 trillion for the private sector over the same period)."[53] These improvements will be spawned by the IoT's contribution to the more efficient management of resources and personnel, the development of new business and revenue models, and of agency-specific innovations as the IoT is adapted to meet the data-gathering requirements of different government departments.

The IoT also has significant potential for cities and the managing of urban spaces, where the majority of the world's populations now live. The evolution of so-called "smart cities," which link people, processes and data, will be greatly enhanced by the IoT. And it is already beginning to happen. Chicago has introduced a number of Smart+Connected

Community initiatives, which are helping to introduce "smarter working practices, incubating technology innovation, and promoting multi-stakeholder collaboration to investigate and enhance the social life of the city."[54]

"City 24/7" is a joint public-private partnership initiative in New York, using smart screens that incorporate touch, voice and audio technology. Anyone at a street corner or a subway station can access information in real time and learn more about the services that are available within two square city blocks. The same information can be retrieved via a smart screen app on a smart phone, tablet, or laptop computer.[55]

Another study, for the McKinsey Global Institute, aimed to assess, in the aggregate, the economic potential of the IoT. Their top-line finding is that the IoT could add as much as US$11.1 trillion to the world economy by 2025[56] (Figure 3.2). The precise figure could be more, depending on the adoption of new technologies and the ability of creative people to innovate on top of the new interconnected platforms.

Of course, the economic potential of the IoT hinges on people trusting the IoT enough to use it in a widespread way in their homes, workplaces and cities (as we point out in chapter eight). But the IoT also has a potential downside in terms of personal privacy and security that is now coming to be widely understood. How you live, eat and breathe can be watched, monitored and exploited by others through the smart devices you use in your car or at your bedside. And it is not just your cellphone, already a treasure-trove of information about your habits and behaviour, that will broadcast your daily activities, thoughts, fears and personal habits, but everything else you own, including what you use and wear, because they will be connected to the Internet.

A Frictionless Universe

With ongoing technological change, one of the most profound consequences will be the continual reduction of the costs of doing business, what might be called the "third revolution" brought on by

Figure 3.2: Economic Potential of the IoT

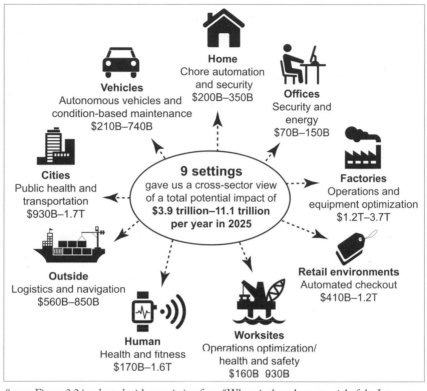

Home
Chore automation
and security
$200B–350B

Vehicles
Autonomous vehicles and
condition-based maintenance
$210B–740B

Offices
Security and
energy
$70B–150B

Cities
Public health and
transportation
$930B–1.7T

9 settings
gave us a cross-sector view
of a total potential impact of
**$3.9 trillion–11.1 trillion
per year in 2025**

Factories
Operations and
equipment optimization
$1.2T–3.7T

Outside
Logistics and navigation
$560B–850B

Retail environments
Automated checkout
$410B–1.2T

Human
Health and fitness
$170B–1.6T

Worksites
Operations optimization/
health and safety
$160B 930B

Source: Figure 3.2 is adapted with permission from "Where is the value potential of the Internet of Things?" in James Manyika, Michael Chui, Peter Bisson, Jonathan Woetzel, Richard Dobbs, Jacques Bughin and Dan Aharon, 2015, *The Internet of Things: Mapping the Value Beyond the Hype,* June, McKinsey & Company, iii, www.mckinsey.com/business-functions/business-technology/our-insights/the-internet-of-things-the-value-of-digitizing-the-physical-world.

Internet, after the IoT. A staple of trade and commerce has always been that the cost of transacting in goods and services is real. Think about trying to move oil from the Middle East to Europe via a massive supertanker. The journey itself costs money. You need to pay for the crew, fuel and various tariffs or duties along the way. These transactions all add up and contribute to the not-so-hidden costs of conducting business that will, one hopes, return a profit at the end of the day.

One benefit of the Internet — and some of its new digital technologies — is the driving of transaction costs down to near zero. Before the widespread availability of email, for example, long-distance communications were conducted by telephone or snail mail, which always cost the user something. Before the Internet, the telegram was the fastest and cheapest means of written communication, but it too had user fees. Before that, people had to use courier pigeons. With each technological advancement, the costs of communications fell. And now, of course, you can download Skype or Facetime on your computer and chat to friends and colleagues on the other side of the planet without paying a cent.

As we move ahead with the digital revolution, transaction costs — and not just for long-distance communication — will fall further as nearly costless bits and bytes are used in the place of real-world objects, especially in trade and commerce. As discussed, bitcoins are one example of an innovation that eliminates the need for banking intermediaries and lowers the cost of doing business across different currency jurisdictions. Although the application of blockchain technology has been largely focused on bitcoin, its potential uses are much wider and could include the delivery of financial services, government services such as health care and education, and the overall operation of institutions in both the private and public sector where data storage and transfer require greatly enhanced security.[57]

3D printing technology is another example of a "frictionless" innovation that will also change the world. It promises to dramatically reduce the transaction costs of production in the textile, manufacturing and medical industries. The technology of 3D printing basically involves sending a blueprint, as bits and bytes of course, from one computer to a printer located somewhere else in the world. The printer then prints, through a series of microscopic additions of the requisite material, a 3D version of the object in question. Already, some remarkable things have been printed by this technology. People have printed working guns, guitars, flutes, shoes and bikinis. Others have printed 3D replicas of children's two-dimensional drawings and life-like models of a fetus from an ultrasound image.[58] In some of the more extreme instances, people have even printed six-storey-tall office buildings, a working prosthetic arm and a functioning lawn mower.[59]

The long-term implications of Internet-enabled technologies like this is that transaction costs will fall to nearly zero. Greater wealth will be generated because those involved in production and consumption will be brought closer together, while intermediaries, such as the postal service, are eliminated. A frictionless universe will change the world — that is, it will if trust in the system can be maintained and the Internet works as it should.

Both Winners and Losers

As in every story of economic transition, there are winners and losers in the transition to the Internet. Centuries ago, the flying shuttle was invented to quickly allow a single weaver to process more cloth. The economic and social ramifications of this simple change in technology were far-reaching. Consumers benefited, because they now had access to less expensive clothes. Yet the old producers in the cottages lost out. Old-fashioned manual weaving could no longer provide people with a living. Inequality, population movement into cities, and social and economic turmoil followed. The same story fits with the later invention of the cotton gin, which was able to card and bat cotton bolls at a much quicker pace than any human could achieve. Adopters of the new technology and consumers won, but producers using the old ways who failed to adapt lost a lot.

This process embodies what the "prophet of capitalism" Joseph Schumpeter called "creative destruction," which is a "process of industrial mutation that incessantly revolutionizes the economic structure from within, incessantly destroying the old one, incessantly creating a new one."[60] The Internet, with its enormous potential for both consumers and producers, is having a similarly creative, yet destructive, effect.

In early 2016, the World Bank released its annual World Development Report. This edition was entitled *Digital Dividends*. The report is pragmatic: rather than simply trumpeting the many benefits of the network, it also shows that there are always losers to any major technological change. As the report puts it, growth, efficiency gains and greater interconnection are certainly occurring with the spreading reach of the Internet, and these developments are generating economic growth. However, the "digital dividends" that the network produces are not evenly spread: "Firms are more connected than ever before, but global productivity growth has slowed. Digital technologies are changing the world of work, but labor markets have become more polarized and inequality is rising — particularly in the wealthier countries, but increasingly in developing countries. And while the number of democracies is growing, the share of free and fair elections is falling. These trends persist, not because of digital technologies, but in spite of them."[61]

How the digital dividends produced by the Internet are allocated depends upon each particular country's adaptability. Nations that have an educated populace, high worker and capital mobility and a safety net for their citizens are more likely to capture the benefits and ameliorate the costs of the economic transition brought on by the Internet. Nations that fail in these basic categories will be generally unable to capture the economic potential of the Internet and are also likely to suffer more from the social and economic disruptions that the Internet brings.

Take a simple example. Imagine a world where everyone who drives for a living loses their jobs in the span of a few years. According to Statistics Canada, there were some 18,009,600 people employed in Canada across all industries and sectors of the economy. Of this total, 909,600 people — nearly a million — were employed in the transportation and warehousing industry.[62] Expressed in percentage terms, driving and warehousing makes up around 0.05 percent of the entire Canadian labour force. With current trends toward automation and the integration of the Internet into the analogue economy, all of these jobs could easily disappear in a few years.

In such a scenario, those who drive for a living will be especially vulnerable. Driverless cars are already being tested and on the horizon. Very soon, it is likely that driving down a major highway you could look over to see a car cruising down the road beside you with no one in the driver's seat. The passenger might be perched in the back seat enjoying a cup of coffee while reading the newspaper on a tablet. Just as easily, the passenger could be sleeping or playing Angry Birds on her mobile device. It is even possible that the car would not have any passengers, as it would simply be *en route* to pick someone up.

America is really the heart of the driverless car industry. Companies like Google have made great strides in the development of technology to allow vehicles to pilot themselves. So far, they have a pretty good record. In October 2015, Google reported that its driverless car had been in 11 accidents over the course of its six years of operation. In each case, those at fault were other error-prone human drivers. Paradoxically, Google attributed even these small accidents to the interaction of the choices made by risk-averse computer-driven cars and the aggressive, corner-cutting and rule-breaking behaviour of human drivers.[63] Their response is to make their cars drive more like humans, which oddly means the program will now break some rules by driving more aggressively.

Still, once all of the bugs are worked out, the driverless car has great potential. The major car manufacturers the world over are all developing their own version of the driverless car. And now the US government is planning on throwing money behind the technology. In January 2016, for example, the Obama administration tabled a nearly US$4-billion plan to boost the production and adoption of driverless cars, citing the potentially salutary effect of driverless cars on carbon emission production.[64] With industry and government aligned, adoption of the driverless car could happen very quickly.

Returning to the Canadian example, we can speculate about what might happen if driverless cars, taxi cabs, limos, buses and trucks went mainstream. Long-haul trucking across the country (especially one the size of Canada) is extremely trying on the human body. For a computer, it is not. The computer would never need to stop; humans would not be able to compete. The same logic applies in other industries, such as taxi and bus transportation. Driverless cars are just more efficient and probably more pleasant for the rider as well. Switching from human to computer drivers can eliminate human error and reduce costs. Like the weavers in the old cottage industries, those who rely on driving for their livelihood will soon lose their work. Insurance companies might also lose, as the number of traffic accidents goes down, forcing insurers to dramatically lower premiums, at least for those who ride in driverless cars. Interestingly, those who wish to retain their "right to drive" might actually be forced to pay higher premiums because they would be deliberately incurring more risk and uncertainty (factors insurance companies price highly) into the process. This is Schumpeter's creative destruction in action. As technology changes, there are both gains and losses.

For Canada, a driverless transition could mean that upwards of 0.05 percent of the Canadian workforce, some one million people, would suddenly find themselves unemployed (minus the amount engaged in warehousing, of course, which could also be automated in the near future). At the same time, the cost for the goods and services provided by drivers would go down, so consumers would benefit. Owners of transportation companies would also earn higher margins and reap larger profits.

There will always be winners and losers in all the stories of economic transformations being generated by the Internet and its ever-growing integration with the analogue economy. Growth and further innovation will certainly result (and, as a whole, we may all be better off), but we should also recognize that the distribution of gains and losses will not be evenly spread across society.

Conclusion

For numerous reasons, the Internet is already foundational to our daily lives. More than that, the Internet is potentially going to become even more important in the future. Certainly, the Internet promises still more innovation, economic development, efficiency gains and new ways of expressing ourselves individually and culturally.

This bright future hinges, however, on us trusting the network enough to allow it to operate openly and freely. This trust is not guaranteed. As the remaining chapters of this book explore, there are many current and potential sources of mistrust that are causing people to change their behaviour in ways that risk eroding the great potential of the Internet as a lush and bountiful ecosystem.

Four

Big Brother in the Internet Age

I n the wake of Edward Snowden's disclosures of NSA surveillance, many have said that the Internet has enabled a world eerily similar to George Orwell's dystopian vision of the future as depicted in his famous book *Nineteen Eighty-Four*. On the novel's opening page, Orwell sets the scene. "On each landing, opposite the lift shaft, the poster with the enormous face gazed from the wall," he writes. "It was one of those pictures which are so contrived that the eyes follow you about when you move. BIG BROTHER IS WATCHING YOU, the caption beneath ran."[1]

Imagined in the late 1940s, Big Brother in Orwell's world is very last century. In at least one important respect, Orwell's dystopia is a mere shadow of the reality of the new millennium. A poster *broadcasting* that someone is watching you? Clumsy and blatant! If only the real big brother watching today were that obvious. Today, governments — our own and others — and private corporations spy on us using sophisticated and subtle methods and surreptitiously shape and control our access to information. Those watching us don't usually broadcast their activities — at least not intentionally — but operate behind a curtain of secrecy. Some governments and companies are more restrained than others, but one lesson that we all must come to grips with is that everyone has turned to the Internet as a tool to achieve wider social and political objecives.[2]

This chapter looks at people's reactions to the big brothers of the Internet age, both governments and companies. We'll consider how their various actions have severely undermined people's trust in the Internet ecosystem, and how they cause or risk real damage to the rich potential of the technology.

Privacy and Freedom of Expression Still Matter

In an era of countless Tweets, Facebook posts, Instagram photos and Snapchats, it is fair to wonder if privacy really is something people still care about. Those in charge of the major Internet companies say that Internet users no longer care about online privacy, while they simultaneously work hard to protect their *own* personal privacy. (However, a few companies, such as Google and Apple, are taking steps to provide more built-in privacy for users of mobile devices and messaging services, and even going to bat against law enforcement in an effort to keep people's data private — for example, as Apple did in the case involving a warranted FBI request to unlock an iPhone belonging to one of the San Bernardino terrorists.)

An example of this took place in late 2009, when Facebook changed its privacy settings to make more information more public by default. Soon after that, in early 2010, Facebook's CEO and founder, Mark Zuckerberg, argued that privacy is no longer a valued social norm. As Zuckerberg put it, "People have really gotten comfortable not only sharing more information and different kinds, but more openly and with more people."[3] Yet, at the same time, Zuckerberg bought four houses surrounding his mansion in Palo Alto for some US$30 million, to give his personal life a physical buffer, suggesting that privacy *does* still matter — at least to him.[4]

In December of 2009, Google CEO Eric Schmidt showed a similar disregard for privacy. He responded to a CNBC interview question about whether people should trust Google to maintain their privacy with the flippant remark that "if you have something that you don't want anyone to know, maybe you shouldn't be doing it in the first place."[5] Yet, earlier in 2005, Google blacklisted reporters writing for a popular technology news blog called CNET after they published a story containing detailed information on Eric Schmidt's neighbourhood, his salary, his political donations and some of his hobbies. The kicker is that all the information on Schmidt was found through normal Google searches. The story was meant to illustrate that companies like Google, which amasses so much personal information, could easily violate people's privacy.[6]

At the same time, people cannot seem to get enough of sharing their private information online. Could it be that the heads of the major Internet companies got it right — people really *don't* care? Looking at the results of first the 2014 and then the 2016 CIGI-Ipsos surveys provides an answer. The responses leave no doubt that people *do* still care a great deal about online privacy.

As a first cut, consider that in the 2014 survey a solid majority of people responding — 64 percent — said they were more concerned about online privacy than they had been the previous year. Another 30 percent were about as concerned as before, leaving only six percent less concerned as time went by. In the CIGI-Ipsos 2016 survey, the majority of people — 57 percent — were again more concerned about privacy than they had been earlier. Only 15 percent of people were less concerned about privacy. These numbers do not support the idea that privacy matters less and less to people.

Internet users' privacy concerns span a range of areas, with people seeing dangers from companies, hackers and governments. And, contrary to what Eric Schmidt or Mark Zuckerberg might like us to think, 74 percent of the people surveyed by CIGI-Ipsos in 2014 had serious concerns about the amount of information private companies collect and how they are using it. And 77 percent of the respondents also cared strongly about the possibility of hackers stealing their

Figure 4.1: Privacy — People Still Care

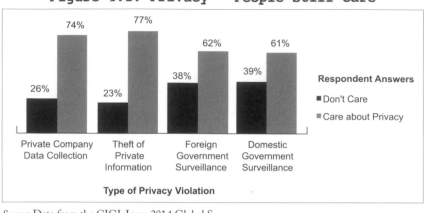

Respondent Answers
■ Don't Care
■ Care about Privacy

Type of Privacy Violation

Source: Data from the CIGI-Ipsos 2014 Global Survey.

personal information. Further, over 60 percent of people said that they were worried about online surveillance, whether conducted by their own government or other countries. No other conclusion can be drawn from these numbers: people care deeply about online privacy (Figure 4.1).

In the same vein, people care about their ability to access information via the Internet. In any discussion of censorship, it is important to first recognize that all societies have a vested interest in controlling access to information. Every society engages in censorship to some degree, often allocating the role of censor to governments, companies or social groups such as churches or clubs. For example, most, if not all, countries restrict child abuse images. Other countries restrict more idiosyncratic things — for instance, Thailand restricts any material that mocks their king. Some countries, such as China, restrict access to all sorts of political or religious content. Some countries practise censorship in a targeted way, restricting certain groups or themes. For example, South Korea restricts favourable references to North Korea. Other countries — Pakistan being a good example — apply censorship with broader strokes, restricting a range of content.

All of this adds up to the idea that the censorship practices of states and companies fall along two continua, as shown in Figure 4.2.

One axis plots the nature of the censorship — whether it is driven by politics or not. The other continuum plots the degree of censorship — is it targeted or applied only under certain conditions only, or a mass approach to the conduct of online life? On the one hand, liberal democracies, such as Canada, the United States and the United Kingdom, tend to fall in the top-left quadrant, where few political things are censored and where the censorship that does occur is targeted. On the other hand, authoritarian regimes, such as China, fall in the bottom-right quadrant, where much more political material is censored and in a mass fashion.

It's a given that all societies some of the time restrict what is said online. But to jump from that fact to the notion that people are unconcerned about online censorship is a stretch. Far from it. Again, the CIGI-Ipsos 2014 survey provides some useful numbers

Figure 4.2: The Continua of Online Censorship

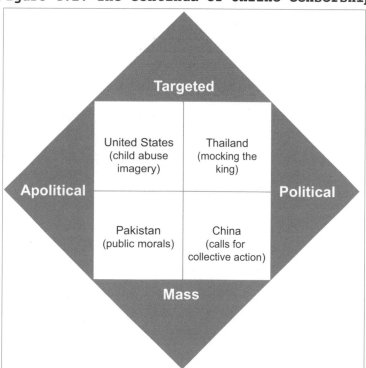

Source: Authors.

Figure 4.3: The Internet as a Tool of Expression and Communication

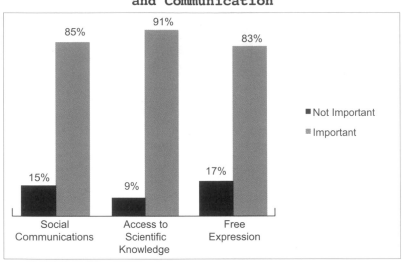

Source: Data from the CIGI-Ipsos 2014 Global Survey.

to pinpoint exactly how *much* people care (Figure 4.3). Generally speaking, people clearly recognize that the Internet is a necessary tool in the expression of political points of view, a crucial means of obtaining information and increasingly important for social communications.

Yet, even as people think that an open Internet is an important tool in the process of free expression, invaluable to the sharing of information and immensely useful as an instrument of social communication, they are also deeply troubled by state censorship of the Internet. As Figure 4.4 shows, roughly two-thirds of people are concerned with the prospect of online censorship — or the restriction of the potential of an open Internet.

But, as you might expect, the level of concern that people express varies considerably, depending on where they live. Nonetheless, the results can be surprising. For example, one might expect that the more authoritarian states would top the list of the countries most concerned with censorship — after all, censorship and autocratic rule tend to go hand in hand. For instance, China's so-called "Great Firewall"

Figure 4.4: General Concern over Censorship

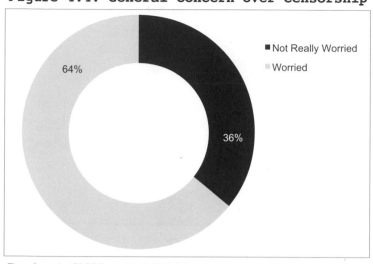

Source: Data from the CIGI-Ipsos 2014 Global Survey.

routinely censors online content. And Egypt, during the Arab Spring, actually pulled the country's plug on the Internet to try to stop the spread of dissent.[7] Pakistan banned YouTube in 2008, 2010 and again in 2012, and places stringent restrictions on Facebook content.[8] Yet these countries' citizens actually express levels of concern over online censorship that are comparable to those expressed by citizens in liberal democracies such as Canada, Australia, the United States and the United Kingdom.

Why? We asked ourselves this when we first received the 2014 poll results. Chinese citizens may be reluctant to express direct criticism of their government on the issue of censorship, although it is clear that many have found ways to express themselves online and work around government censors.

When the countries and territories from the 2014 survey are ordered by their level of political freedom — from autocracies (zero) to liberal democracies (20) — using a common measure of democracy in the social sciences called the Polity IV index, an inverted-U shaped relationship appears (Figure 4.5). The responses show that concern over censorship is highest in mixed regimes such as Mexico, South

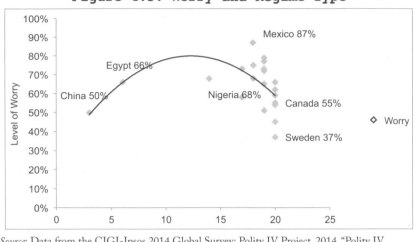

Figure 4.5: Worry and Regime Type

Source: Data from the CIGI-Ipsos 2014 Global Survey; Polity IV Project, 2014, "Polity IV Individual Country Regime Trends, 1946–2013," www.systemicpeace.org/polity/polity4.htm.

Korea, Turkey and Tunisia that are neither wholly free (like the United States) nor highly repressive (like China).

When you think about it, this seemingly peculiar result makes sense in that fear and ignorance are the factors that drive the level of expressed concern over online censorship. The partially or nearly free countries in the middle of the range (such as Mexico and India) create an environment with three characteristics: first, their governments are not completely restrained by the protection of human rights and the rule of law, which potentially leads to abuses; second, their people are free enough to express their real opinions; and third, information is plentiful enough that people know what their government is doing. Middling repression appears to create a perfect environment for incubating a high level of concern about online censorship.

In the end, as with privacy, people across the world do care about free expression and the occurrence of online censorship. Internet users widely recognize that the network is a valuable tool of political expression, social communication and a crucial way to access information in our wired world. Censorship threatens all of that and people are worried.

Overall, the results of the 2014 survey show that people are concerned with both online privacy and Internet censorship. As we will see, when governments and businesses impinge upon user privacy and censor information, they erode the correctness and reliability of the information obtained online. People lose trust in the system, the network's social capital wanes as a result, and users change their behaviour, undermining the economic potential of the Internet.

State Surveillance and a Loss of Trust

All states conduct surveillance on their populations. Often, these efforts are facilitated by Western firms selling surveillance technologies such as deep packet inspection tools that allow governments and ISPs to see what you are sending and saying online. Estimates put the market for these technologies at US$5 billion in 2011.[9]

Governments have a number of legitimate reasons to watch what people do so as to maintain order in society and protect their citizens. Sometimes, this watching can get excessive. The obvious examples are in authoritarian regimes such as in China, Russia, Iran and many other countries. The more surprising cases of excessive surveillance are found in the liberal democracies of the West. And nowhere is excessive watching more prevalent and shocking than in the United States, where strong constitutional protections exist alongside one of the largest and most capable online surveillance systems in the world. So, while we focus here on the NSA's programs and their effects, it is important to recognize that all governments spy. Indeed, the NSA — like other agencies in liberal democratic countries — is far more constrained in its activities than many intelligence agencies round the world.[10]

One of the most remarkable things about the chain of events that Snowden set off is that it affected both the actions of individuals and the politics of nations — even if some believe that the global reaction was not proportionate to the scale and scope of NSA activities.

The NSA's reach was global and the details of its surveillance apparatus has filled many books already.[11] For our purposes, we will consider, as a case in point, a flashy-sounding NSA program launched in 2007 called PRISM. Strictly speaking, PRISM is a program that allows the NSA — subject to the approval of a Foreign Intelligence Surveillance Act (FISA) courts authorization — to access data stored on the servers of major US technology companies such as Google, Yahoo!, Microsoft, Apple and Facebook.[12]

The program is pretty clever, in a Machiavellian kind of way. The major US technology companies that the NSA accessed control a huge share of the global online marketplace. In April of 2015, Google, Yahoo! and Bing (owned by Microsoft) accounted for a little over 96 percent of search engine traffic.[13] In 2014, there were around 1.79 billion social media users across the world. Facebook alone had some 1.42 billion active users in 2014, meaning that 79 percent of all social media users are on the American technology giant.[14] In April 2015, Litmus Email Analytics tracked the opening of 1.01 billion emails. Of that amount, four American companies (Apple, Microsoft, Google and Yahoo!) made up 90 percent of all the email clients.[15] These numbers paint an obvious picture showing that most of the world's online activity flows through these major American Internet companies. PRISM is ingenious because, rather than having the NSA go out to get the data that it needs from the far reaches of the Internet (a process known in the NSA as upstream collection), it simply lets the data come into a few more central locations that it has access to, and then peruses the data at its own leisure (downstream collection). Bringing the mountain of data to Muhammad, as it were.

What the NSA is doing with PRISM is certainly something that could be taken straight from the pages of Orwell's dystopian Big Brother future. One key difference between the omnipresent totalitarian state dreamt up by Orwell and the activity of the NSA — and it is a crucial distinction — is that the NSA could only access corporate data via PRISM if it received a FISA warrant. The FISA court, while secretive and operating outside the bounds of normal judicial process, does provide an important check on the potential overreach of the NSA.

In 2012, the NSA submitted 1,856 requests for data to the FISA courts. The court did not deny any of these requests. It did, however, modify 40 of them. The following year, the government submitted 1,655 cases to the court. Once again, the court did not turn down a single request, but, as before, they did require the modification of 34 submissions.[16]

A more transparent process could likely lead to more requests being denied, but it could also hinder the effectiveness of foreign intelligence collection, which is an integral part of keeping society safe from all manner of harms.[17]

When they become public, programs like PRISM raise the level of public concern about online privacy and contribute to a loss of trust. Accordingly, people may adapt by using the network either less often or differently. Behavioural change is exactly what we see in this case.

Think about one of the most basic online activities that people undertake every day: simple web searches. Everyone's search habits are different. Some people might search only for specific things related to their daily lives. Others, like one of the authors (Eric), might watch programs on Netflix and randomly Google things mentioned in the shows. During a stint watching the TV medical drama *House*, for example, this sort of behaviour leads to web searches of every sort of medical condition from lupus to necrotizing fasciitis to HIV/AIDS. Watching episodes of the counterterrorism thriller *24* could lead to searches for anything from torture techniques to terrorist plots.

Personal search patterns would not be an issue if the major Internet companies didn't retain user-generated search data, creating a massive reservoir of data that the NSA can then access. Unfortunately, retaining data is a core part of the business model of the major Internet search companies such as Google, Yahoo! and Microsoft. Access to a large quantity of data provides a gateway to what people are like, what they want and how they are likely to behave. Knowing this much about someone is tremendously valuable for advertisers and other companies that rely upon a mass base of consumers. But not all search engines operate in the same way. One web search company, DuckDuckGo, is based upon the opposite idea. Their explicit policy is to not track or store data on your web searches.

So, with its greater privacy protections, did people flock to companies like DuckDuckGo in the wake of what Snowden revealed? Let's take a look at some of the numbers. DuckDuckGo operated before word of NSA's surveillance hit the media, and continued to operate afterwards. In social science terms, we have sort of a natural experiment, where a discrete event occurs that can fundamentally change the way people behave.

To illustrate this idea, a parallel example would be looking at the effect of a new law mandating the use of seat belts on traffic fatalities. If fatalities remained roughly the same before and after the law came into effect, then it is likely ineffective. If traffic fatalities fall to a significant extent after the law comes into force, then it is likely having a demonstrable effect on the outcome of traffic accidents. That is a natural experiment in action.

The Snowden revelations and the use of privacy-based search engines like DuckDuckGo is the same — a natural experiment in action. Take a look at Figure 4.6. In the 11 months preceding the Snowden disclosures in June of 2013, DuckDuckGo averaged about 48 million direct web queries (web searches) per month. In the 11 months after people learned of what the NSA was doing, DuckDuckGo had an average of 129 million searches per month, or almost three times as many queries.

The plotted line in Figure 4.6 says it all. DuckDuckGo's usage rates were plodding along, maybe increasingly gradually, before word broke of NSA's activities. Enter Snowden and new public knowledge of NSA snooping in June 2013 and, mirroring a sudden eruption, there is a massive and nearly immediate jump (following a three-day lag, according to the daily numbers) in the number of DuckDuckGo searches. While other events can certainly cloud these numbers, it certainly appears that NSA surveillance eroded trust and prompted

Figure 4.6: DuckDuckGo Users Before and After Snowden Revelations

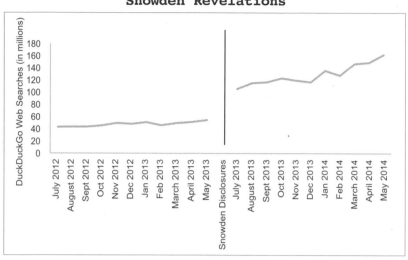

Source: Data from DuckDuckGo.

people to switch from companies such as Google, Bing or Yahoo! to search engines services that were more likely to protect their privacy (Box 4.1).

In a further effort to keep what they do online free from prying eyes, people also flocked to other technologies in the wake of Snowden's disclosures, and not just to private search engines like DuckDuckGo. Many also turned to the anonymous web browser known as The Onion Router — or Tor for short.

Tor is a system that encrypts and then relays a person's Internet traffic to a website via a series of volunteered computers hosted all around the world. As we discuss in chapter six, it is often used by criminals to avoid the prying eyes of law enforcement, but it is also a very useful system for ordinary people who want to maintain their privacy online or those who seek to circumvent censorship impositions to gain access to restricted content, especially in repressive regimes.[20]

In a pattern that mirrors DuckDuckGo usage, use of the Tor network took off in the months following Edward Snowden's

Box 4.1: Small Changes, Huge Effects

Individually, the act of changing a search engine might not seem like a big deal. But even a simple action such as this — a user changing their preferred search engine to better protect privacy — takes effort that person would otherwise not need to spend. A new search engine needs to be found. The privacy and profile settings need to be understood and adjusted. The new interface requires adaptation by the user. These things take time.

The accumulation of small events when spread over hundreds of thousands of people can have large consequences. When aggregated, the number of lost hours for people who changed their behaviour because they lost trust in the Internet ecosystem due to state surveillance is significant.

A simple thought experiment gives a rough sense of the magnitude of the aggregate costs that are involved. According to Statista research, Europeans did an average of 138 web searches in December of 2012 (the most recent year for which data is available).[18] The European average works well as a gauge for online behaviour in the West in general, because it gives us a sense of normal Internet search patterns across many different developed countries.

So, if we take the average monthly number of DuckDuckGo *searches* both before and after word of the PRISM program broke, and divide those numbers by 138, we can get a general approximation of the average number of monthly DuckDuckGo *users* both before and after Snowden's disclosures leaked out. Crunching these numbers, we get an average of roughly 346,000 users of DuckDuckGo per month before Snowden and an average of 935,000 users per month after Snowden.

Now, subtracting the two from each other, we get an increase of, on average, 590,000 DuckDuckGo users per month. For simplicity's sake, let's say each person took, on average, one hour to set up DuckDuckGo as an alternative search engine. So 590,000 hours of wasted time for those people who switched to DuckDuckGo alone (and there are many similar options out there, so we can imagine these hours are just the tip of the iceberg).

We can also monetize this time investment. In Europe in 2013, the average hourly labour cost across the core 18 EU members was €28.9. The average hourly labour cost across the full 28 EU members was €24.2.[19] Working the numbers, we find that — if all of DuckDuckGo's new users were like average Europeans in the core 18 EU member countries — the changed behaviour in response to a loss of trust of the Internet ecosystem would cost the economy roughly €17 million or US$19 million. Working through the numbers for the full 28 countries of the European Union, we get a drag on the economy of €14 million or US$16 million.

Even this amount — about US$19 million at the high end — is very small change in global terms. But these are the estimated costs for just those people who switched to DuckDuckGo — and only those who switched in the 11 months immediately following the disclosure of NSA surveillance. Ixquick, Privatelee, StartPage, Qrobe.it and Gibiru are other search engines that emphasize privacy. If each had a similar growth in the number of new users after the Snowden leaks, then we are actually looking at around five times the cost estimated above — or roughly US$95 million in the year following Snowden's news. Although this figure might not be enough wasted money to stop an entire economy, the cumulative small actions undertaken by individuals because they lose trust in the system do build force. And such estimates don't capture other behavioural changes — such as self-censorship or simply electing to use the Web less often.

disclosures. In the 11 months leading up to the first story on the NSA's activity, people accessed the Tor anonymity network an average of 46,949,418 times per month.[21] What is telling is that the average number of monthly users was relatively constant in the months preceding Snowden's disclosures. All that changed when the story of NSA surveillance broke.

Figure 4.7 reveals Tor usage rates in the months following Snowden's disclosures. In July of 2013 — the month following the initial disclosure in June — there were 49,149,255 Tor network users, only slightly above the preceding 11-month average.

In August, word broke of another surveillance program being operated by the NSA, known as XKeystroke.[22] The presentation slides

Figure 4.7: Tor Before and After Snowden

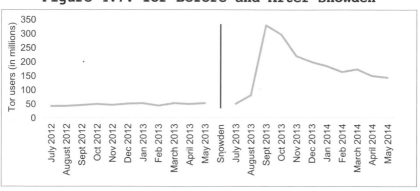

Source: Data from The Tor Project, "Tor Metrics — Estimated number of clients in the Tor network," https://metrics.torproject.org/clients-data.html.

released by Snowden indicated that it was one of the NSA's "widest-reaching" programs, providing near "real-time" interception of a person's Internet activity. With plenty of room for the possibility of exaggeration, the presentation goes on to suggest that it provided intelligence analysts with access to "nearly everything a typical user does on the internet."[23]

Typical users did not take this latest news lying down. In August, the number of people using Tor, which would be one of the best possible protections against NSA snooping, had increased to 79,832,280. Come September, the number jumped to 328,475,740.

From that high point, the number of Tor users began to slowly decline (likely due to Tor's limited functionality, which probably put many Internet users off). Nevertheless, one year after the first media story covered Snowden's disclosures, the number of monthly Tor users was still far higher than it was before word broke. Indeed, the number of monthly average users of the network for the 11 months following Snowden's leaks was 180,149,042 — or an increase of 284 percent.

The downside is that Tor enables the Dark Web, which is home to a host of social ills, ranging from child abuse imagery sites to illegal marketplaces such as Silk Road.[24] The irony here is that NSA efforts to use the Internet as a surveillance system to keep people safe instead eroded people's trust after the story broke. That loss of trust induced many people to start using Tor to ensure that their web traffic was secure and private. That swelled the number of signals entering and exiting the Tor network, making it harder for law enforcement to police the Dark Web and making the network less safe overall, as crime spills from the bytes and bits online into the real world.

Since word of the PRISM program broke, some aspects of NSA surveillance have been reined in. In the immediate aftermath of the revelations, organizations ranging from the American Civil Liberties Union to Republican Senator Rand Paul and Freedom Works Inc. have sued the government in attempts to stop the program. By all indications, the program is still operational, although others, such as the NSA's bulk phone data collection program, which collects

Figure 4.8: Most Users Would Trust the Internet More if Governments Guaranteed They Were Not Monitoring Them

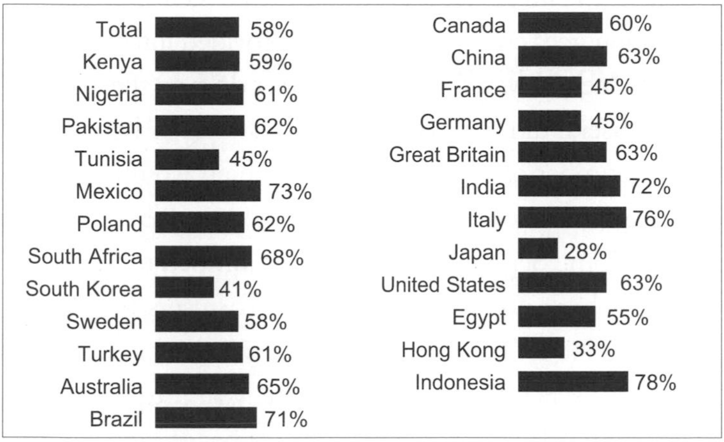

Total	58%	Canada	60%
Kenya	59%	China	63%
Nigeria	61%	France	45%
Pakistan	62%	Germany	45%
Tunisia	45%	Great Britain	63%
Mexico	73%	India	72%
Poland	62%	Italy	76%
South Africa	68%	Japan	28%
South Korea	41%	United States	63%
Sweden	58%	Egypt	55%
Turkey	61%	Hong Kong	33%
Australia	65%	Indonesia	78%
Brazil	71%		

Source: Data from the CIGI-Ipsos 2016 Global Survey.

telephone numbers and call duration, have been shuttered.[25] Whether PRISM is active or not today, the trust of Internet users has taken a hit and that trust will be hard to rebuild.

Clearly, the loss of trust at the level of the individual user following Snowden's revelation of the PRISM program incurred costs as people adapted their behaviour to better protect their privacy. However, Snowden's revelations caused even greater ripples at other levels. Word of NSA snooping created considerable international concern, with some countries going so far as to threaten to hive off their own Internets (we take up the discussion of these national-level pushes for data localization and their economic costs in the next chapter).

When people were asked directly if they would trust the network more if they could be guaranteed that their Internet usage was not being monitored, a clear majority, 58 percent, said yes. While the numbers went from a low of 28 percent in Japan up to 78 percent in Indonesia, the general association is clear: users base their trust on their perceptions of their privacy online (Figure 4.8).

The bottom line is this: people care about privacy, so state surveillance leads to costly losses of trust through a simple chain of cause and effect. Government snooping violates Internet users' privacy, causing people to trust the Internet less, as clearly shown by the data.

Private Companies — Not So Private Users

We cannot merely focus on how Big Brother peeps into our personal lives because private companies do much the same as governments, although for different reasons. But, surveillance is surveillance. And when Internet users think the network lacks privacy, they take actions that are costly, both individually and collectively.

Most companies that provide a web-based service, and many others as well, collect their users' data. Target, Facebook, Amazon, Google and many of the smaller applications that we install upon our mobile devices collect data only tangentially related to the service they provide. This data is often collected, aggregated, sold, combined, split and recombined, anonymized and de-anonymized to give a picture of what people are like, what they want, where they have been and even what they are likely to do in the future.

Brightest Flashlight is one app that does this. The app provides a really bright means of illumination. But, to use the program, users also need to give it access to their devices' GPS locations. In late 2013, the Brightest Flashlight app collected this GPS data and then sold it to third-party vendors of big data and to marketing and advertising firms, so that these companies could figure out those users' movements and more efficiently sell them products. In total, 50 million users of the Brightest Flashlight app had their personal data collected and sold.[26]

The Brightest Flashlight app is not the only company collecting and selling their users' data. In 2012, the information technology (IT) research company Lookout conducted a study to pinpoint the proverbial "genome" of the app industry as found on Apple and Android devices. Looking into the numbers, they learned that 34 percent of free apps in the Apple store and 28 percent of all apps for Android devices were able to access user location data, just as the Brightest Flashlight app had done. In addition, 11 percent of Apple apps gained access to their users' contact lists, while 7.5 percent of Android apps did likewise.[27] Far from being an isolated phenomenon, the overreach of private companies into our private realms — through apps and other forms of digital data collection — is widespread.

Take the big box store Target as another example. Like most retailers, Target collects detailed data about its shoppers, through both online and off-line means. To sift through it all, Target has what is known as a predictive analytics team. This team is shockingly good at what it does and the result is an invasive breach of privacy. Consider the following cautionary tale.

In 2012, an angry father walked into a Target store on the outskirts of Minneapolis. As the story goes, the father demanded to see the store manager. The enraged father confronted him, waving a flyer: "My daughter got this in the mail! She's still in high school, and you're sending her coupons for baby clothes and cribs? Are you trying to encourage her to get pregnant?"[28]

The father would have been right to be upset, if that was indeed what Target was trying to do. In fact, some time after the father's visit, the store manager (unconnected from the corporate marketing arm) called the father to apologize again for what seemed like clearly inappropriate advertisements. But, to the manager's surprise, the father was no longer angry — rather, he seemed embarrassed. "I had a talk with my daughter," the father told him. "It turns out there's been some activities in my house I haven't been completely aware of. She's due in August. I owe you an apology."[29] Thanks to its big data analytics, Target had a hunch that the teen was pregnant, and got it right, even before the girl's family knew.

Target reportedly got so good at predicting what consumers might need that it actually started to intersperse its advertisements with decoys and dummies. As Frank Pasquale explains in his masterful book on how secret algorithms are coming to rule our lives, "Not surprisingly, some customers found it creepy to start receiving pregnancy-related ads. Target responded, not by explaining to customers how it came to its conclusions, but by mixing more non-pregnancy-related ads into the circulars targeting expectant mothers."[30] Target's strategy was to create a smokescreen for its surveillance.

While companies can be duplicitous about what kind of data they are collecting and how they use it, some of the blame for the current state of affairs must fall on individuals. Companies often do tell users in their terms of service that they will collect and even potentially sell user-generated content. Most of us scroll down to click the box saying we agree to the terms of service and move on to downloading and then using the product without a second thought.

This habit can get us into some real metaphysical trouble, as one amusing case from 2010 illustrates. An online company, GameStation, changed its terms of service on April 1 so that users conferred onto the company the ownership of their immortal souls. The terms of service read:

> By placing an order via this Web site on the first day of the fourth month of the year 2010 Anno Domini, you agree to grant Us a non transferable option to claim, for now and for ever more, your immortal soul. Should We wish to exercise this option, you agree to surrender your immortal soul, and any claim you may have on it, within 5 (five) working days of receiving written notification from gamesation.co.uk or one of its duly authorised minions.[31]

The terms of service laid out the company's "right to serve such notice in 6 (six) foot high letters of fire, however we can accept no liability for any loss or damage caused by such an act. If you a) do not believe you have an immortal soul, b) have already given it to another party, or c) do not wish to grant Us such a license, please click the link below to nullify this sub-clause and proceed with your transaction."[32] Some 7,500 people turned over their souls to the company without a blink in this elaborate April Fool's Day joke. As ridiculous as this example is, it proves that many people do not bother to read the terms and conditions of the online services they use.

These examples show that companies can violate people's online privacy in their quest to collect user data to try to turn a buck. Interestingly, as shown in the 2016 CIGI-Ipsos survey, a slim majority of people — 51 percent — do not actually know that companies collect and sell user-generated data. Another interesting fact from the 2016 survey is that younger users are far more ignorant than older users of how their data gets used by companies providing free online services (Figure 4.9).

Income and education are two more factors that drive individual understanding of what private companies are doing with data generated by their customers. More income and more education — variables that tend to run together — are also associated with greater data awareness. Poorer and less well-educated individuals are less aware of what companies are doing with their data. At the low end of the household income scale, only 48 percent of people realize that their data is being bought and sold. Once a family's income moves into the highest income bracket, the relationship switches decisively, with 60 percent of respondents aware of corporate practices. A similar story emerges when considering users' educational levels. Among those on the lower end, only 46 percent understand that their data is being

Figure 4.9: Do You Know that Free Online Services Collect and Sell Your Data?

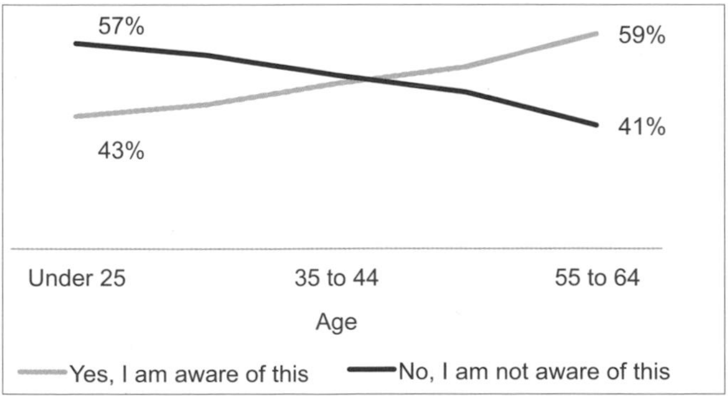

Source: Data from the CIGI-Ipsos 2016 Global Survey.

Figure 4.10: Are You Aware that Companies Collect and Sell Your Data? Income, Education and Data Awareness

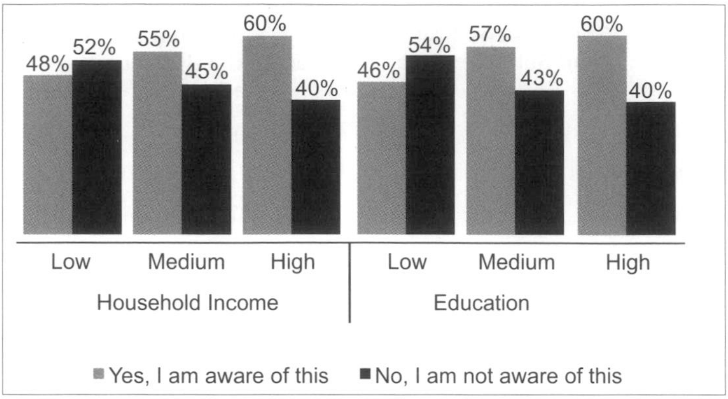

Source: Data from the CIGI-Ipsos 2016 Global Survey.

used by companies to turn a profit. At the higher end, the number again swings up significantly, with 60 percent of people realizing that their data is being collected, analyzed and sold by private companies (Figure 4.10).

Another set of telling differences emerge if you look at the issue geographically. Overall, the percentage of people in the CIGI-Ipsos 2016 global survey who are aware that their data is used for commercial purposes by companies providing free online services is pretty much the same as the percentage of those who are not aware: 49 percent and 51 percent, respectively. However, looking beneath these top-line trends to the difference in the level of data awareness per country reveals some stark differences.

Probably one of the most notable is that the level of awareness people have of corporate data practices is positively correlated with each country's GDP per capita. We already saw that income tends to drive up people's awareness of corporate data awareness at the individual level. When you rank the countries and territories in the survey according to their GDP per capita and then plot their level of awareness of corporate data practices, a clearly positive association between the ranking and the level of awareness emerges. Nations such

Table 4.1: Country Wealth and People's Level of Awareness over Corporate Data Practices

	Know that Many Corporations Collect and Sell User Data (%)	Do Not Know that Many Corporations Collect and Sell User Data (%)	GDP Per Capita (US$)
Kenya	34	66	2,818
Pakistan	29	71	4,590
India	53	47	5,439
Nigeria	36	64	5,639
Indonesia	43	57	10,033
Egypt	39	61	10,046
Tunisia	33	67	10,910
South Africa	52	48	12,446
China	57	43	12,599
Brazil	34	66	15,110
Mexico	37	63	16,284
Turkey	48	52	18,869
Poland	64	36	23,976
Italy	63	37	33,039
South Korea	68	32	33,629
Japan	39	61	35,635
France	76	24	37,214
Great Britain	66	34	38,178
Canada	58	42	42,778
Australia	59	41	43,219
Germany	62	38	43,602
Sweden	62	38	44,034
United States	63	37	52,118
Hong Kong	57	43	52,552

Source: Data from the CIGI-Ipsos 2016 Global Survey; World Bank, n.d., "Data — Indicators," http://data.worldbank.org/indicator.

as the United States, Great Britain, France, Hong Kong, Canada and Sweden have both a high GDP per capita and relatively high data awareness (Table 4.1).

Of course, a simple association cannot tell us much about precisely why income matters so much, and it is possible that it is not income per se, or income alone, that causes higher levels of data awareness. High income tends to be correlated with higher education levels, democracy and higher Internet penetration levels, to name but a few factors. Each factor might be contributing in its own way to the association witnessed across the sample of 23 countries and Hong Kong.

These data leave us in an interesting spot. A slim majority of people do not know how their data is being used. But that majority grows far more pronounced among poor, uneducated and young Internet users, which is problematic. At one level, the descriptive results from the 2016 CIGI-Ipsos poll suggest that the people who are least well off, both within and across societies, tend to be the ones who are most blind to what online corporations are doing with the data they generate. The trouble is that not only can people living in ignorance be exploited, but also that they tend to react very strongly when their ignorance is shattered.

So What? Snooping, Privacy and Trust

What happens when people grow wise to the idea that private companies are violating their privacy? As we saw with the data about attitudes to government surveillance, people change their behaviour — in ways that are personally and economically costly.

The social media giant Facebook provides a great example of what happens when privacy concerns compel a behavioural change that in turn causes economic harm. People reveal a lot about themselves on Facebook. "Liking" a post (or choosing another of the new response buttons available) shows support for a particular cause or way of thinking. Facebook status updates reveal a great deal about the poster's personality and even provide a record of what he or she is doing on any given day. The photos people upload to their page, or ones that they are tagged in, put their physical images out into the world, sometimes in compromising circumstances (a drinking binge, for example) and often paired with others (be they friend or foe), marking out the boundaries of their social networks. Embedded or integrated applications such as Foursquare, which has users sign into a location that is then publicized on the Facebook newsfeed, provide a GPS-specific record of where those individuals go throughout the day. With all this personal information on the social media platform, privacy concerns loom large.

Year over year, the number of Facebook users has certainly continued to grow, but the aggregate numbers mask a changing profile of who is actually using the site. A recent study in the journal *Cyberpsychology, Behavior, and Social Networking* entitled "Who Commits Virtual Identity Suicide?" delves into the twin questions of who uses social media sites like Facebook and who leaves them. Comparing Facebook quitters with current Facebook users, the authors found that 48.3 percent of those who quit the social media site were extra privacy-conscious. Interestingly, the quitters also tended to be older (over 30) and male.[33]

People who care about privacy are increasingly committing "virtual identity suicide" because they think Facebook (and likely other social media companies) are too invasive a presence in their personal lives. Abandoning their online lives in this way can be costly.

At first glance, the immediate personal costs of deleting one's profile and signing out might seem minuscule — namely, the nuisance of deleting the account. But the problem is the hidden costs can be greater than this, because social media is increasingly a tool of opportunity. As a result, those who leave social networking sites because of concerns about personal privacy are potentially hurting their employment prospects and professional advancement. Economists refer to this loss as an opportunity cost — the price paid in giving up one thing in order to do or have something else.

The key to a better future, for most people, is a better job. The numbers show how integral social media has become to the hiring process. According to one 2012 study, 92 percent of companies are using social media as a core tool in the hiring process, up from 78 percent in 2010 and 87 percent in 2011. These numbers don't just refer to the use of sites explicitly geared to connecting employers and employees, such as LinkedIn. Sixty-six percent of companies also use Facebook — another 54 percent use Twitter — as means of finding and then vetting potential employees. Companies are likewise enthused over the potential of social media: 42 percent indicate that social media recruiting has helped improve employee quality and 20 percent report that it takes less time to hire new employees with social media recruiting.[34] In places that still allow the practice, some employers even go so far as to ask potential employees for their Facebook passwords, so that they can check out a potential employee's personal life.[35]

Even in jurisdictions where privacy protections preclude employers from insisting upon access to their prospective workers' social media lives, an insidious hidden pressure might still mean that those who don't volunteer their personal information get blacklisted. Imagine that you are an employer faced with a slate of potential candidates and are looking for any details that can help you in picking someone who will fit well with the company, work hard and follow the rules. Some potential employees, really wanting the job, are willing to provide access to their social media accounts without being asked. Right away, those who are not willing to turn over all the details of their personal lives are at a disadvantage in the hiring process.

As a potential employer, you might also have this niggling concern that those who are privacy conscious feel that way for a reason. *Maybe they hold radical political opinions. Maybe they like to drink, then take photos and post them online. Or, maybe it is drugs...who knows?* Those in the job market basically face what is known as a prisoner's dilemma. They can all agree to refuse to share their private social media accounts so that their privacy is intact, thereby allowing a level field for the job competition. That would be best for all, but it is less likely to happen, because some might choose to defect by sharing their social media accounts in order to get ahead and land the job. One solution is to just not have *any* social media accounts and avoid the dilemma altogether.

Here we have pressures that pull in opposite directions. People's privacy gets violated as companies collect user data, resulting in a loss of trust that causes some users to take extreme actions such as quitting social media sites. At the same time, companies are increasingly turning to social media as an essential tool in the hiring process. The result of these two trends is that those concerned with privacy face an uncomfortable choice: either give up your privacy or accept that you will be increasingly disadvantaged in the job market. You could call this "the online job privacy dilemma." And across the places surveyed in the 2016 CIGI-Ipsos survey, users routinely undertook behavioural changes in response to the data practices of companies. Most starkly, 20 percent of users use the network *itself* less as a result of corporate data practices (Figure 4.11).

Finding that 20 percent of Internet users use the network less often because of online companies' data policies might not immediately seem like a huge issue. But, if you frame the matter in absolute terms — as a count of *people* rather than as a percentage — that 20 percent adds up very quickly. Using population and Internet penetration data from the World Bank[36] and the country-level details from the 2016 CIGI-Ipsos survey on the percentage of respondents who changed their behaviour as a result of companies' activity with user-generated data, we can pinpoint how many people now use the Internet less often.

Figure 4.11: Corporate Data Collection and User Behaviour

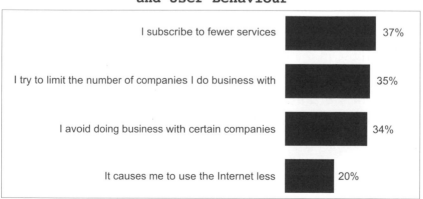

Source: Data from the CIGI-Ipsos 2016 Global Survey.

The final number is huge. As Figure 4.12 shows, almost *400 million people* have reduced their Internet use because they distrust the activities of online companies that collect, aggregate and sell consumer-generated data. With around three billion Internet users in the world, that works out to one in seven Internet users pulling back from using the network because their trust is eroded.

Despite the assertions of Zuckerberg and Schmidt, referred to earlier, it is clear that many people still care a great deal about online privacy. With states peeking into our lives via our computer screens and companies recording everything we do online, it is no surprise that nine out of 10 Americans want to have greater control over who has their data and how it is collected and used. It is also not surprising that more than two-thirds of users don't think current government restrictions are adequate to protect online privacy, and that a similar two-thirds lack faith in the ability of large American companies to protect their information.[37] It is, in short, no surprise that people are increasingly distrustful of the operation of the Internet ecosystem.

Figure 4.12: The Effects of Corporate Collection and Sale of User-Generated Data on Internet Use

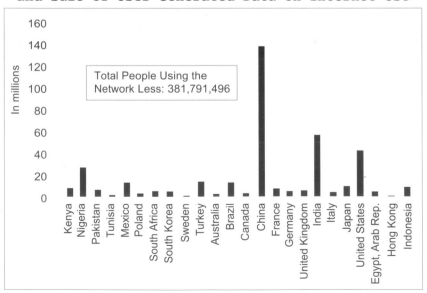

Source: Data from the CIGI-Ipsos 2014 Global Survey; World Bank, "Data — Indicators."

As user trust has waned due to privacy violations by states and companies, people have begun to adjust their behaviour and the cumulative effect of these behavioural changes has a significant impact on the social capital of the network. Moreover, as people lose trust in the network and take steps to opt out of modern digital life, the economic, innovative and developmental potential of the Internet correspondingly falls.

Governments and Censorship

Censorship basically means that others are controlling the quality, quantity and type of information that network users can access. It has the effect of undermining people's trust in the Internet ecosystem by shaking people's sense of confidence in the reliability and correctness of the information provided by the Web. Government censorship can take many different forms, ranging from the outright forbidding of access to certain content to making access too slow to be worth it. A few examples illustrate the point.

Governments in predominantly Muslim countries in the Middle East, South Asia and North Africa routinely censor the content of the Web according to a principle of *Hisbah*, which can be defined as "the duty of enjoining good when it is neglected and forbidding evil when it is prevalent in society."[38] Homosexual content, pornography and unfavourable references to Islam, to name a few examples, fall within this category. Sudan, Saudi Arabia, Egypt, Kuwait, Oman, Yemen, the United Arab Emirates and Indonesia all have some degree of faith-based online censorship.

One of the biggest culprits is Iran. Iran has even gone so far to propose building its own *Halal* — or pure — Internet that would be distinct from the rest of the World Wide Web. Content on the *Halal* Internet would be strictly controlled and limited to only that information deemed acceptable by the Iranian government. Efforts in this direction began as early as 2001, when Internet regulators took over control of all the Internet access points into the country.[39] The calls got further support in 2012, when the Iranian Telecommunications Minister, Reza Taghipour, was quoted as saying, "Supporting local software and creating secure communication infrastructure are among the most important strategic decisions in the field of cyber defense, and in this regard the first phase of this network will become operational in the month of Khordad."[40] This call would have corresponded roughly to the late May or early June 2012 launch of Iran's *Halal* Internet. It has yet to happen.

While it has not yet created its own Internet, Iran remains one of the most heavily censored digital environments in the world. The forms of censorship in Iran are many, and cumulatively quite effective. For instance, Iran routinely employs a censorship technique called deep packet inspection, where an ISP can see the content of the data that a person sends around the Web in order to track and block anything it deems impure. Complementing this technical method, Iran also has legislation mandating that Internet cafes need to install cameras and take down photo identification details for anyone using the Internet, leading to extensive self-censorship. In 2006, Iran also mandated that ISPs were not allowed to provide download speeds in excess of 128 kilobytes per second to consumers. Slow download speeds can affect a person's ability to access certain web content, such as YouTube videos, Facebook or even some more data-heavy websites, leading to censorship by inconvenience. The ban has been gradually eroded over time and download speeds in 2015 were higher, but still hovering at about one-fifth of the average global download speed.[41]

Pakistan is another predominantly Muslim country that has engaged in fairly extensive censorship. Pakistan has, for instance, a rather storied history with YouTube. In February 2008, Pakistan banned the video sharing website, citing concerns over the increasing number of "non-Islamic objectionable video[s]."[42] Later that month, the ban was lifted. In May of 2010, Pakistan again banned YouTube, over objections that the website contained "blasphemous" depictions of the Prophet Mohammed that are considered offensive in Islam.[43] The ban was lifted later that same month. In 2012, Pakistan moved once more to ban YouTube in protest over the website's refusal to remove the amateurish film *Innocence of Muslims*.[44] Breaking with the previous pattern, the ban was not promptly lifted, inspiring the *The New Yorker* writer Ali Sethi to nickname Pakistan "Banistan."[45] The ban has since been lifted.

Another country with a history of Internet censorship is Turkey. According to the OpenNet Initiative, in 2010 Turkey had several Internet censorship technologies at its disposal and selectively filtered social and political content.[46] In 2014, these selective efforts grew just a bit more pointed when Turkish Prime Minister Tayyip Erdoğan obtained a court order to ban the social networking giant Twitter. At a campaign rally in Bursa, Erdoğan bellowed to a crowd of supporters that "we now have a court order. We'll eradicate Twitter. I don't care what the international community says. Everyone will witness the power of the Turkish Republic."[47] The move was not a complete surprise, as it epitomized a growing trend in Turkey (and in Erdoğan's Justice and Development Party, in particular) to greater levels of Internet censorship and was in line with an earlier statement by the Turkish prime minister in 2013 during the Gezi Park protests, where he described Twitter as "the worst menace to society."[48]

As restrictive as these counties are, the People's Republic of China is far more thorough at censoring online content. The OpenNet Initiative again provides some of the details.[49] China's main line of censorship is something known colloquially as the Great Firewall. The Great Firewall is much like the personal firewalls that many of us install on our own desktops, laptops and mobile devices, but it works on a society-wide scale. Firewalls are basically programs set up to detect web activity that has certain predefined identifiers (viruses or vulnerabilities — or, in the case of China, content that is politically unacceptable) and then prevent access. This is China's primary defence against external content deemed inappropriate by the regime. To restrict access, the Great Firewall blocks access to sites with certain sensitive key words, conducts deep packet inspection to see what people are sending across the Web, endeavours to block virtual private networks (VPNs) that are often used to circumvent government-imposed content restrictions, and resets connections when people try to access prohibited material, generating delays and inconveniences.[50] It also outright blocks certain websites and has expelled a number of Western Internet platforms. In 2015, the list of major Internet companies that are banned in China included Google, YouTube, Facebook, Reddit, Instagram and Twitter, and the list continues to grow.[51]

Controlling the type of information that people have access to from the outside world is only half the battle. China has a huge and active Internet population of around 640 million people in 2015, which generates its own vibrant domestic cyberspace that the government then needs to monitor and censor. As a first measure, China has a huge Internet censorship bureaucracy that Harvard political scientist Gary King and his co-authors have described as what "may be the most extensive effort to selectively censor human expression ever implemented."[52] To give a sense of scale, in 2012 and 2013, China had somewhere between 20,000 and 30,000 Internet police and as many as 250,000 to 300,000 active Internet monitors. If Orwell was alive today, he might recognize these battalions as his "thought police."

To help control what is said on domestic blogs and websites, China has also decentralized its censorship to the companies themselves. As a result, "providers must install filters that prevent positing of thousands of keyword combinations, delete or conceal posts with sensitive comments, and cancel the accounts of bloggers deemed to have posted too many troubling posts."[53] Some of these companies then employ as many as 1,000 people to monitor Internet activity and restrict visible content, particularly as it pertains to potential collective action — phrases like "meet me in Tiananmen Square."[54]

Backing up these technical methods and the veritable army of online censors are the draconian rules of an authoritarian regime. Internet users have to conform to rules laid out by the National

People's Congress Standing Committee on Safeguarding Internet Security, which impose punishments ranging from fines to imprisonment and hard labour for those who violate the dictates of the regime. In 2010, for example, Zhao Lianhai's activist blog was shut down and he was sentenced to two-and-a-half years in prison. A punishment of that length brings to mind some truly nefarious things: vitriolic hate speech, inciting violence or maybe the dissemination of illegal pornography. But his crime was nothing of the sort. All he did was call attention to the problem of widely available tainted milk that had given babies kidney stones across China.[55] The trend continues: in late 2015, Pu Zhiqiang, a Chinese human rights lawyer, was charged with "inciting ethnic hatred" and "picking quarrels and provoking trouble."[56] He had done these things over the span of 2011–2014 and in the form of seven (yes, just seven) tweets on Weibo, the Chinese version of Twitter.

Clearly, state censorship of the Internet is pervasive and takes different forms. Content can be restricted outright. Websites can be forbidden. And content can be removed from social networking sites. Sometimes the tricks of online censorship are subtler and aim to frustrate rather than dictate. Making websites too cumbersome to be functional can cause people to look elsewhere for their information, creating the same effect as censorship.[57]

The Costs of Online Censorship

Censorship is costly in addition to being dehumanizing. It reduces how people use the Internet both directly by restricting what users can do and indirectly by eroding trust. Internet censorship and blocking by states is a major cause of Internet fragmentation. If you were on the Internet in Saudi Arabia, Iran or China, for example, a whole range of sites would not be accessible on your computer. That is because these countries have imposed restrictions on the flow of content and information through various kinds of censorship, filtering and blocking techniques.

In October 2013, Saudi national Hisham Fageeh had the equivalent of a runaway pop hit in the Kingdom of Saudi Arabia. His YouTube video "No Woman, No Drive" — a parody of the famous Bob Marley song — had reached over three million views after only two days online.[58] In the video's introduction, Fageeh said he had adapted the song to reflect "lyrics relevant to my culture."[59] He posted it to YouTube the same weekend that more than 60 women took to the wheel in Saudi Arabia's largest protest to date against the ban on women driving.[60]

Fageeh's success exemplifies the growing popularity of YouTube in Saudi Arabia. In fact, Saudis are among the world's most avid users of the site.[61] Young Saudi viewers in particular are disinterested in bland state-sanctioned television programming and instead prefer locally produced YouTube content made by contemporaries who know their audience.[62]

Some of this content walks a very fine line between humour, satire and political commentary. *The Wall Street Journal* in 2014 noted that some web-based shows produced in Saudi Arabia had been allowed a significant amount of freedom when compared with traditional media.[63] But this has begun to change.

In 2014, the Saudi Government directed the Saudi General Commission for Audiovisual Media to monitor online content produced in Saudi Arabia for objectionable content.[64] The same year, the Kingdom, for the first time, began enforcing e-publishing legislation passed in 2011 and shut down at least 35 news websites for failing to register with authorities, according to Freedom House's 2014 "Freedom on the Net" report.[65] The same report noted that many Saudi Internet users heavily self-censor, particularly in the wake of high-profile arrests of several activists.

Even before these developments, Reporters Without Borders and Freedom House considered Saudi Arabia among the worst countries globally in regard to Internet censorship and freedom. The Kingdom already had strict controls over Internet use, and authorities use a

Figure 4.13: Iran's Censorship Double Standard

Jack @jack · 1 Oct 2013
@HassanRouhani Good evening, President. Are citizens of Iran able to read your tweets?

↰   ⇄ 1.5K   ♥ 927   •••

Hassan Rouhani
@HassanRouhani   ☼   ⊕ Follow

Evening, @Jack. As I told @camanpour, my efforts geared 2 ensure my ppl'll comfortably b able 2 access all info globally as is their #right.

4:24 PM - 1 Oct 2013

Source: https://twitter.com/jack/status/385056531269427201.

content filter to block websites deemed "morally reprehensible" or politically objectionable.[66] In 2014, the Internet in the Kingdom of Saudi Arabia was already circled by walls — and the efforts to crack down on YouTube have only reinforced them.

The Iranian government is a master of irony. Despite legal bans against Twitter and other social media sites, Iranian President Hasan Rouhani has not one, but two Twitter accounts (in Farsi and English), which he claims he uses to connect with constituents on foreign and domestic policies. Foreign Minister Javad Zarif uses both Twitter and Facebook (also banned) frequently, and his page has almost one million likes. Even Grand Ayatollah Khamenei has an active Instagram account with thousands of posts and hundreds of thousands of followers. Iran's censorship of Facebook, Twitter and many other sites is part of its efforts to create its own *Halal* self-contained Internet, but policy and practice are not in sync.[67] The irony is not lost on outside observers (Figure 4.13).

Despite Rouhani's claims on Twitter that he sees access to the global Internet as his people's "right," Iran marches on with its censorship in new and creative ways. In February 2015, Iran attempted to circumvent Western Internet sanctions by unveiling Yooz, its own search engine. Iran claims that Yooz, which means "cheetah" in Persian, is faster and more secure than Google, Bing or Yahoo! and can support up to one billion Persian websites.[68] Detractors say Yooz merely provides the Iranian government with another opportunity to censor "objectionable" material and monitor Internet traffic.[69] In addition, the Iranian government continues its aggressive attacks against websites it deems dangerous, which include arresting bloggers, journalists and activists, according to Reporters without Borders' most recent report. In February 2014, a revolutionary court sentenced Arash Moghadam Aslani to eight years in prison in response to material he posted on, ironically, Facebook.[70]

Another ironic twist is that Iran's censorship of the Internet has unintentionally resulted in a booming Internet industry: of anti-censorship software companies. Allegedly, almost 70 percent of young Iranian Internet users have installed VPNs that allow them to access the entire Internet without restriction. They are easy to find and one can even use government-sanctioned payment services (basically the Iranian equivalent of PayPal) to pay for the service. This sector is so lucrative that some observers claim that government authorities — despite publicly condemning the services — are tacitly allowing sales of the software in order to line their pockets and might even be using the services themselves.[71] Iran's heavily restricted environment makes such allegations hard to prove, but the blatant use of social media by Iranian leaders suggests there could be some merit to the claims.

China's Great Firewall is another example of the lengths that authoritarian regimes will go to in restricting their citizens' access to the Internet. But sometimes even that firewall is breached. On January 22, 2014, the news exploded with reports that 500 million online users in China had been redirected to a site in the United States. The reality was less sensational but still historic; for several hours, due to a routing error, half a billion Chinese Internet users were able to access webpages in what *The New York Times* dubbed the biggest Internet breakout in history.[72]

Cyber analysts and bloggers outside of China gleefully touted their theory: that China's Great Firewall had malfunctioned and redirected users to banned websites instead of blocking them. Millions of Chinese Internet users, they explained, were sent to an IP address owned by a company registered to a physical address in Cheyenne, Wyoming.[73]

In reality, reporters at the time were not actually sure where the company's servers were physically based.[74] Nonetheless, the company in question found itself on the wrong end of Chinese censors because it offered services to help mask Internet addresses, and because its founder was a practitioner of Falun Gong, a banned group in China.[75]

China vehemently denied any allegations that the outage was self-inflicted. "This again shows that China is a victim of hacking," declared Chinese Foreign Ministry spokesman Qin Gang.[76] The editors of the often pro-government Chinese daily, the *Global Times*, cast responsibility on the United States, writing, "if the US fails to deal with the incident properly, Chinese trust toward the US over the Internet will be damaged."[77]

The outage's aftermath suggests further Internet fragmentation is on the way. *The Beijing Times* argued that the incident showed why China needed to host more Internet infrastructure on its own soil.[78] Dong Fang, an Internet engineer at 360 Security Solution, elaborated further. "All the root name servers are located in the United States, Japan and European countries," he explained. "A problem with them would affect all the domain name processes and website visits in China. We need to establish a monitoring system over DNS [Domain Name System] and response system for accidents. Building root domain name servers in China should be completed as soon as possible."[79]

Polling data from the 2014 CIGI-Ipsos survey points out the locus of flagging trust. Surprisingly, it aligns with the sentiment expressed in China's *Global Times*. As shown in Figure 4.14, only 34 percent of respondents agree that their government would restrict access to the Internet. Fully 43 percent, however, strongly think that other governments might endeavour to do so. A difference of nine percentage

Figure 4.14: Government Restriction of Access

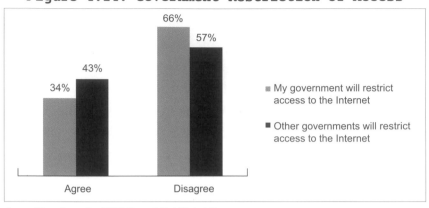

Source: Data from the CIGI-Ipsos 2014 Global Survey.

points might not seem like a huge divide, but looking more closely at how each of the 23 countries and Hong Kong responded, you get a picture with a much starker contrast.* In aggregate, 16 of the 24 were more concerned about other governments restricting access to the Internet than about actions by their own government. That proportion works out to about 66 percent of all countries sampled.

But, whether foreign or domestic, censorship erodes user trust. Users trust the Internet because it provides them with correct information and is reliable in a pinch. Censorship undermines these technical

---

* A rudimentary statistical test known as a t-test further supports the idea that there is a real difference here. T-tests compare the averages of two groups of people, countries or other samples to see if the differences between them are genuine or just the product of the simple fact that things vary. In this case, comparing the percentage of respondents that are concerned about their government restricting Internet access against the percentage concerned with other governments restricting access produces a statistically significant result. In other words, it is 99 percent likely that people are genuinely more concerned about *other* governments restricting access to the Internet than about restrictions imposed by their own political authorities. The t-test retuned a statistic of 0.0092, for those who are interested.

features. Additionally, when they spill over into the real world and lead to arrests, charges and detention in prisons, censorship practices also have direct safety implications for Internet users and their families.

Users are certainly not immune to the effects of censorship and are readily willing to link these activities to broader issues of trust. Two numbers from the 2016 CIGI-Ipsos survey show this relationship in sharp relief. Sixty-nine percent of respondents indicated that being able to express their personal opinions online free from fear would cause them to place more trust in the network. Mirroring this notion, 59 percent of Internet users felt that they could trust the Internet more if governments could guarantee that it was not censored. The implication is clear. Trust fails when the network is censored.

What is also increasingly apparent is that censorship and blocking harm economic growth and innovation, as even the Chinese are beginning to discover. Chinese Premier Li Keqiang was reported in the *Financial Times* as saying to a committee meeting of China's legislature that "I have visited some developing countries that have faster Internet connections than Beijing."[80] China's firewall and special routing and filtering/surveillance mechanisms contribute to slower Internet speeds, sometimes by design and sometimes as a result of censorship practices. As the *Financial Times* story noted, this was "the first time this problem had been publicly acknowledged by such a high official — and crystallized a dilemma facing China's leaders. As economic growth begins to sag from double digits to what Mr Li calls a 'new normal' — 7 per cent GDP growth expected this year — the government is talking up the power of the Internet to transform the economy and avoid a hard landing."[81] A recent EU Chamber of Commerce survey in China discovered that 86 percent of Chinese companies have complained about the negative impact that Internet blocking has on their business.[82]

A major study by the Dalberg Global Development Advisory Group concludes that there is "a strong correlation between the degree of Internet openness in a given country (as measured by its Freedom on the Net score) and the degree to which the country has economically benefited from the Internet (as measured by the 'Economic impacts' score of the World Economic Forum's Networked Readiness Index)."[83] It also finds "a similar relationship when the analysis relies on measures of the Internet's contribution to overall GDP." It notes that "[r]estrictions on openness increase the risks and costs of doing business for firms that rely on the Internet, and therefore inhibit investment and innovation, resulting in lower levels of economic activity." In the case of Turkey, for example, one entrepreneur "estimates that the cost of complying with an arcane and restrictive set of rules regarding website content accounts for 15% of his total operating costs." In Thailand, "the 2007 Act on Computer Crime, which included broad provisions concerning intermediary liability, has led many service providers to conclude that the burdens of doing business outweigh the benefits."[84] Basically, contrary to common practice in many parts of the world, ISPs and content providers in some jurisdictions can be held liable for what was done via their platforms and services.

Of course, it is not just authoritarian states that try to block content and restrict certain kinds of access on the Internet. Liberal democracies will sometimes attempt the same in the name of copyright protection or to prevent criminal behaviour.

In January 2012, visitors to Wikipedia and Reddit found that the sites were down — but this was no technical glitch. Wikipedia and Reddit had embarked on a voluntary self-imposed blackout in protest of a proposed US law, the Stop Online Piracy Act (SOPA).

In short, SOPA strengthened the United States Justice Department's ability to go after websites that hosted disputed copyright material, prosecute them for violations and block US citizens from visiting the sites, among other restrictions.[85] Critics claimed it was tantamount to controlling and censoring the Internet. The backlash was severe. Thousands of other sites joined Wikipedia and Reddit in their shutdown. Google blacked out its logo, Mozilla added a black "stop censorship" banner across its logo, and sites such as Craigslist and *Wired* set up anti-SOPA landing pages.[86] Craigslist sent a pointed message to lawmakers on its front page: "Corporate paymasters, keep those clammy hands off the Internet!"[87]

Internet giants such as Mark Zuckerberg, tech entrepreneur Gene Hoffman, Twitter founder Jack Dorsey and Arianna Huffington of *The Huffington Post* railed against the bill.[88] Hoffman derided SOPA for attempting to turn the United States into the world's copyright police and explained SOPA would kill small firms and start-ups.[89] Google's chief legal officer argued that SOPA would "censor the web."[90] Zuckerberg explained that SOPA damaged the Internet's power as a "tool…for creating a more open and connected world."[91]

A group of 83 prominent Internet inventors and engineers sent an open letter to the US Congress arguing "we, the under signed have played various parts in building a network called the Internet…[and SOPA] will risk fragmenting the Internet's global domain system (DNS) and have other capricious technical consequences."[92] *The Daily Show*'s Jon Stewart succinctly summarized the complaints by declaring that SOPA could "break the Internet."[93]

In the face of such resistance, the US Congress shelved the bill, although other worrisome siblings continue to be raised. Indeed, WikiLeaks revelations suggest that the intellectual property chapter of the Trans-Pacific Partnership Agreement contains provisions that echo those in SOPA, just wrapped up in a different cover.[94]

The OECD has addressed the issue of intermediary roles, including the problems of copyright enforcement and take down regimes in some depth in a series of carefully researched studies and reports. It has recommended that governments adopt clear principles and a set of "best practices" in legislation that clearly delineate appropriate protections and any limitations to Internet intermediary liability.[95]

Google has also weighed in on the issue by urging governments to "honor existing international obligations including under the World Trade Organization (WTO) Agreement, prevent trade barriers created by information regulation, and develop new international rules that provide enhanced protection against these trade barriers of the 21st century."[96] Google has also outlined an ambitious three-point agenda to "publicly highlight as unfair trade barriers those practices by governments that restrict or disrupt the flow of online information services; take appropriate action where government restrictions on the free flow of online information violate international trade rules; [and] establish new international trade rules under bilateral, regional, and multilateral agreements that provide further assurances in favor of the free flow of information on the Internet."[97]

Conclusion

In this chapter, we have looked at the surveillance and censorship practices of states and corporations. Surveillance tends to undermine people's trust in the Internet by violating their desire for privacy. Censorship undermines the quality of information that people can obtain and their perceptions of the network's reliability and can raise some real-world safety concerns, thereby eroding trust and social capital. Once again, as trust wanes, users change their behaviour, often compelling them to use cumbersome technological solutions that harm an economy's potential for innovation and level of economic health.

The big lesson? The social capital of the network is tenuous. People's trust can be eroded remarkably quickly. States and private actors can damage that trust with serious consequences for how Internet users behave. When people lose trust in the system due to state or corporate surveillance, they change their behaviour to try to make their information more private. Sometimes, as we can infer from the results of the 2016 CIGI-Ipsos poll, hundreds of millions of people simply use the network less — or at the very least less productively. More obviously, but just as important, the costs of lost opportunity accrue quickly as individuals and states change their behaviours — and those numbers can run into the billions.

Five

One or Many, Internet or Fragnet?

Vinton G. Cerf is one of the rock stars of the Internet. Although his is not exactly a household name, it should be. He is the co-founder of the Internet. No one would be able to get online and surf to their heart's desire without his invention. Along with his University of California colleague, Robert Kahn, Cerf created the Transmission Control Protocol/ Internet Protocol (TCP/IP), which assembles packets of data for transportation across the Internet, as well as many of the Internet's other key design features. Much of this inventing was done in the early 1980s, when Cerf worked at the US Defense Department in its highly secretive Defense Advanced Research Projects Agency (DARPA). It was at DARPA that he had a major hand in developing the data packet and security technologies that are so central to the Internet's basic operations.

Today, Cerf is vice president and chief Internet evangelist for Google. He is also one of the leading champions of an open, accessible, safe and secure Internet and very much in demand as a public speaker at gatherings of Internet junkies, who will crowd around him to pose for selfies and get his autograph. Lately, he has been warning his audiences about the looming danger of

Internet "fragmentation." At a May 2015 conference at Columbia University, Cerf's remarks drew worldwide attention to the prospect that the Internet might break apart. "In my view, fragmentation is destructive of the basic functioning of the Internet," he said. "Fragmentation would be a terrible outcome [and] destroy the value [of the Internet]....we have to work to make sure that there is no reason to fragment."[1]

What exactly is fragmentation? As we'll discuss, it has many nuances and complexities. The word itself conjures up images — a child's errant baseball shattering a suburban picture window or perhaps a medieval landscape of castles, drawbridges and moats where travellers and traders are not only threatened by bandits and hooligans, but burdened by taxes and tithes as they cross from one fiefdom to another. Certainly, in the context of Internet governance, the word suggests something radically different from the interconnectedness we assume is at the heart of the network. There are some countries that want to throw that baseball into the window by disconnecting themselves from the Internet and creating their own parallel, national-level networks. Others want to regulate and tax activities on the Internet, much like those medieval lords and barons.

Fragmentation is fundamentally a matter of degree. Some fragmentation is actually a good thing, under some circumstances. Limiting the ability of people to view child pornography, for example, fragments the flow of data on the Web, but it is morally the right thing to do. More generally, differences in local laws effectively fragment the content available on the Internet, so that videos, websites and blogs are accessible in some jurisdictions and not in others. In the extreme, fragmentation based upon content is problematic, although many would be firmly in agreement that different cultures ought to have the right to express themselves online and have a say about what content is available in their countries. So, while too much fragmentation (or fragmentation of the wrong sort) is very bad indeed, as with many things in life, there is a middle zone where some fragmentation actually produces more benefit than harm.

As all this suggests, different people use the term fragmentation to mean very different things. As William J. Drake, Vinton G. Cerf and Wolfgang Kleinwächter[2] point out in their white paper on the subject for the World Economic Forum, the technical community might take it to mean messing with the infrastructure and protocols of the network, while businesses might see fragmentation as different regulatory rules across countries, while civil society might interpret it to mean restrictions on the ability of users to access content. Varying conceptualizations can, of course, result in confused policy.

Nuance and degree make it challenging to describe the full reality and the complex nature of the Internet fragmentation problem that is concerning Vint Cerf, but in this chapter we take a look at some of the factors and forces at play, in particular, some of special interest not only to policy makers but also to Internet users. Box 5.1 provides an overview of some forms of fragmentation and their potential costs and benefits, as well as policies that might help to address them.

The breakdown of public trust — specifically, three of its components: correctness, privacy and security — is creating its own political and regulatory dynamic to fragment the Internet. Eroded public trust plays a role in demands for data localization, requirements for territorial routing and the development of different legal regimes, which all have the potential to undermine economic growth, innovation and free expression. Propriety protocols and traffic prioritization on the Internet are having their own separate impacts on trust, especially as trust pertains to correctness — reliability of access and content — namely, the user being able to access the proper information from a trusted site when he or she goes online.

Box 5.1: Fragmentation Matrix

Legal Fragmentation

Different countries have different legal rules and it is not clear which rules apply in which cases. For example, does the location of the user, the server or the company matter?

Costs
- Coordination problems can undermine economic growth and the spread of the Internet.
- Costs include questions of jurisdiction and cumbersome and expensive legal processes (mutual legal assistance treaties [MLATs]).

Benefits
Limited legal interoperability may provide benefits through:
- its respect of state sovereignty as well as local social and cultural perspectives; and
- creation of comparative advantages to do with data protection.

Potential Policy Solutions[3]
- Harmonization
- Standardization
- Mutual recognition
- Reciprocity
- Cooperative solutions

Caveat
Not all issue areas need the same type of policy response. For example, the harmonization needed to maintain the DNS is not the same as the reciprocity or mutual recognition needed to limit privacy violations across countries.

Data Localization

Occurs where countries require that data be stored locally to avoid certain parts of the Internet.

Costs
- More costly management of corporate IT platforms.
- Delays or cancellations of IT projects due to legal uncertainty.
- Withdrawal of corporations from some jurisdictions due to high costs.

Benefits
- Local IT firms that are protected by data localization laws.
- Organizational innovation among firms as they try to adapt to these regulatory realities.

Potential Policy Solutions
- Limit the root cause of broad-based surveillance of foreign nationals by the United States and other governments.
- Include data localization laws in trade agreements to effectively open national borders, as was done with other areas of commerce in the twentieth century.

Caveat

Data localization laws cause distributional shifts in wealth. Some actors win from data localization, while others lose. Not everyone will want to give up these policies, even if more GDP growth could be obtained overall.

Proprietary Protocols

The Internet functions due to open, interoperable protocols such as Wi-Fi and TCP/IP. With the growth of platforms such as Facebook, Twitter and Skype that are based on proprietary protocols, a market has emerged for application programming interfaces (APIs) that allow different programs to talk to one another.

Costs
- Needing to rely on APIs to enable different programs to communicate results in transaction costs and the potential for other inefficiencies.
- Proprietary protocols may stifle innovation and the development of the best protocols possible because they are not open to public scrutiny. They can lead to monopoly competition, which is economically inefficient.

Benefits

Proprietary protocols can result in large profits for certain firms and industries.

Potential Policy Solutions
- Maintain the universality of the Internet's protocols.
- Maintain the openness of the standard development process (so that everyone who wants to can contribute to the development process).
- Maintain open standards in order to promote maximum economic competition.

Caveat

Large content providers and content intermediaries benefit from their proprietary protocols. Owners of APIs also do well interfacing between siloed systems. These corporations will resist policies to maintain universally open and interoperable protocols.

Territorial Routing Requirements

Costs

- These requirements create inefficiencies by working against the logic of the Internet, which finds the optimal data route.
- They risk generating monopolies and cartels in the data-transit space.

Benefits

Some nations would claim that routing traffic in certain ways hinders the surveillance efforts of foreign governments, particularly the NSA, making citizens safer.

Potential Policy Solutions

Since the structure of the Internet works against territorial routing requirements, the main focus should be to allow the Internet to function as it was designed.

Caveat

To be effective, such efforts will require the cooperation of governments, content intermediaries and ISPs.

IPv4 to IPv6 Transition

Currently, most devices use the IPv4. These addresses are becoming depleted as more devices and individuals come online. The replacement protocol, IPv6, will vastly expand the number of addresses and allow the Internet to continue growing. However, the protocols are not strictly interoperable.

Costs

- Without an effective transition, the number of Internet users will either be capped at the limited number of available IPv4 addresses or there will be effectively two Internets, one based upon IPv4 and one based upon IPv6.
- There are tremendous economic costs to a failed transition, as the Internet's potential to continue to foster economic growth will be hindered.
- Users of one protocol might also be unable to access content hosted on the other protocol system.

Benefits

Those Internet registries that control the unused IPv4 addresses can benefit from a slow transition because they can sell these addresses to others. High demand for scarce addresses should make this business practice profitable.

Potential Policy Solutions

Policies to effectively manage the transition need to be coordinated and broad-based. For the Internet to continue growing, governments may need to compel companies to build ICT systems based upon the IPv6 protocol. To minimize the pains of the transition, translation programs that allow IPv4 devices to communicate with IPv6 devices should be promoted. Crucially, such efforts are only likely to be effective if paired with a forced transition to IPv6. Otherwise, translation services hinder the transition by making it unnecessary for people to change.

Caveat

Metcalfe's law indicates that the value of a network is proportional to the square of the number of users of that network. There will be very little market incentive to transition to IPv6 until the number of IPv6 users surpasses the number of IPv4 users.

Traffic Prioritization

Often referred to under the banner of net neutrality, traffic prioritization refers to limiting either a user's ability to access content and services or the ability of different networks to effectively share data and communicate.

Costs

* Traffic prioritization can be costly for consumers, who might find that their ability to access certain services or content is impinged due to the behaviour of an ISP.
* Traffic prioritization can also inhibit innovation by raising the start-up costs of firms needing to pay extra to gain quality access to consumers.

Benefits

Well-established ISPs, particular those that also own content generators such as sports teams, can benefit economically from slowing the traffic of services that are in competition with their own.

Potential Policy Solutions

* Maintaining network neutrality is more or less a vote for maintaining the current system. Not taking policy action will serve to maintain the current system to some measure.
* Policies could be undertaken to limit the anti-competitive activities of some ISPs that own both content and the networks that deliver it.

Caveat

Previous rulings in favour of network neutrality in the United States are under challenge. Given the dominance of the United States in the ICT and content spaces, the US policies will have impact everywhere.

Creation of Alternative Networks

The most salient case is Iran's plan to develop its own Internet.

Costs

Developing country-based intranets effectively partitions one part of the Internet off from the remaining whole. Both sides lose out, but not necessarily by equal amounts:

- Users within the intranet could not access content and service outside of the local network.
- Those on the broader network could not access the content and services provided on the local network.
- Local intranets could also facilitate a state's surveillance of its population.

Benefits

- Local intranets would protect citizens from foreign surveillance in some measure.
- Having a closed intranet could also be a benefit to local businesses.

Potential Policy Solutions

- Pressure should be applied to countries that are contemplating the development of intranets.
- The drivers of intranet development, such as broad-based foreign surveillance, could also be reformed to limit the incentive for intranet development.

Caveat

Broadly, this area of concern should focus on restrictions to the general Internet only. Many countries, do require that certain sensitive material, such as government communications, remain on an intranet or effectively stay within the originating country. Companies and individuals also do this. Financial service industries rely upon private networks to capitalize upon microsecond latencies. Individuals also use VPNs to share content.

Restrictions on Digital Flows

Flows in information and data make up some 3.4 percent of GDP in 13 economies that together represent 70 percent of the world's GDP.

Costs

- Restrictions on digital flows will cause significant economic loss.
- Failure to liberalize the data flow restrictions in more closed economies will result in a further loss of missed GDP growth.

Benefits

- As with the other forms of international flow restrictions, some businesses will benefit from limited digital flows because they will be shielded by public policy from global competition.

Possible Policy Solutions
- Preventive policy tracks are needed to limit any new barriers to the flow of digital data.
- Proactive policy tracks are needed to remove barriers to data flow among countries, through trade negotiations and the like.

Caveat

Economics cannot be considered in isolation from security concerns. Free-flowing data makes economic sense, but it also generates security concerns:
- States are concerned about their data and their citizens' data falling into the wrong hands.
- Individuals are concerned about differing rules governing use, distribution and storage of their data. For example, some jurisdictions might have weak privacy laws, which can put people's privacy in jeopardy.

Content Fragmentation

Many parts of the Internet are effectively fragmented from each other due to linguistic and cultural barriers. One way in which these social barriers overlap with the technology of the Internet is via internationalized domain names (IDNs), many of which do not use the Latin alphabet.

Costs

Costs accrue to all users — those using IDNs and those using other domains. Both sides suffer from content restrictions and the potential loss of opportunities for economic growth:
- Main cost is the inability to meaningfully access content that exists in other languages.
- IDNs do not interoperate perfectly with other services such as email, browsers and certificate authorities that use other domains.

Benefits

IDNs and other culturally or linguistically specific parts of the Internet allow for local socio-cultural expression.

Potential Policy Solutions
- Develop translation services that allow users of one type of script (for example, Latin) to access content hosted in another (such as Mandarin or Cyrillic).
- Strengthen interface programs that allow for services hosted on one domain name to be used by IDNs, and vice versa.

Caveat

Barriers to interaction across socio-cultural lines should be minimized, but the choice of interaction across boundaries should remain voluntary and user driven.

Stepping on the Garden Hose: The Breakdown of "Net Neutrality"

The Internet was designed to allow packets of information to flow freely and at the same speed across the network, regardless of the information's content or characteristics. That is to say, traffic was not prioritized, so, when a consumer downloaded a movie or television program from, say, Netflix, the ISP would treat that large data file no differently than a smaller file, such as email. Put simply, the ISP can't play favourites among its users.

This principle, "net neutrality," means that large firms like Netflix or YouTube have access to the Internet on the same terms as smaller firms. It's supposed to be a level playing field.

In some countries, though, the ISPs, which are either monopolies or have few competitors in their local market, have sought to levy additional fees on content providers or to block or slow down the delivery of content by competitors over their networks. That was the case with Verizon, the US telecommunications giant, which challenged the Federal Communication Commission's rules on net neutrality in US courts. In early 2015, a number of US companies also challenged Federal Communications Commission policies under Title II of the Communications Act, which does not allow companies to pay for faster broadband access.

In April 2014, the European Parliament passed legislation supporting the principle of net neutrality. For many, the move was seen as a victory for the champions of an open Internet, although it has yet to become actual law. Under the proposed legislation, major European ISPs such as Vodaphone or Deutsche Telekom will not be allowed to block content and will have to offer services over their networks that do not discriminate against their competition. But the proposed legislation still has yet to be ratified by the European Parliament and, even then, the rules will have to be thrashed out with the European Commission before they can be implemented.

Figure 5.1: Percentage Change in Netflix Download Speed Since January 2013, by ISP

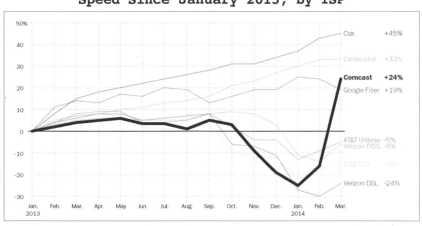

One well-publicized case of what violations of net neutrality can do involves the popular video streaming service Netflix and its battle with Comcast in the United States. In late 2013 and early 2014, in a clash of titans, the two got into a tussle about Netflix download speeds over Comcast's network. Comcast wanted Netflix to pay more for the use of its cables and wireless signals because Netflix was eating up lots of bandwidth but didn't have to pay for it. Comcast thought that was unfair.

In the midst of the dispute, Netflix released data showing the download speed of their services over the Comcast network. The numbers are striking. Amid the fray, Netflix download speeds slowed precipitously (Figure 5.1). From October 2013 to the depth of the trough in January 2014, Netflix download speeds fell almost 30 percent. Shortly after Comcast and Netflix reached an agreement in February 2014, Netflix streaming speeds on Comcast networks increased even more dramatically, rising almost 40 percent.

What happened? Some allege that Comcast clamped down on the delivery of Netflix's content — an action known technically as throttling. Throttling is like standing on a running garden hose —

Figure 5.2: Measurement Lab's Take on the Netflix Slowdown

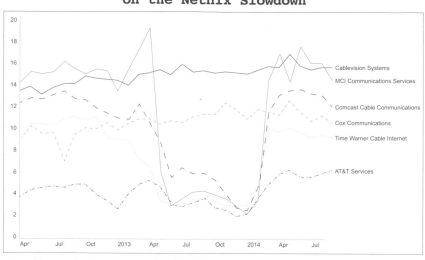

Source: Reprinted with permission from Dan Rayburn, 2014, October 29, "New Study From M-Lab Sheds Light On Widespread Harm Caused By Netflix Routing Decisions," *Business of Video* (blog), October 29, http://blog.streamingmedia.com/2014/10/mlab-netflix-routing-decisions.html.

the volume of water/data out the other end slows to a trickle. If so, Comcast's response was just as unfair and as damaging to the interests of consumers as any advantage Netflix might have had at the outset.

Of course, like all stories, there are two sides. While some blame Comcast, others place the blame for the slowdown of Netflix downloads at the feet of Netflix's intermediate network, Cogent.[4] Cogent carried Netflix content to other ISPs, including Comcast and Time Warner Cable. But, in early 2013, Cogent began to *prioritize* the traffic of retail users over the content of wholesale customers (such as Netflix). Netflix download speeds fell to all the networks that did not have a direct interconnection agreement with Netflix (basically just Cablevision Systems and Cox Communications).

As Figure 5.2 shows, Measurement Lab, the world's largest source of open Internet data, caught Cogent red-handed in this practice. Around February or March, Netflix speeds across a number of networks (not just Comcast, the one it was battling with) declined precipitously. It appears as though Cogent may have had a hand in the slowdown.

For our purposes, who did what and who should take the blame is really of secondary concern. More important is the impact such disputes have on consumers' perceptions of the reliability of the network. Throttling services may cause people to trust the network less, as it makes the system slow and unreliable. Being unable to consistently stream videos on demand falls into this category, even if it might seem like a small problem compared to other forms of eroding trust such as breached computers and stolen records.

Without net neutrality regulations, the Internet could become akin to those fiefdoms of old, or a modern-day toll road with fast-track carpool lanes — placing some companies at a competitive disadvantage vis-à-vis rival firms that get preferential access to the network. Consumers, too, would suffer, either because content was blocked or because they would have to pay more to access certain kinds of services. Small start-up companies offering new products and services online would also be hit hard if they had to pay more to deliver video or other high bandwidth services to consumers. Larger companies could probably absorb this cost, but start-ups and smaller firms that lack a revenue base could easily find themselves disadvantaged when up against their more powerful and better-financed competitors.

If countries go their separate ways on the principle of net neutrality, the costs of navigating a patchwork of global networks could skyrocket and the Internet could fragment. A major study of US and European net neutrality debates and regulations conducted for the GCIG identifies four types of fragmentation that could occur if countries fail to harmonize net neutrality policies and legislation: "further divergence between the US and the EU regarding the competitiveness of their Internet industries; increased barriers of market entry for new innovative start-ups in the EU that seek to challenge Silicon Valley tech titans; divergence of customer experience of the Internet; and [use of] discriminatory interconnection practices...to undermine the global Internet marketplace of information and services."[5]

Some countries, such as the United States and the Netherlands, have solid net neutrality protections. Others are debating the rules (including the United States until quite recently) and some, such as India, have no rules at all. Should the side of the debate advocating against the equal flow of data online win the day, the Internet will become far less reliable. As a result, people will trust the network less, and the digital social capital that allows for tremendous innovation on top of the platform will fall away.

Boundaries vs Walls: Considering Free Speech and the Right to Be Forgotten

Back in 1998, a Spanish lawyer named Mario Costeja González was in some financial trouble. As a result of mounting debts, his property was to be auctioned off, and a newspaper in Spain published two notices about the upcoming forced sale.[6]

By 2010, González had long resolved his credit problems, but he remained concerned that Google searches on his name continued to link to the old newspaper notices. He appealed to Spanish authorities to force the newspaper to remove the notices from its website.[7] A writer for *The Atlantic* described the resulting court case, ultimately decided by the Court of Justice of the European Union (CJEU), as one that "could change the Internet as we know it."[8]

The CJEU ruled that the newspaper could keep the notices on its website, but ordered Google to remove any links to the notices during searches of González's name.[9] The court argued that González's right to privacy overruled "not only the economic interest" of Google, "but also the interest of the general public in having access to that information."[10]

Many derided the judgment. The British House of Lords' EU Committee issued a report claiming the CJEU's judgment was "misguided" and "unworkable."[11] The founder of Wikipedia compared the European ruling to something one would expect from a totalitarian state.[12] Jules Polonetsky, executive director of the Future of Privacy Forum think tank, lamented to *The New Yorker* that "the decision will go down in history as one of the most significant mistakes that Court has ever made."[13]

The Atlantic sardonically titled its story on the ruling "Will Europe Censor This Article?" The magazine highlighted how, ironically, the ruling explicitly mentioned González's name and auction notices, asking, "Will the Court order that its own decision be made unsearchable online?"[14]

However, not all requests to censor search results inspire as much scorn. When nude photos of actress Jennifer Lawrence were leaked online without her consent, Lawrence told *Vanity Fair* to much acclaim that the event was no less than a sex crime. "Just because I'm a public figure, just because I'm an actress, does not mean I asked for this," she said, elaborating that "it should be my choice."[15] The United States has no equivalent to the European Union's "right to be forgotten" (RTBF) policy. Lawrence and her lawyers relied on the Digital Millennium Copyright Act to successfully justify demands that Google remove links to the sites hosting the pictures. Some believe that those who take selfies also own the copyright to their photos, although a photo uploaded to Instagram was recently sold for US$90,000 without the knowledge of the photographer.[16]

Others in the United States cannot resort to copyright legislation, no matter how sympathetic their situation may be. In 2006, 18-year-old Nikki Catsouras was horrifically decapitated in an auto accident, and gruesome photos of the scene began to circulate online. Her family later learned that two California Highway Patrol officers had emailed official investigation photos to their family members for their shock value on Halloween. The photos were subsequently forwarded, went viral and ended up on thousands of websites.[17]

Nikki's family began to fear accidentally stumbling across the photos online. Eventually they sought legal assistance. Because the United States had nothing equivalent to Europe's RTBF legislation, the family was forced to appeal to individual websites to take down the grisly photos. Nearly 2,000 websites complied, but many more continue to host the vivid reminder of the Catsourases' daughter's death.[18]

Catsouras's father told *The New Yorker* that, after six years of legal battles, a similar RTBF ruling in the United States could have saved him much grief. "What a great thing it would have been for someone in our position…I would do anything to be able to go to Google and have it remove those links."[19]

Most of us would support the right to have a modicum of privacy online, particularly in the kinds of situations described above. And some level of privacy is essential if citizens are to trust the Internet and not feel threatened by the prospect of extremely personal (or simply wrong, hurtful or slanderous) information finding its way online. However, if every country develops its own legislation to enforce privacy standards, and if those standards differ substantially from one jurisdiction to the next, compliance with all these different rules will present major challenges to companies providing services across different jurisdictions. Privacy laws, therefore, also factor into the issue of fragmentation.

For example, in 2014, the European Commission proposed a number of key changes to the 15-year-old "Safe Harbor" agreement, which gives roughly 3,000 US companies the right to repatriate the personal data of Europeans as long as they allow users to opt out and limit collection to "relevant" information.[20] The agreement was subsequently invalidated by a decision of the CJEU, prompting months of intense negotiations and the eventual conclusion of a "political" agreement on a new EU-US Privacy Shield, which will protect the rights of Europeans when their personal data is transferred to the United States.[21] Although the actual details of the agreement are subject to further negotiations, it will impose rigorous obligations on companies as to how to handle the personal data of Europeans, raising compliance and reporting costs for US companies. Even more controversial is the as yet unenumerated right to know who holds one's personal big data, as well as the right to own it. As Will Marshall argues in *The Wall Street Journal*, "Some US companies have indeed failed to be responsible stewards of customer data. But the privacy rift is more a matter of cultural differences: Europeans regard privacy as a 'fundamental human right,' while Americans are more inclined to let companies collect personal data in exchange for access to the Internet's boundless information. US tech companies are especially worried that a too rigid approach to privacy threatens the use of 'big data' analytics to improve services and raise productivity."[22]

Carl Bildt, a former prime minister of Sweden, warns about an "open hunting season across much of Europe" where, in his words, "the prey [is] big American companies that, in the eyes of many, are too dominant in internet-based services ranging from search and social media to shopping and online television."[23] Bildt's point is that there are clearly digital protectionist tendencies arising in Europe, and elsewhere for that matter. These tendencies are manifesting in both the rhetoric of politicians and in recent moves by regulators to try to compel largely American Internet companies to keep the data of Europeans in Europe. As with all forms of protectionist policies, these efforts distort markets and make everyone less well off, even if they are superficially at least appealing on privacy grounds.[24]

Jonah Force Hill at Harvard University concurs: "While increased legal protections for personal data may be a necessary part of the solution to the online privacy problem, there are mounting concerns that if many countries adopt their own unique privacy requirements, then every firm operating on the Internet could potentially be subjected to a multiplicity of inconsistent laws. If companies are unable to meet each country's differing requirements, either because those requirements are in conflict with one another or because of the added costs associated with meeting multiple disparate rules, then we could see firms pulling out of particular markets entirely."[25] Ultimately, these differences are bridgeable, although they are likely to be the subject of protracted negotiations among governments.

Data Localization

We can now return to the interrelationship of lost trust due to eroded privacy, data localization and the national-level economic costs these incur. Data localization is defined as "storing data in a datacenter on the Internet that is physically situated in the same the country where the data originated."[26] Pressure for data localization is driven by concerns about privacy and data security. Before anyone had ever heard of Edward Snowden, American expatriate and European resident James Kinsella saw the writing on the wall. He predicted that consumers were growing increasingly concerned about their privacy and that stricter data protection rules in the European Union would soon follow. In response, he challenged a software engineer in 2012 to prove that a cloud-based team-sharing platform could operate as cost-effectively in Europe as in the United States.[27]

From this challenge emerged Kinsella's brainchild, Zettabox, an entirely European cloud storage company that Kinsella founded along with partner Robert McNeal. With its catchy slogan, "It's better in Europe," Zettabox describes itself as a world-class cloud service, with data housed entirely within the geographical borders of Europe. Zettabox stores customer data in leased centres in Amsterdam, Berlin, Frankfurt, Milan, Geneva, Paris, London and Madrid.[28]

With much fanfare, including a supportive mention in the European Commission's "EU Data Protection Reform and Big Data Factsheet,"[29] the start-up came out of beta in June 2015. *The New York Times* hailed Kinsella as "an unlikely champion for European technology," and many have applauded the transformation of the former Microsoft and MSNBC.com executive into a staunch supporter of Europe's tough data privacy rules.[30] Observers admired the start-up's willingness to go head-to-head with industry giants Google, Amazon and Microsoft. "Europe needs a European service," Kinsella told *The New York Times*. "Europeans have no say over where their data is held by American companies. We're offering an alternative to that."[31]

Many other nations have also jumped on the data localization bandwagon, including, most notably, Brazil. The problem with these calls for what are colloquially known as data localization requirements is that they are costly for everyone, and probably not even that effective at preventing state agencies from getting access to personal data. For example, the cost of building a single new data centre in Brazil, several of which would be needed to store the user-generated data of Brazil's roughly 101 million Internet users, is roughly US$60.9 million. Monthly operational costs for a *single* data centre come in at around US$950,000.[32] With costs like these, many Internet companies would not even be able to operate in Brazil. Excluding companies from the Brazilian market would both hinder domestic investment and harm corporate bottom lines in the rest of the world. Isolating the market would also limit the possibilities for innovation, cultural expression and economic growth in Brazil.

At the same time as countries contemplated new restrictions on the flow of data, US firms suffered directly from lost business as a result of Internet users' loss of trust. One study puts the cost of the PRISM revelations for the US-based cloud industry (where user data is stored on remote servers located all over the world) at between US$22 to $35 billion over the next few years.[33] The German government initiated plans to change its procurement policies to exclude American technology firms with ties to the NSA and other intelligence agencies from bidding on lucrative public contracts.[34] Cisco Systems has also talked publicly about the negative effect of the NSA's activity on its bottom line, stating that, as a result of the NSA disclosures, its worldwide revenue would fall by as much as eight to 10 percent in the fourth quarter of 2014 due to weak global sales.[35]

More generally, the loss of trust that results from state surveillance is also a harbinger of significant economy-wide costs. When data flows less freely across the borderless world of the Internet, innovation and economic productivity are undermined. For example, one study modelling minimalist and maximalist data localization policies across a number of countries finds that distrustful responses from Brazil to the Internet ecosystem could cost the entire Brazilian economy between US$4.7 and $15 billion, or a GDP reduction of 0.02 percent, in 2014. The costs are even higher in Europe, speaking to advanced economies' greater dependence on the Internet infrastructure. Here, data localization could cost anywhere between US$80 and $193 billion and reduce the European Union's GDP by as much as 0.04 percent.[36] Brazil and Germany are not alone in their contemplation of data localization legislation. China, India, Indonesia, South Korea and Vietnam also have proposed laws in the works. At the root of it are concerns about surveillance, privacy and foreign competition.

Another study carried out by McKinsey for the GCIG finds that global financial institutions, which "have leveraged the Internet to establish private communication networks and capture efficiencies from global technology" are now struggling with myriad different national rules and restrictions about how to manage and transmit customers' data, even across their own private networks.[37] Based on interviews with senior financial executives, the study points to degrading operational efficiencies and the rapidly rising costs of doing business as banks struggle with the challenges of interpreting literally thousands of regulations and the costs of having to invest in new technology in order to adapt to privacy and data handling requirements in different national jurisdictions. In some countries, regulations have become so onerous that exit is becoming a serious option.[38]

What is perhaps surprising is that results from the 2014 CIGI-Ipsos poll paint a mixed picture about the level of the individual consumer's desire for data localization. When asked if they want to have their data stored on a secure server, 73 percent of respondents polled indicated that they did. But, when asked if they wanted their data stored on a secure server that was also housed in their own country — what Zettabox proposed to do in Europe — the results are, as a whole, statistically indistinguishable. Here, only 72 percent of respondents wanted data to be stored on a secure server that was also in their own country.

One interpretation of this result is that people care a lot about security of data storage, but not about its location per se. The 72 percent of respondents who want to have stored data secured in their own country is statistically indistinguishable from the 73 percent who just want security.* According to these numbers at least, most people don't seem to care about location so long as the data remain secure (Figure 5.3).

However, these totals obscure some telling regional differences. One of the most notable trends is that physical location matters more for those living in the rich, liberal democracies in North America and Europe than for those in most other regions of the world. Nine percent more of the respondents in North America and four percent more of respondents in Europe want their data to be both secure and physically stored in their own country.

The other interesting finding revealed by the regional data is that Hong Kong and South Korea don't actually want data stored locally, much preferring instead that it be stored securely (that is, elsewhere). Table 5.1 shows public preferences in the surveyed Asia-Pacific nations regarding secure data storage and data location. The difference between secure and secure-and-local is 17 percentage

---

* The 73 percent figure is essentially a baseline measure. It tells us how many people want their data to be stored securely. Deviations from this baseline of secure storage tell us how much more or less people value storage in their own territorial jurisdictions. So, if 91 percent of people wanted data stored securely and in their own country, then the difference between that number and 73 percent would be the extent to which location matters, assuming that people answer consistently across questions. In this hypothetical example, about 18 percent more people would be motivated to choose security and location over just security alone. According to the actual numbers, there is no such difference.

Figure 5.3: How and Where User Data Is Stored — Public Perceptions

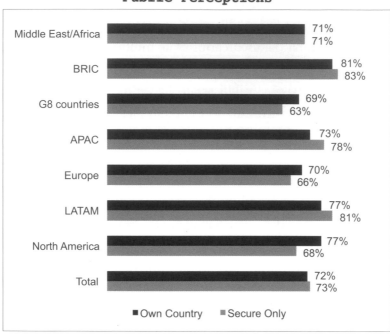

Source: Data from the CIGI-Ipsos 2014 Global Survey.
Note: BRIC = Brazil, Russia, India and China; G8 = Group of Eight; APAC = Asia and Pacific; LATAM = Latin America.

Table 5.1: Asia-Pacific Preferences About Data Localization

	China	Hong Kong	Indonesia	Japan	South Korea
Secure	87%	82%	83%	61%	73%
Secure and in own country	85%	65%	82%	59%	53%
Difference	-2%	-17%	-1%	-2%	-20%

Source: Data from the CIGI-Ipsos 2014 Global Survey.

points for Hong Kong respondents and 20 points for South Korean respondents.

While we need to be careful about ascribing motives to these differences, it is possible that individuals in both Asian jurisdictions are hesitant to even allow for the possibility that data stored primarily within their own respective political jurisdictions is actually secure.

South Korea has been subjected to a constant barrage of cyber attacks emanating from neighbouring North Korea, including attacks directed at its major financial institutions, which have incurred major losses. The country is also fearful of a military invasion from the north. This may be one of the reasons why South Koreans feel less confident about the physical location of their data and put a premium on making sure that the data is secure and less vulnerable to attack. South Korea also has the National Security Act, which allows the government to summarily arrest anyone who has ever voiced an opinion that could be construed as supportive of North Korea. The enforcement of restrictions like these can require spying (although not always) on personal data, which could make South Koreans uncertain about what their government is doing.

Hong Kong, given its generally pro-democratic culture and integration with Communist mainland China, may also place a higher premium on security because of the territory's perceived vulnerabilities to pressure and manipulation by Chinese political authorities. In 2014, these perceived vulnerabilities even came to a head when mainland China became involved in the pro-democracy rallies in Hong Kong.

The main lesson to draw from these results is that there are interesting cross-national variations in public attitudes about data localization and in the degree to which the public feels that privacy and security are enhanced if data is stored in centres located within their own national borders. While pretty well everyone wants their data stored securely, North Americans and Europeans, by a small but significant margin, believe that secure local data storage is even more desirable. Some companies might want to take advantage of this by marketing a national (or regional) as opposed to a world-based cloud service. But territorial solutions are not necessarily what everyone wants. Some countries doubt that local security is possible and prefer that data be stored securely, regardless of the physical location of the servers.

It is worth noting that some governments are having second thoughts about imposing data localization requirements. For example, after much internal debate, the Brazilian government decided to drop data localization requirements in its new Marco Civil legislation — which we will discuss later — because of strong opposition from ISPs and social activists, who correctly argued that such restrictions would be damaging to business and small start-ups.[39]

Yet, at the same time, other nations have moved ahead with their data localization plans. Data localization is certainly costly in economic terms for a country that decides to do it. But there are other motives — for example, security. The idea that you can control your own data better in your own jurisdiction is not fanciful. The United States is in a legal battle with Microsoft over data of a US citizen that was generated by use of an American company's service but stored in Ireland. The United States says it can access that data as a part of a legal proceeding. Microsoft says it has no legal claim to the data. The battle rages on. If the United States had data storage requirements, it could easily access this data. That ability is motivating for many nations.

The other motive for increased data localization is distributional. Data localization disadvantages foreign companies that are trying to operate in a given jurisdiction, while it favours local firms. Like the old mercantilist protectionism of the nineteenth century, data localization can be seen as a move to pick domestic winners at the expense of foreign competition. Short-sighted, perhaps, but it won't stop those politicians looking out for quick political gain by implementing otherwise poor policy.

Territorial Routing and Rerouting

Territorial routing is a form of fragmentation, in that it dictates how data flows over the Internet. Usually, data is sent by the fastest possible route. That is the design principle behind how the Internet is built. It is highly efficient.

Sometimes, however, limitations to infrastructure mean that data flows in weird ways that can affect users' perceptions of privacy and, by extension, the level of trust that they invest in the system. Take a few examples gathered by IXmaps, a research project based at the University of Toronto.[40] Imagine that someone from Toronto, Ontario, sends an email to Health Canada, headquartered in Ottawa, Ontario, about her health coverage for some sensitive illness. The shortest route in physical terms might be a straight line, but this particular email travels first to New York and then to Montreal, before it heads back east to its final destination. As another example, imagine an email sent from an aspiring university student from Abbotsford, British Columbia, to Lakehead University in Thunder Bay, Ontario. Again, the shortest distance is to head straight east. This particular email, however, first heads to San José, then to San Francisco, and then to Kansas City and Chicago, before heading north and back across the border into Canada. Or, even more surreally, imagine an email sent by a young hockey fan in Toronto, Ontario, to the Hockey Hall of Fame, also in Toronto. The email is sent to an address within the same city, and yet it detours through the United States before returning to the land of hockey and maple syrup.[41]

At first glance, these examples might seem so bizarre as to be fantastical. But they are remarkably representative of a broader trend in the online data flow of Canadians. While the precise amount of Canadian data flowing to the United States is anyone's guess, Ronald Diebert, the director of the University of Toronto's Citizen Lab, places the number somewhere around 90 percent of Internet traffic.[42]

These data flows emerge because of a lack of infrastructure, but they have clear privacy ramifications. It is far easier for authorities to peer at data that transits or comes to rest within their own national jurisdiction. Canadians might not be too concerned about their traffic routing through the United States, but other nations in the world certainly would be. These privacy concerns have even generated policy changes that will have implications for how data flows and how commerce and economics unfold. Consider, for example, the case of Brazil.

Meetings between US presidents and foreign leaders are carefully scripted events, and planned months, if not years, in advance. The sheer logistics are overwhelming. In 2013, the Brazilian President Dilma Rousseff's meeting with President Obama was the only state visit scheduled that year — a fact Brazil touted as a sign of its growing global importance.[43] So Rousseff's decision to cancel her meeting with President Obama, just a month before the planned visit, was a very big deal. It sent a pointed message: Brazil was deeply unhappy with the Snowden revelations that the United States was intercepting confidential information about its citizens and government, and was willing to interrupt bilateral relations over the issue.[44]

Currently, a lot of Brazil's Internet traffic routes through the United States before reaching Europe.[45] Snowden's leaks revealed that the United States was collecting personal data on Brazilian citizens, businesses and government officials. Brazil's reaction was fierce. In addition to cancelling the state visit, Brazil decided to push forward on a massive infrastructure project — building a 3,500-mile fibre optic cable across the Atlantic Ocean to Portugal, at an estimated price tag of US$185 million. Brazil's objective was both technological and political: it sought to prevent the American NSA from spying on its citizens, while also distancing itself from US technology companies.

Brazil's efforts are part of a larger strategy of Internet self-reliance. In 2009, Brazil began drafting the Marco Civil law, also known as the Brazilian Civil Rights Framework for the Internet, which was approved by Brazil's Chamber of Deputies in 2014. The legislation regulates Internet usage in Brazil and covers privacy rights, net neutrality, freedom of speech, Internet security and Brazilian jurisdiction over Internet companies. The Brazilian justice minister dubbed it Brazil's "Constitution of the Internet." As noted above, the government also had tried to require companies to store Brazilian data on servers physically located within Brazil, so that information was available to Brazilian courts, but backtracked in the face of intense domestic opposition.

Proprietary Protocols: Sometimes Even Walled Gardens Get Personal

The Internet functions due to open, interoperable protocols such as Wi-Fi and TCP/IP. With the growth of platforms such as Facebook, Twitter and Skype, which are based upon proprietary protocols, there has been an emerging market for APIs that allow different programs to talk to one another. However, reliance upon APIs to facilitate communication across different programs results in high transaction fees, which can run up to 10 percent to 15 percent of total cost. Proprietary protocols can stifle innovation and the development of the best (that is, most efficient) protocols, because they are not open to wider scrutiny. They can also lead to monopolies, which are economically inefficient, and they have an adverse impact on trust and Internet reliability because they slow down data transfers and create latency problems. Proprietary protocols also stifle the "generative Internet," that is, a platform on which technologists can build new things, to use the phrase of Harvard's Jonathan Zittrain.[46]

Sometimes the clash is not between open standards and proprietary protocols, but between two separate bastions that refuse to work together. Personal rivalries among the kings and queens of Silicon Valley are sometimes just as important.

The late Apple CEO Steve Jobs's hatred of Adobe Systems' Flash software is legendary, and the Apple vs. Adobe feud became one of the tech industry's most visible — and visceral — disputes over proverbial walled gardens. According to biographer Walter Isaacson, Jobs felt personally offended in 1999 when Adobe would not develop video software for Apple. He funnelled his ire onto Flash, later describing it to Isaacson as a "spaghetti-ball piece of technology that has lousy performance and really bad security problems."[47]

Jobs banned Flash from iPhones, iPads and iPods, and any users attempting to view videos using Flash received an error message. Adobe argued that the ban prevented Apple mobile device users from accessing the full Web, because at that time, almost three-quarters of videos on the Web required Flash.[48]

In an open letter published in April 2010, Jobs attempted to justify Apple's ban of Flash by claiming he preferred more open and interoperable systems. "Adobe claims that we are a closed system, and that Flash is open," he wrote, "but in fact the opposite is true."[49]

Industry critics were quick to point out the hypocrisy of Jobs's arguments, claiming that Apple was equally culpable of trying to defend its walled garden and stringently control users' end-to-end experience.[50] Steve Sullivan, a writer for the technology website Ars Technica, described the feud as a "pot, meet kettle" idiom, and wrote that Jobs "doesn't want users to freely wander and creatively explore the Web or their own computers; he wants them to move from the fenced-off 'Freedom Zone' based in San Jose [Adobe] to the one based in Cupertino [Apple]."[51]

The CEO of Adobe responded to Jobs's attacks by calling his reasoning a "smokescreen" and Adobe took out multiplatform ads saying "We love Apple...what we don't love is anybody taking away your freedom to choose what you create, how you create it, and what you experience on the Web."[52] Despite Adobe's defence, the force of Jobs's personality and the commercial clout of Apple had prevailed. Adobe capitulated in 2011 and announced it would no longer be developing Flash for mobile devices.[53] Jobs — posthumously — had won.

The Jobs-Flash battle is a microcosm of a large problem. Many other privately operated programs refuse to work together. Microsoft Word tends to work less well on Mac computers than on PCs. Microsoft Outlook does not allow users to upload attachments if they access it via the Google Chrome web browers (or, ironically, via Microsoft Edge). It is a mixture of business decisions and inherent technical design flaws that results in these failures. User trust, however, is tenuous, and the clash of proprietary protocols can easily lead people to think that the network is less reliable than they would like. Expecting most people to be able to sort out who is doing what is unreasonable. When computers fail, most people just throw up their hands and bemoan the whole darn thing.

Conclusion

In this chapter, we have probed the concept of Internet fragmentation and assessed how it is both caused by, and has consequences for, trust. The concept of trust is multidimensional, and thus addressing trust deficits with isolated policy measures can be ineffective and even counterproductive. Social capital, reliant as it is upon user trust, can be easily disrupted. Sometimes policies that can fragment the Internet are actually developed because governments are responding to a perceived loss of trust. However, these policies can have negative unintended consequences and undermine trust further. Network fragmentation can occur for other reasons, such as for business motives or reasons of political correctness. It is somewhat of a Gordian knot, but the point is plain: a loss of trust and fragmentation are extremely damaging to harnessing the potential of the Internet ecosystem.

Dealing with fragmentation is also a common-pool resource problem that cannot be solved by any one nation, company or stakeholder, as in the so-called "tragedy of the commons." As Michael Chertoff and Paul Rosenzweig put it, "[S]overeign unilateralism will come with significant costs — both economic and social ones. Global companies will be subject to competing and inconsistent legal demands, with the inevitable result that consumers will suffer diminished access to the network overall."[54]

One solution, as proposed by Chertoff and Rosenzweig, is the idea of legal harmonization. Again, like fragmentation itself, harmonization is really a matter of degree. States can usefully begin to address the trust deficit that is spurring calls for fragmentation of the

Internet by harmonizing their laws to some extent, making them work together to bolster people's confidence in the system as a whole. Trust can thereby be sustained and maybe even rebuilt, but it will be the outcome of a prolonged process of negotiation by those countries that are committed to having a free, open, accessible and secure Internet.

Six

Crime, Punishment and the Deep Dark Web

Hacks and data breaches abound. It seems like almost every day we tune into the news only to learn that another company's servers have been breached. Each time it happens, our personal information — our credit card numbers, social insurance or social security numbers, our addresses, details on our tastes, our names and our birthdates — are stolen away by digital bandits. A data breach involves a violation of the boundaries of our personal and private lives.

A lot of old-fashioned crimes have also shifted online, particularly into the recesses of the Dark Web. The next sensational story in the news lineup might be the arrest of dozens of individuals linked to an online child abuse site, or an illegal online marketplace selling drugs or offering hackers or assassins for hire, or the suicide of some poor soul after pictures of her involved in sexual acts were shared via online platforms with her friends, colleagues and strangers.

The Internet is a fantastic device, but it remains a tool of those who wield it.[1] As we have shown already, the Internet has great potential for good, but it can also be used as a tool by those who want to harm society. Unlike other tools, the Internet is both a vehicle and a platform. As a vehicle, it can be used to transit criminal activity to a target. Hacks and data breaches fall into this category. As a platform, it is also the medium on top of which crime occurs. Online pornography and illegal marketplaces are in this group. But whether it's conveyed by a vehicle or promulgated via a platform, crime in cyberspace has the effect of eroding our trust.

This chapter looks at how crime unfolds both via the Internet and on top of it — at the social level. Crimes of all types affect user trust in profound ways, with enormous consequences for how people use the network. And whether the actual incidence of cybercrime is as widespread as we might fear, our perceptions also affect our behaviour in significant ways.

The State of Cyber Security

To get a full sense of the security of the Internet, we need to go back to 1969. It might come as a surprise that the first networked computers came online as early as the late 1960s. The Internet was developed by researchers (including Vint Cerf, whom we met in chapter five) at DARPA as a way to share their research and ideas. The early network quickly expanded to include academics at several universities, most of them American. The aim of the network was to facilitate communication between like-minded individuals and to promote the sharing of research. The Internet of old was largely used by professionals for professional reasons.[2] Those using it knew whom they were talking to and for what reason. It was a safe, secure scene, and filled with trusting users.

In this sort of environment, security or verification procedures to ensure that someone was who they said they were, and that the material they were sending you was as it was advertised, were not really needed. Generally speaking, security and verification procedures are inefficient and impede the flow of information, so why use them if you don't have to? Just trusting that things will work out can be easier and cheaper — or so we used to think.

From today's vantage point, the level of blind trust that existed during the heady days of the early Internet might seem naïve. But consider that although the Internet first emerged as a networked system of computers in 1969, it wasn't until 1988 — 19 years later — that the *first* Internet worm was introduced. The worm was designed by a Cornell graduate student named Robert Morris, then 23 years old.

The story, now legendary, is that in a show of Ivy League rivalry, Morris launched the malware from a computer at the Massachusetts Institute of Technology (MIT) to mask its intellectual origins at Cornell. (Ironically, Morris is now a professor at MIT.) The worm was designed to rapidly propagate itself, causing a widespread infection that eventually affected approximately 10 percent of the entire Internet.[3] But, even in this first case of a widespread worm, the malware did not carry a payload that could permanently damage the infected computer systems. And, according to Morris, the worm's release was not meant maliciously, but was instead intended as a means to plot out the size of the Internet, similar to the way contemporary web crawlers constantly rummage around the Web to map its crevasses and summits. In short, compared to some of the malware of today, the Morris Worm was downright friendly.

It took nearly two decades of Internet activity for the first infection, so the basis of trust that infused the founding of the Internet was not totally unwarranted. But, old habits die hard, and the trusting approach to the initial design of the Internet has lived on in some of its later technical developments. However, online security can no longer be assumed — and in fact safeguarding it has become a huge problem.

After the Morris Worm, cyber attacks continued to proliferate throughout the network. Increasingly, the nature of the system was revealed for what it truly was: a vulnerable bunch of interconnected devices that could be targeted from anywhere else in the network. IT security firms began to take notice of how bad things were getting. Each year, in an effort to track the insecurity of cyberspace and to drum up business, these companies began to publish Internet security reports.

Figure 6.1: Web-based Attacks (Absolute Number), 2008—2014

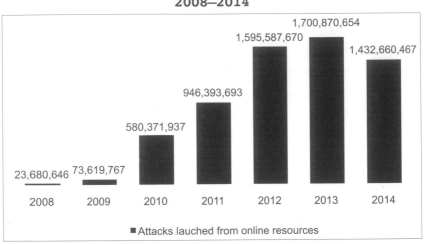

Source: Data from Kaspersky Lab, annual "Kaspersky Security Bulletins — Statistics" for the years 2008–2014, https://securelist.com/all/?category=437.

The IT security firm Kaspersky Lab, for example, provides an estimate of the number of web-based attacks that occur each year. Figure 6.1 shows the trend from 2008 to 2014. Web-based attacks occur via the Internet, as opposed to hacks delivered via Universal Serial Bus (USB) keys carrying viruses or fraudulent payment systems. Using their data, we can see that web-based attacks have risen from a low of about 24 million attacks in 2008 to a high approaching two billion attacks in 2013, amounting to a 7,000 percent increase in just six years!

These numbers seem really bad, but it is important to factor in the growing size of cyberspace in order to have a realistic sense of how safe the Internet actually is.[4] It would be logical to expect crime to go up as the population increases. It would be logical, too, to expect more cybercrime in a large, active cyberspace than in one that no one uses. So, to realistically compare events across different-sized populations, we need to "normalize" the numbers — which basically means we need to express the crime as a proportion of the size of the population. We do this all the time with crime statistics in the real (non-cyber) world — for example, "a murder rate of one murder per 100,000 people."

Normalizing the statistics matters because it puts the likelihood that a particular person is going to be affected by a crime into perspective. Imagine two scenarios: first, a town of 1,000 people with 100 crimes and, second, a city of 100,000 people with 1,000 crimes. In the town, one out of every 10 people will be the victim of a crime. In the city, in contrast, only one out of every 100 people will be a victim of crime. Basically, even though the city has as many violent crimes as the entire population of the town, crime is actually less of a problem.

When the number of web-based attacks in cyberspace from Figure 6.1 is normalized in relation to the amount of data flowing across the network or the number of Google searches undertaken each year (both recognized measures of how busy cyberspace is), a different picture emerges (Figure 6.2). The absolute number of web-based attacks hit their peak in 2013. The normalized number of web-based attacks, expressed as a proportion of either online data flows or the

Figure 6.2: Web-based Attacks (Normalized Number), 2008–2014

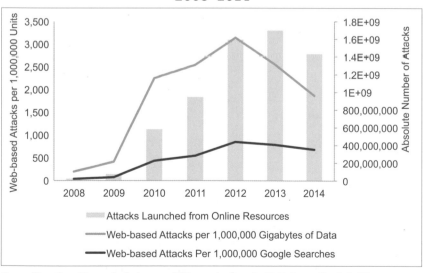

Source: Data from Kaspersky Lab, annual "Kaspersky Security Bulletins — Statistics" for 2008–2014, https://securelist.com/all/?category=437; Cisco Systems, "Cisco Networking Index: Forecast and Methodology" for 2008–2013 (www.cisco.com/web/BR/assets/docs/whitepaper_VNI_06_09.pdf) and 2009–2014 (http://large.stanford.edu/courses/2010/ph240/abdul-kafi1/docs/white_paper_c11-481360.pdf); Statistics Brain, 2015, "Google Annual Search Statistics," www.statisticbrain.com/google-searches/.

number of Google searches, hit its peak in 2012, one year earlier, and has declined faster than the absolute numbers ever since. In short, the situation in cyberspace is certainly worse than it was in 2008, but it is better than the impression we get from looking at the absolute or year-over-year change in the total number of web-based attacks.

In fact, so long as cyberspace continues to grow each year (akin to a constantly growing human population), absolute numbers on the occurrence of cybercrime will always paint a worse picture than the normalized numbers. One of three misrepresentations will always occur: first, the absolute numbers will say things are worsening, while the normalized numbers say that things are getting better; second, both sets of numbers will say that things are improving but the normalized numbers will say things are getting better at a faster rate; or third, both sets of numbers will say the situation is worsening but the normalized numbers will say that things are deteriorating more slowly than the absolute numbers.[5] Informed trust requires a real sense of the security of cyberspace, which can only be had if the crime statistics are normalized. But, as we said before, perception often rules the day.

The Moral Hazard of Data Breaches and IT Security

While normalizing cybercrime statistics is a useful and necessary corrective to how we think about security in cyberspace, popular perceptions matter a lot. And even if people merely think that crime is endemic to cyberspace, regardless of any evidence, they will often act as if it is. The link between perceptions of trustworthiness and the actions of Internet users has a long lineage.[6]

The story of data breaches, eroded trust and economy-wide effects paints a stark picture of how cybercrime can undermine perceptions of security and cause people to change their behaviour in collectively maladaptive ways. Companies of various stripes get hacked all the time. Target was breached in 2013, with 110 million records being

Figure 6.3: Data Breaches per Year in the United States

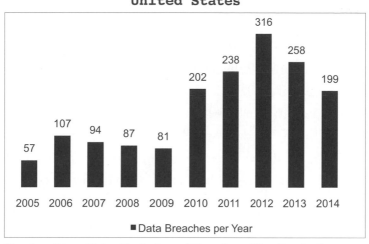

Source: Data from Privacy Rights Clearinghouse, "Chronology of Data Breaches."

compromised. In 2014, eBay was hacked and details on all 145 million account holders were compromised. The list goes on.

The breaches that we usually hear about are often the large and sensational cases, but they are just the tip of the iceberg. Privacy Rights Clearinghouse maintains a running list of all data breaches in the United States.[7] Figure 6.3 shows the total number of data breaches due to external hacks and insider fraud against all sectors of the economy, including businesses, health care and government institutions. The quantity of breaches varies from a low of 57 in 2005 to a high of 316 in 2012 (note that this data does *not* include data breaches due to insider theft or fraudulent payment systems, for example). Working out the math, these yearly numbers amount to an average of 164 data breaches per year in the United States alone, due to either someone hacking into the system from the outside or the fraudulent behaviour of employees on the inside.

Not all data breaches are created equal, so a simple average per year does not tell the full story. Sometimes the records taken involve crucial pieces of private information like our social security numbers. At other times, they include only more trivial details such as our email addresses.

The smallest data breach in this range affected only four records; the largest breached as many as one billion records! Sometimes breaches are highly publicized, such as the hacks of Target, Home Depot and eBay. But, although it sometimes seems that a major breach is in the news on a daily basis, most data breaches pass right under the radar of public knowledge.

In fact, the vast majority of people have not had their personal data stolen through a data breach (or at least do not know about it, even if their data *has* been compromised). In the 2016 CIGI-Ipsos survey, we asked people directly if they had ever been notified that their data had been compromised by a data breach. Despite the publicity surrounding the high-profile hacks of companies like eBay, a surprisingly low number of people actually reported being notified of any compromised data. Only 27 percent of respondents surveyed in the 2016 poll said that they had received a notice of some kind. The remaining 73 percent, or most people in most nations, indicated that they had not been contacted about breached personal data (Table 6.1).

Again, as we have seen with many examples in the preceding chapters, people in different countries appear to have different rates of exposure to data breaches. While in none of the surveyed nations has a majority of the population been notified that their personal data has been compromised, a few do come close. South Korea is the best example, as 48 percent of the population indicated that they had been notified about a breach of their personal data. In Kenya, which has a comparatively low Internet penetration rate but a burgeoning IT sector and a robust mobile banking system, 43 percent said they had been notified. In Nigeria, home of the Nigerian Prince email scams, 48 percent said that they have been notified of a problem with their personal data.

Other countries swing wildly in the other direction. Only four percent of Internet users in Pakistan, which has a very low level of Internet access and a relatively low income level compared to those

Table 6.1: Respondents Who Have Been Notified of a Data Breach

Total: Yes: 27%   No: 73%

Country	Yes	No	Country	Yes	No
Kenya	43%	57%	Australia	17%	83%
Nigeria	48%	53%	Brazil	18%	82%
Pakistan	4%	96%	Canada	18%	82%
Tunisia	36%	64%	China	39%	61%
Mexico	27%	73%	France	15%	85%
Poland	19%	81%	Germany	21%	79%
South Africa	28%	72%	Great Britain	19%	81%
South Korea	48%	52%	India	39%	61%
Sweden	9%	91%	Italy	19%	81%
Turkey	16%	84%	Japan	19%	81%
United States	40%	60%	Hong Kong	23%	77%
Egypt	26%	74%	Indonesia	33%	67%

Source: Data from the CIGI-Ipsos 2016 Global Survey.

surveyed, reported that they had been notified about personal data breaches. And in Sweden, only nine percent reported that their data has ever been breached.

Another interesting aspect of this story is that the *personal* costs of data breaches do not appear to be that high in absolute terms, at least relative to the cost often faced by those companies that have been breached. In the survey, those individuals who had been notified that their data was breached were asked to estimate what the loss of their data cost them personally, in strictly monetary terms. The great majority of people estimated that data breaches cost them either nothing (47 percent) or between $0.01 and $999.99 (44 percent). The costs to the remaining respondents are spread in descending order from $1,000 and more than $500,000 (Figure 6.4).

There are two ways to look at these numbers. One way is to focus on how much data breaches, spread through time, have cost in the aggregate. The other is to focus on how much data breaches

Figure 6.4: Respondents' Estimated Personal Cost of Data Breaches

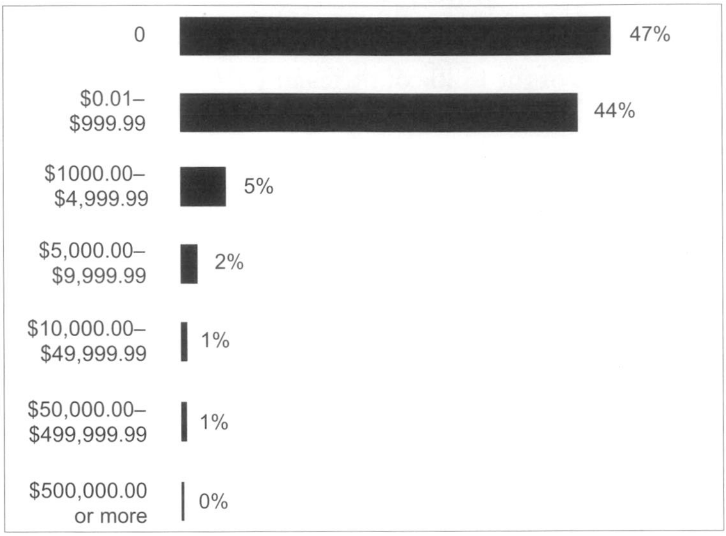

Range	Percentage
0	47%
$0.01–$999.99	44%
$1000.00–$4,999.99	5%
$5,000.00–$9,999.99	2%
$10,000.00–$49,999.99	1%
$50,000.00–$499,999.99	1%
$500,000.00 or more	0%

Source: Data from the CIGI-Ipsos 2016 Global Survey.

cost each individual person. Depending on the view you choose, the implications for behaviour in the Internet ecosystem diverge considerably.

As we have seen before (with people changing their behaviour in response to Edward Snowden's revelations about NSA surveillance), the accumulation of small costs to individuals in different countries can produce a very big number when added together.

Given that respondents put their estimated personal financial losses due to data breaches into different monetary ranges, we end up with three potential scenarios. One is the best-case scenario, where every individual's personal costs were at the low end of the selected range. Another is the worst-case scenario, where each individual's personal costs fall at the high end of the range. The third is a middle-ground scenario, where the individual costs due to data breaches fall halfway between the two extremes. As estimates, each is likely incorrect.

Regardless of the scenario you favour, a truly dismal picture emerges. In the best-case scenario, the accumulated personal costs due to data breaches for Internet users in those countries for which we have data add up to over US$5.4 trillion.* That number works out to a sum greater than the estimated contribution of the Internet to the economies of the G20 countries in 2016 alone. The mean cost scenario comes in at an extraordinarily large sum of US$10.6 trillion or roughly two and a half times the economic contribution of the Internet to the Group of Twenty (G20) economies in 2016. As if these two scenarios were not bad enough, the worst-case scenario is simply jaw-dropping, even though we used $500,000 for the top cost bracket. When all the numbers are crunched, the end result of the apocalyptic worst-case scenario of accumulated personal costs due to data breaches is an astronomically high pricetag of US$15.7 trillion.

It is important to bear in mind that these estimated costs cover the entire history of people discovering that their online data was breached and not just the cost of data breaches in a single year or a single country. And they are based on user perceptions and memories, which are fallible, and so our calculations have to be taken with a grain of salt. Nonetheless, they give the reader a potential sense of accumulated costs of cybercrime to the global economy.

---

*   To estimate the total cost of data breaches, we used population data for each country from the World Bank. We then multiplied this number by the percentage of the population using the Internet in each country, to give us the population of Internet users. From there, we used the responses from the CIGI-Ipsos 2016 survey to find out how many Internet users had been affected by a data breach. We did this by multiplying the percentage of users in each nation who had been notified that their data was breached. We took this number and multiplied it by what people thought data breaches had cost them personally (for example, 90 percent of people in the United States think breaches cost them between $0 and $999, so 90 percent of the breached population in the United States fall into this bracket). We repeated the process for each nation and then summed the values together, arriving at the estimated costs provided.

Table 6.2: The Poor State of Basic Digital Hygiene

Percentage of Internet users who fail to ...	
Avoid certain Internet sites and web applications	54%
Change password regularly	59%
Avoid opening emails from unknown email addresses	45%
Use commercial antivirus software	61%

Source: Data from the CIGI-Ipsos 2016 Global Survey.

Indeed, small things do add up. The Center for Strategic and International Studies, in collaboration with McAfee, estimated the costs of cybercrime anywhere from US$300 billion to $1 trillion in 2013 alone.[8] The World Economic Forum's *Global Risks Report 2016* puts the cost of "crimes in cyberspace" at US$445 billion annually.[9] Finally, Juniper Research projects the annual cost of data breaches at over US$2 trillion by 2019.[10] If you imagine adding up these costs year over year, you can see how we can get to the total figures given above.

While the overall numbers seem bad, the individual-level cost of a data breach is really not too onerous for most people. For many (47 percent), data breaches are estimated to cost nothing at all. For many more (44 percent), they only cost between $0.01 and $999.99. When you think about it, the way these numbers shake out makes a lot of sense. Many people have had their credit card defrauded or something of that sort. The banks and the credit card companies expect it and even insure for it. Users don't have to pay.

However, even these low personal costs can sometimes have an adverse effect on how people behave. Low personal costs generate what economists call a "moral hazard." Basically, because people are not paying for the full costs of their activity, they tend to take more risks and protect themselves less than they otherwise would. This tendency manifests in the IT space as what could be called poor digital hygiene. Or, put another way, as behaving in risky and ill-advised ways online.

We see this in the 2016 polling data. People were asked some questions about their basic level of digital hygiene. We found that most people still fail to take the steps necessary to adequately protect themselves online (Table 6.2). With the solitary exception of not opening emails from unknown addresses, a majority of people still don't avoid certain websites or applications (54 percent), fail to change their passwords regularly (59 percent) and do not use commercial antivirus software to prevent malware infections (61 percent).

The consequences of these bad behaviours are pretty clear. A few numbers really tell the story well. In 2014, an IT security firm called Balabit IT Security investigated how many network breaches across a number of companies were the result of hackers exploiting the technology (hacking the system) versus manipulating the people involved. What they found was that upwards of 84 percent of breaches could be directly attributed to the failings of the people involved rather than the exploitation of the technology.[11] The lesson is that if people were more careful, many cyber attacks could be prevented.

A number of other studies show that people do not take appropriate measures to secure themselves online and that better digital hygiene could really improve the state of cyberspace. In 2009, for example, a report to a US Senate panel showed that if network administrators followed proper procedures in setting up their networks and monitored their systems correctly, 80 percent of cyber attacks could be prevented.[12] In the *2015 Verizon Data Breach Investigations Report*, the number of preventable attacks is even greater. As the report puts it, "We found that 99.9% of the exploited vulnerabilities had been compromised more than a year after the associated CVE [common vulnerabilities and exposures] was published."[13] In other words, 99.9 percent of cyber attacks could have been prevented if people actively updated their operating systems, programs and antivirus software.

Better digital hygiene would clearly have a positive effect on the level of security in cyberspace, preventing the exploitation of many systems by malicious hackers of every stripe and political persuasion.

In contrast to individuals, the corporations that collect and hold user-generated data are on the hook for much larger sums, although those costs may still be lower than the cost of investing in better IT security.[14] For example, Target paid a final bill of around US$162 million when it was hacked in 2013 and lost 70 million records.[15] Home Depot, which lost credit card details for 56 million people, had to pay US$63 million for the breach — $30 million of which was offset by an insurance reimbursement.[16] Anthem, a health care company that had a breach compromising the records of 80 million people, may ultimately face costs in excess of US$100 million.[17] Insurance, tax deductions and other factors will offset the total impact of data breaches on the corporate bottom line, but the picture is plain. Companies are paying a lot for breaches of user data, but ultimately what may be more serious are the reputational costs of poor digital hygiene, especially if consumers decide to vote with their feet and take their business elsewhere to more trusted sites.

Data Breaches, Trust and Social Capital

Some data breaches are large, others are small. Some have high individual costs, others do not. Some users likely care about aggregated total costs, while others likely only care about how much a data breach costs them in particular. With all this variation, pinpointing the link between data breaches, which violate people's perceptions of privacy and security, and the trust that users place in the system is a bit nebulous. But, at the end of the day, we can expect that data breaches of all sorts impinge upon people's security and erode their trust, to a greater or lesser degree. Caveats aside, we should still be able to observe the sort of average effect of a data breach on user trust.

One way for us to measure change in trust is to look at how people modify their behaviour after data breaches occur — for example, do people stop shopping online or stop shopping at particular websites?

It turns out that they do. According to one survey of 2,000 respondents, when credit cards or other financial information is involved, 87 percent are unlikely to do business again with the company that experienced the data breach. The numbers hold up fairly well

Figure 6.5: Respondents Vow to Never Use a Financially Breached Company Again

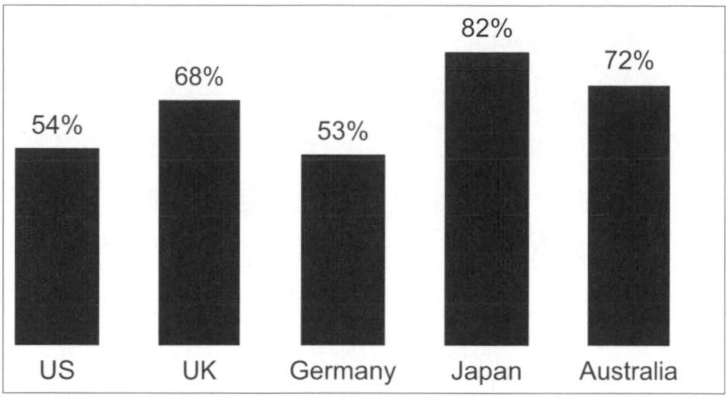

Source: Data from SafeNet, "Global Survey Reveals Impact of Data Breaches on Customer Loyalty."

across different types of breached information. The compromise of a home address results in 83 percent of people stating that they would not return to the breached business. Even at the lowest possible end of personal information, telephone numbers and email addresses, a full 80 percent and 76 percent, respectively, would stop frequenting a hacked company.[18] The telling thing about these results is that a person's own records do not necessarily need to be breached for them to change their behaviour. Simply hearing that a company has some IT security problems is often enough for people to shy away from doing business with it.

In another example, a majority of people surveyed by SafeNet in the United States, the United Kingdom, Germany, Japan and Australia indicated they would never again use the services of a company that has had the personal financial data of its users stolen.[19] In this case, like so many others, the violation of the privacy and security of user data leads directly to changed behaviour. The numbers range from 82 percent of people in Japan saying they would not patronize a company that had been breached, to 53 percent (still a majority) of Germans saying that they would stop shopping at compromised stores (Figure 6.5).

These behavioural consequences have a clear effect on the corporate bottom line, which captures the cost of eroded trust. The Ponemon Institute produces an annual study on the cost of data breaches, where

Table 6.3: Data Breaches, Consumer Trust and Lost Business Costs

2008	$4,592,214	2011	$3,010,000
2009	$4,472,030	2012	$3,030,814
2010	$4,536,380	2013	$3,324,959

Source: All figures are in US dollars. Data from Ponemon Institute, *Cost of Data Breach* studies (Ponemon Institute Research Report series) published in 2012 (www.ponemon.org/local/upload/file/2011_US_CODB_FINAL_5.pdf), 2013 (www4.symantec.com/mktginfo/whitepaper/053013_GL_NA_WP_Ponemon-2013-Cost-of-a-Data-Breach-Report_daiNA_cta72382.pdf) and 2014 (www-935.ibm.com/services/us/en/it-services/security-services/cost-of-data-breach/).

they identify how much data breaches cost companies in the United States and other countries. Obviously, data breaches can directly cost companies a lot of money, involving costs of replacing lost credit cards, litigation, repairing damaged IT infrastructure, higher insurance and other financial burdens.

The Ponemon Institute also collects data on what they call "average lost business costs" — basically, the average costs that firms must absorb after a data breach because customers have lost faith in them. The advantage of using the *average* lost business cost is that it explicitly captures the idea that some breaches will be highly costly for a company in terms of lost business, while others are going to be far less costly. Table 6.3 details these costs from 2008 to 2013. These indirect, trust-mediated costs are not inconsiderable, ranging from an average of US$4.6 million in 2008 to a low of US$3 million in 2011.

From these numbers, it is straightforward enough to conclude that flagging trust due to the occurrence of cybercrime is costly in economic terms. But, we can actually get more precise than that. If we take the average lost business cost provided by the Ponemon Institute and multiply those numbers by the total number of American data breaches against businesses (including health care) each year, we can get a rough picture of how costly eroded trust due to cybercrime is for the American economy. Table 6.4 presents all the data, including the final product detailing the total economy-wide cost of a loss of trust. The costs of a loss of trust due to a company

Table 6.4: Economy-wide Effects of Crime and Erosion of Trust

Year	Number of Breaches of Businesses (Including Health Care Providers)	Average Lost Business Cost	Total Economy-wide Effects
2008	49	$4,592,214	$225,018,486
2009	48	$4,472,030	$214,657,440
2010	140	$4,536,380	$635,093,200
2011	178	$3,010,000	$535,780,000
2012	219	$3,030,814	$663,748,266
2013	209	$3,324,959	$694,916,431

Source: Data from Privacy Rights Clearinghouse, "Chronology of Data Breaches"; Ponemon Institute, *Cost of Data Breach* studies (Ponemon Institute Research Report series) published in 2012 (www.ponemon.org/local/upload/file/2011_US_CODB_FINAL_5.pdf), 2013 (www4.symantec.com/mktginfo/whitepaper/053013_GL_NA_WP_Ponemon-2013-Cost-of-a-Data-Breach-Report_daiNA_cta72382.pdf) and 2014 (www-935.ibm.com/services/us/en/it-services/security-services/cost-of-data-breach/).

being breached are quite large, reaching a high of US$695 million in 2013 alone. Cumulatively, over this six-year period, flagging trust due to cybercrime has likely cost the US economy at least US$2.96 billion. Globally, the costs would be even higher and other more intangible benefits would be lost as well, especially since American consumers appear to be far more forgiving than their British, Japanese or Australian counterparts.

DDoS Attacks and Network Reliability

In 2013, a middle-aged Briton named Ian Sullivan used his skills as a hacker to launch a series of devastating distributed denial of service (DDoS) attacks against "social services, social housing and crime prevention websites."[20] A DDoS attack is a form of web-based attack that floods a website with requests for data. The effect is to knock the site off-line. Think about it this way. It is a common scene in movies involving alien attacks or large-scale natural disasters to have the protagonist frantically trying to make a phone call to a loved one only to be greeted with a recorded message, "All our circuits are busy right now. Please try again later."

The basic way in which a DDoS attack disrupts user Internet access is like these overwhelmed phone lines. When your computer sends a request for information to a website, the website responds with the desired content. Each website has a finite ability to respond to these queries. If too many queries come in all at once, the website gets overwhelmed and cannot retrieve and deliver the requested information. DDoS attacks harness the power of tens of thousands of computers linked together in what is known as a botnet to send millions of requests to a website, effectively overwhelming its capacity to respond, slowing it down or even knocking it completely off-line.

The most common target for DDoS attacks are IT, financial services, media and e-commerce websites, but any site can be affected. DDoS attacks are also incredibly common. Thirty-eight percent of businesses operating public-facing websites (that is, ones that can be accessed via Google or Yahoo!) suffered from DDoS attacks between April 2013 and May 2014.[21] DDoS attacks have real effects on user perceptions of the reliability of the Internet.

Bucking the common trend of targeting the wealthy and powerful, our British antagonist Ian Sullivan decided to target government websites that are there to provide services to the most vulnerable in society. As Steven Pye of the UK's National Cyber Crime Unit put it, "Many DDoS attacks are little more than a temporary inconvenience but in this case Sullivan's actions are likely to have deprived vulnerable people of access to important information, ranging from where to get support on family breakup, to reporting crime anonymously."[22]

DDoS attacks are always disruptive, as that is their intent, but they don't really have a lasting impact, since they don't steal or damage any information. The length of time that a DDoS attack will keep a website down depends upon a number of factors, including most notably the size and duration of the attack itself and the counteractions undertaken by the targeted organization, such as blocking the IP addresses of computers that are engaged in malicious activity. Some attacks knock websites down for only a few hours; in rarer instances,

DDoS attacks can even take sites down for several days. One 2014 survey, for example, found that the average amount of time that a DDoS attack kept a website down was 2.3 hours.[23]

In the broad scope of our day-to-day lives, 2.3 hours of disruption can seem like a pretty minor inconvenience. Depending on when the attack happens, a majority of Internet users might not even notice that it occurred. The problem is, if you shift the frame of reference even a little, DDoS attacks can start to have some serious implications for Internet users. Imagine that a DDoS attack targets a service when it is needed most (such as during a natural disaster) or if a series of attacks targets the same organization over and over so that it is knocked off-line for 2.3 hours each day, month after month. Suddenly the potentially minor effects of DDoS attacks start to have more serious implications for the reliability of the network.

One surprising trend is that the locus of botnet activity is not spread evenly around the world. Internet traffic is sent from computer to computer via ISPs. In 2010, a group of researchers decided to look for a pattern in the traffic crossing the networks of the Internet to try to see if certain ISPs were safe harbours for those operating the botnets used to launch spam email campaigns and DDoS attacks.[24] What they learned was that there are definitely a few bad apples among the crop of global ISPs. In fact, just 10 ISPs accounted for 30 percent of all IP addresses found to be launching spam. The worst 50 ISPs accounted for fully half of all the spam. These numbers are astonishing in "light of the fact that," as the authors note, "there are... anywhere between 4,000–100,000 ISPs" worldwide.[25] Cleaning up these few swamps of malicious activity could have huge benefits in reducing occurrences of some forms of online crime, especially since the cumulative cost of DDoS attacks is estimated to be as high as US$920 million a day.[26]

By affecting the reliability of the system, DDoS attacks directly erode people's trust. The aim of DDoS attacks is to literally take a website off-line, meaning users cannot access it at all. People who experience a DDoS attack can come to trust the Internet ecosystem less, because they know it is possible that in a crunch time it might not be there for them.

As with other types of breaks in trust, we can look for evidence to assess to what extent this sort of loss of trust matters. To begin with, what do companies think DDoS attacks cost them in terms of eroded trust? One Kaspersky Lab report finds that 33 percent of companies are concerned that DDoS attacks will cause others to lose confidence in them, resulting in lost contracts and business opportunities. And 38 percent of companies are also concerned that having their webpages slowed or completely knocked off-line will damage their reputations.[27]

DDoS attacks are growing more frequent and the attacks are getting more severe, although defences and counteractions are also getting more sophisticated. These attacks make the network less reliable. People trust a networked system like the Internet because they think it will provide them with reliable service. If people cannot be sure that a website will be there when they need it, they will shift their behaviour, which could translate as a company losing out on their repeat business, or in the extreme, that they refuse to rely upon the Internet for important daily activity. Such actions clearly limit the Internet's potential to provide economy-wide efficiency gains and hamper innovation.

The Dark Web and Real-World Safety

Remember the rainforest analogy from chapter two? There we described the Internet's vibrant top-level canopy of publicly accessible websites and its secretive, shadowy underside — the Dark Web, or Dark Net, accessible by specially configured browsers such as Tor.

While Tor rides upon the same globe-spanning Internet infrastructure as the World Wide Web that we all use daily, the way in which the two put users into touch with content is totally different. When we access the top level of the Internet, we send a request via our ISP to the website that we want to visit and the site returns that information to us. The connection is direct.

This directness entails that our web surfing is well known by a variety of actors. The websites we visit know what we are viewing and how long we linger on a particular page. Our ISPs know all the sites we visit and the amount of information that we are viewing. The directness of the typical Internet connection also creates clear, detailed records that allow law enforcement to check in after the fact to see if anyone has broken any laws.

The Dark Web is different. Anonymized web surfing is what creates the Dark Web. The Tor browser, for example, operates much like a normal web browser, except that rather than sending the request for content directly to the intended target, it relays the signal through a series of three interconnected devices that are among the all-volunteer army of computers that comprise the Tor network. The nature of the connection is a bit like a digital version of the children's game of Telephone, only without the laughter and confusion.

The process by which Tor creates anonymity unfolds in a fairly straightforward way. Sitting at home, a person can fire up the Tor browser and send a request to view a website. This signal is sent to the first relay computer in the Tor network. This computer then sends the request on to a middle relay. The middle relay computer does the same, sending the signal on again to what is known as an exit node computer. The exit node then sends the request to the website that the person wants to view and takes the returned information and sends it back via another series of relays to the computer originating the request.

Breaking up a web user's signal in this way ensures that information on the original user and the content he or she is viewing is diffused. Each system in the chain possesses some of the information needed to identify a user, but not enough to really say who is doing what. The first computer in the relay system, for example, could be used to pinpoint the originating computer, but it doesn't know the content that is being viewed. The middle computer knows the first computer in the relay and the exit node, but not the originating computer or the content being viewed. The exit node computer knows the content being viewed and the middle computer, but not the first relay or the originating computer. The website knows the exit node computer and nothing else. All along the way, the signal is heavily encrypted to prevent the people operating the relays from snooping in on a user's desired content. The end result is the closest thing to online anonymity that you can get.

That online anonymity, however, breeds a dilemma.[28] The anonymity of the network provides cover. Cover can be good. If you live in a repressive regime that actively censors online content, you might need to use a system like Tor to surf the Web freely. It can also be useful if free political expression is outlawed and Internet users need to use surreptitious measures to express their political points of view. These notions are confirmed by statistical evidence on the country of origin of Tor network clients. As countries reach the extreme ends of authoritarianism, political repression does indeed drive people to use certain parts of the Tor browser more frequently.

The trouble is that cover can also be bad. By being able to surf the Web anonymously, people are able to conduct illicit or outright illegal behaviour with only a slim chance of being nabbed by law enforcement. A few examples paint the picture well.

Let's start with the infamous online illegal marketplace Silk Road. The website was purposefully named after the ancient trading route between Europe and the Orient. Back then, all manner of goods and services flowed from the East to the West, and vice versa. The modern online marketplace did the same in cyberspace. It connected ready sellers of things as far-ranging as drugs to guns with eager buyers. Transactions on the illegal marketplace were often done using the anonymous digital currency bitcoin. To put it in terms with which the average web users would be familiar, Silk Road was a lot like an illegal version of a Craigslist, Kijiji or eBay.

The first Silk Road started in February 2011. At the time, it was one such site among many. Yet Silk Road swiftly beat out its rivals, becoming the place to go if you wanted to buy or sell drugs, guns, or other illegal goods and services. Despite the large variety of goods and services available, one study of the sort of things sold on Silk Road characterized the website as a virtual "drug store," noting that "the four most popular categories [of things for sale] are all linked to drugs."[29] With its burgeoning popularity, Silk Road's revenue quickly expanded. By 2012, the site administrator, known popularly as the Dread Pirate Roberts, was earning as much as US$92,000 per month, with the site supposedly clearing as much as US$1.2 billion in revenues.[30]

It was a wild ride for the Dread Pirate Roberts. He was earning over one million dollars a year by simply providing an anonymous forum connecting buyers and sellers. But what was being sold on the illegal marketplace was bad enough that it got the attention of many of the big three-letter agencies in the United States. The Department of Homeland Security (DHS) launched the cleverly named operation Marco Polo in late 2011. DHS was joined by the FBI (Federal Bureau of Investigation) and ICE (US Immigration and Customs Enforcement) and others. The full might of the US government went after Silk Road and the Dread Pirate Roberts.

It took slightly over a year, but eventually law enforcement was able to track down the server that was hosting the Silk Road webpage. Of all the places in the world, the server ended up being nestled in a well-air-conditioned room in the otherwise frigid climate of Iceland. The FBI was able to locate the server by manipulating (the jury is still out about how much "manipulation" was involved) the CAPTCHA* on the log-in screen of the Silk Road website.[31] To hear the FBI tell

---

* CAPTCHA stands for "Completely Automated Public Turing Test To Tell Computers and Humans Apart." CAPTCHAs are the blurry letters and numbers that need to be read by human eyes and entered into a log-in tab. They are designed to prevent computers from being able to access websites, keeping things for humans only.

it, their techies typed a series of miscellaneous characters into the CAPTCHA on the Silk Road log-in page and the website returned the IP address information of a server that was not a known node in the Tor network. Others charge that this is impossible and that the FBI must have effectively hacked the log-in page by inputting lines of code in the CAPTCHA that tricked the website into thinking it was being given administrative commands.

Either way, identifying the server's location was enough of a lead. From there, site administrators began to be identified and arrested (although the actual laying of charges was often delayed so as to avoid tipping the government's hand to the rest of the online criminals). With no honour among thieves, the operators of Silk Road began to turn on each other. One site administrator testified as a witness for the state. Word of the betrayal got back to the Dread Pirate Roberts, who then compounded his eventual legal problems by offering $80,000 to an undercover law enforcement agent to have his erstwhile ally murdered. Law enforcement staged the killing, and the noose drew tighter around the modern-day bandit's neck. The fantastic tale came to a head in October 2013, when Ross Ulbricht, the man behind the mask, was arrested. In 2015, he was sentenced to life in prison for his crimes. It was a victory for law enforcement.

A place where people are free to buy and sell socially damaging drugs or worse is bad. But the shadows of the Dark Web actually get darker still. These deep recesses are exemplified most by the tremendous flow of site visits to child abuse imagery sites. Gareth Owen and Nick Savage of the University of Portsmouth, England, conducted an innovative study that really provides a perfect snapshot of traffic on the Tor network.[32]

There are a bunch of websites housed on the Tor network that are known as the Tor hidden services. Normal websites that are accessible by an ordinary web browser have a suffix like .com or .ca — for example, cnn.com, bbc.co.uk or cbc.ca. The hidden services websites on the Tor network have a .onion ending (as in The *Onion* Router).

Figure 6.6: Websites on the Dark Web

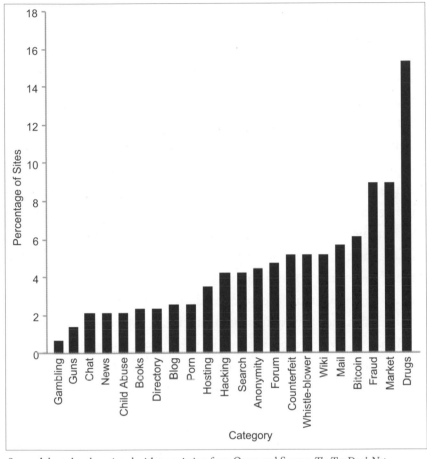

Source: Adapted and reprinted with permission from Owen and Savage, *The Tor Dark Net*.

These websites are hosted on purely volunteered servers. The websites rotate through the available list of volunteered servers around the world, increasing the difficulty of pinpointing who is running what site. These are anonymous Dark Net sites in the purest expression of the term.

Owen and Savage volunteered 40 relays to be a part of the Tor network. Over a period of six months, they used web-crawling bots to categorize the content of the websites that were hosted on the Tor hidden services — that is, the various .onion websites. As Figure 6.6 shows, they found a wide assortment of websites. There were sites dedicated to chat rooms. There were sites for whistle-blowing and sites for buying and selling illegal goods and services. There were also pornography sites. And, in the deepest recesses, there were sites dedicated to the worst of the worst, child abuse.

Once they had characterized the sites on the .onion suffix, Owen and Savage set about to actually track the flow of traffic to the sites. Because of the system's anonymity, they were not able to say anything about who was visiting the various webpages. All they could say was that someone (or something, in the case of a web-crawling bot) was visiting a website at a particular time via the Tor network. So from there they started counting. What they found was extremely disturbing.

In their initial categorization of the Dark Web sites, they found that the child abuse sites made up a very small proportion of all available sites on the .onion suffix, roughly two percent. But disturbingly, Owen and Savage found that 82 percent of all the site visits flowing to all the websites that they had catalogued on the Dark Web were going to that small percentage of sites dedicated to the production, dissemination and viewing of child abuse imagery.

It is a horrifying finding, but one that largely fits with what we see on the news. A few times every year, the media covers a story about how law enforcement officials, often working diligently across national borders and with private companies, have broken up a child abuse ring that was virtually housed upon the Dark Web. In 2011, for example, Europol conducted Operation Rescue, together with partners from 13 nations. Police uncovered 670 suspects in a widespread child abuse ring, leading to the eventual arrest of 184 individuals.[33] Six-hundred and fifty people were arrested in 2014 by the United Kingdom's National Crime Agency on charges related to child abuse imagery.[34] Another 50 were arrested in Northern Ireland in 2015 on similar charges.[35]

Sometimes, the Dark Web is used for more benign, but still troubling and illegal, purposes. In July 2015, Ashley Madison — a site that aimed to connect men and women who wanted to commit adultery — was hacked. As we described in the first chapter, around 32 million records were stolen by hackers calling themselves the Impact Team. After another month or so of waiting, the hackers behind the breach listed the names and email addresses of the site's subscribers on the Dark Net. The hack itself was illegal, so spilling the data had to be done carefully so as to avoid the watching eyes of police.

The leak of the names of Ashley Madison users quickly had huge real-world consequences. People lost sleep, lost their jobs and lost their relationships. In its most extreme manifestation, some people even lost all hope and took their own lives. Just six days after the hackers posted names of Ashley Madison users onto the Dark Web, Pastor John Gibson, a teacher at the New Orleans Baptist Theological Seminary, a husband and a father of two, took his own life. The note Gibson left behind talked about his depression and gave an apology to his family. A representative for Ashley Madison expressed condolence, stating, "Dr. Gibson's passing is a stark, heart-wrenching reminder that the criminal hack against our company and our customers has had very real consequences for a great many innocent people."[36]

Online illegal marketplaces, child abuse websites and the disclosure of the identities of adulterers are obviously the work of different species of owls. Yet all three have two things in common. First, they occur on the Dark Web, and, second, they have real-world safety implications. Dark Web marketplaces might take the sale of drugs off the streets, but they make it easier for people to buy drugs and guns or even to hire a hacker or a would-be assassin. Any one of these activities can easily cause real-world harm to real people. Child abuse rings have innocent victims. Hackers and assassins cause obvious harm to their targets. And, as the case of John Gibson shows, sometimes simply being able to broadcast stolen private information in an anonymous way can lead to suicides and distraught, broken families.

With these sorts of events occurring at the underbelly of the Internet, people certainly are apprehensive about the existence of the Dark Web and often agitate to have it shut down. The emergence of the illegal marketplace Silk Road 1.0 even prompted US Senator Charles Schumer to characterize the site as "more brazen than anything else by light-years."[37] The Digital Citizens Alliance makes the general point even more plainly: online crime on the Dark Web will "slowly erode the trust and confidence we have in the internet."[38]

In the 2016 CIGI-Ipsos survey, questions were devised to get at people's perceptions of whether the Dark Web ought to be shut down. Because people have varying levels of familiarity with the technology (some might have used Tor, while others might not even know what the Dark Web is, for instance), a bit of a preamble to the question was provided, laying out both the beneficial and the negative uses of the system:

> A part of the Internet known as the "Dark Net" is only accessible via special web browsers that allow you to surf the web anonymously. Journalists, human rights activists, dissidents and whistleblowers can use these services to rally against repression, exercise their fundamental rights to free expression and shed light upon corruption. At the same time, hackers, illegal marketplaces (e.g. selling weapons and narcotics), and child abuse sites can also use these services to hide from law enforcement. Do you agree or disagree that the "Dark Net" should be shut down.

Overwhelmingly, people indicated that they agreed that the Dark Web should be shut down — 71 percent of respondents. These findings were also remarkably stable across education, income and age levels. And they are fairly consistent across countries as well, with some of the more repressive regimes in the sample of countries — China and Egypt, for example — actually having more people (79 percent) who want to shut down the Dark Web (Figure 6.7).

From the perspective of user trust, shutting down the Dark Web seems like a sensible idea. Eliminating the Dark Web would reduce crime and help users feel the Internet was safe. The flip side, though, is that despite the clear abuses that go on in the Dark Web, systems like

Figure 6.7: National Perspectives on Shutting Down the Dark Web

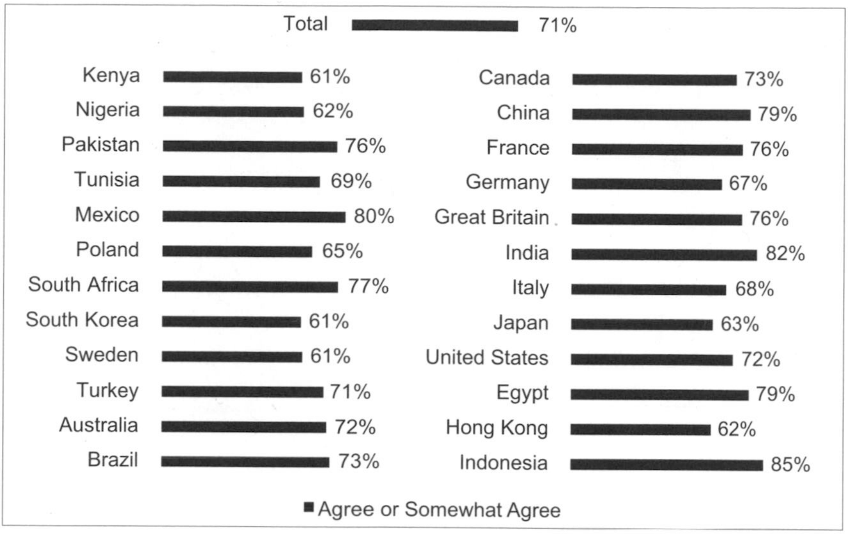

Total	71%			
Kenya	61%	Canada	73%	
Nigeria	62%	China	79%	
Pakistan	76%	France	76%	
Tunisia	69%	Germany	67%	
Mexico	80%	Great Britain	76%	
Poland	65%	India	82%	
South Africa	77%	Italy	68%	
South Korea	61%	Japan	63%	
Sweden	61%	United States	72%	
Turkey	71%	Egypt	79%	
Australia	72%	Hong Kong	62%	
Brazil	73%	Indonesia	85%	

■Agree or Somewhat Agree

Source: Data from the CIGI-Ipsos 2016 Global Survey.

the Tor network are used by some people, particularly those in repressive regimes, for noble — or at least very least benign — purposes.

Shutting down Tor could harm the interests of those who simply value their online privacy. Numbers on the pattern of traffic across the entire Tor network show that 94 to 97 percent of all traffic on the Tor network actually stays on the surface Web and does not go anywhere near the Dark Net websites that Owen and Savage catalogued in their own study (Figure 6.8).[39] What this suggests is that a unilateral move to shut down Tor to take the Dark Web off-line would impinge upon the privacy of many ordinary network users.

Shutting down Tor would also affect the security and personal safety of users in repressive regimes. Tor is often the only available tool for dissidents, human rights advocates and journalists to remain private and access censored information. As we saw in an earlier chapter, repressive regimes tend to restrict online content *in extremis*. Some countries (for example, Pakistan) ban sites like YouTube; others (Turkey, for one) ban Twitter; others (such as China) enforce a ban against a host of Western companies.

Figure 6.8: Pattern of Tor Traffic

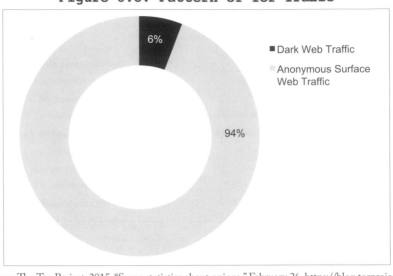

Source: The Tor Project, 2015, "Some statistics about onions," February 26, https://blog.torproject.org/blog/some-statistics-about-onions.

Remember Taylor Wilson, who in his early teens was able to build a nuclear reactor in his garage because he accessed a treasure trove of scientific literature online? That sort of innovation only happens when information is freely shared and available. Additionally, statistical evidence on the pattern of Tor network usage from 2011 to 2013 suggests that when repression reaches its extreme levels, as in China, Russia and other illiberal countries, Tor network usage increases in a statistically significant way.[40] All of this adds up to the proposition that, if the Tor network were to be shut down, it would be damaging to the interests (and trust) of many users in the system. There are no perfect or easy solutions to this dilemma. The best that can be hoped for is to minimize the harms of the Dark Web through, for example, more effective policing by law enforcement agencies around the world.

A New Breed of Vigilante Justice

As with almost everything to do with the Internet, the growing role for non-state actors is not all bad. As we have seen before, what matters is how people choose to use the network. People can choose to try to do ill or they can choose to try to do good.

The online hacktivist group Anonymous is a perfect example of this duality. Gabriella Coleman, an anthropologist from McGill University, has really done more than anyone else to come to grips with Anonymous's multi-faceted existence. The title of her 2014 book, *Hacker, Hoaxer, Whistleblower, Spy: The Many Faces of Anonymous*, sums up the complexity of the group, for it is not really an institution or organization as these terms are typically understood.

Anonymous's decision-making process is driven by a collective assessment of how much and how well people contribute to its activities. Other indicators of status tend not to matter. If you are skilled and willing to work hard, you can play a role in shaping what course Anonymous takes. If a person thinks too highly of themselves, or as special or as deserving of respect, they will get the opposite from the amorphous blob that is Anonymous. It is the ultimate "flat" organization, punctuated by periods of organized cohesiveness during specific operations.

Anonymous started out as a group of individuals from around the world who liked to get up to no good. Over time, though, the leaderless, faceless organization has morphed into something more. With Project Chanology in 2008, Anonymous came onto the scene in a powerful way to protest the efforts of the Church of Scientology to censor the free flow of information. In 2011, Anonymous got involved in the Arab Spring with Operation Tunisia by launching DDoS attacks against government websites in retaliation for the regime's stand against the ongoing protests. In 2012, Anonymous went after the websites of the Government of Syria, again attempting to knock them off-line in retaliation for an Internet blackout and the brutal treatment of dissidents by the regime of Bashir al-Assad. From the early beginnings of the group as a bunch of people who wanted to run pranks and get up to mischief, Anonymous has increasingly taken on the role of political justice warrior, involving itself in conflicts where the downtrodden are standing up to well-entrenched institutional powers like churches and governments.

With Operation Darknet in 2011, members of Anonymous also showed that they were willing to campaign against criminals lurking in the Dark Web, in this case targeting users of online child abuse imagery sites hosted on Freedom Hosting servers. In a statement released by Anonymous at the time of the operation, the group claimed that, "By taking down Freedom Hosting, we are eliminating 40+ child pornography websites. Among these is Lolita City, one of the largest child pornography websites to date, containing more than 100GB of child pornography."[41]

In taking down the Freedom Hosting child abuse imagery sites, Anonymous undertook a quick left-right combination. Their first move was to use something known as an SQL (short for structured query language) injection attack to hack the websites and gain access to the membership records for the child abuse imagery rings. The group then released to the public the identities of 190 suspected child abusers and pedophiles.[42] They followed up this tactic with a DDoS attack that took the illegal websites off-line. Sometimes Anonymous even becomes involved as a private investigator where law enforcement appears too slow or too unwilling to act for justice. In 2011, Rehtaeh Parsons, then a 15-year-old high school student in Cole Harbour, Nova Scotia, was sexually assaulted by four of her classmates. Digital images of the assault were later circulated around the school via social media. As the ridicule of her peers piled on and with justice for the attack seeming impossibly out of reach, Rehtaeh Parsons attempted to hang herself. She eventually succumbed to her injuries and died at the age of 17 in 2013.

Heartbroken, Rehtaeh's mother posted an angry message online. The note got Anonymous's attention. Members of Anonymous began looking for evidence that would identify the four perpetrators of the assault. They quickly found what they were looking for and levelled an ultimatum to the police in Halifax, charging that if the stalled investigation was not begun anew, the hacktivist group would release the names of the perpetrators to the public. The police relented, indicating in a statement that they had "new and credible information" in the case, and started the investigation again.[43]

Three months later, little had changed. Anonymous, dissatisfied with the progress in the case, decided to act. In a statement posted to Pastebin, an online messaging forum, the group revealed the identities of the four attackers, claiming that the decision to point the finger at the suspects was done because "Nothing has happened yet, no charges were laid, no communication with the public and all the 4 accused involved are still running free."[44] A not so small measure of justice was meted out.

Rehtaeh Parsons's father, Glen Canning, points directly to the role of Anonymous in securing justice for his daughter. As he stated to the media in 2015, two years after his daughter's tragic death, "Why go through the courts? Why go through the system? Why be revictimized again when you can write something and get hold of some people online who can really do a hell of a lot more to bring you a sense of justice than the police and the courts can?"[45] Canning went on to explain that the vigilante breed of justice that Anonymous doled out was not necessarily a good thing, only that it made up for defects in the current institutional and political systems governing the social world. "Stuff like this happens because the system is broken," said Canning. "If we can fix the system... then maybe we wouldn't need Anonymous."[46]

With its lack of formal organization, Anonymous generates confusion. Internet users are not really sure whether hacktivist groups are socially constructive, destructive or something else entirely. In the 2016 CIGI-Ipsos survey, several questions were posed to try to determine more precisely what people thought of online hacktivists such as Anonymous. The survey found that people are confused about their role (Figure 6.9).

People seem to generally agree that Anonymous is not a good thing. For example, most people think groups like Anonymous are breaking the law and should be stopped. A majority also hold a negative view of hacktivist groups.

Figure 6.9: The Confusing World of Anonymous

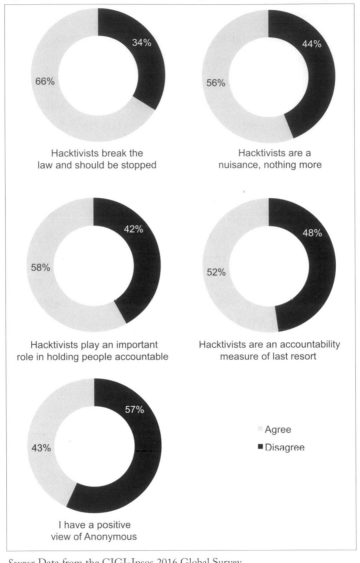

Source: Data from the CIGI-Ipsos 2016 Global Survey.

Although this was not part of the survey, it is likely that these perceptions stem from a combination of the tactics Anonymous uses — hacks of computer systems — and the lack of a clear leadership, not to mention the purposefully disconcerting use of Guy Fawkes masks. No doubt piled on as well is the fear that any person — for almost any reason — could become a target of the shadowy and unaccountable Anonymous.

Respondents were far more confused about whether hacktivist groups like Anonymous, regardless of their methods, might actually fulfill a useful social function some of the time. For example, in one question, a majority of respondents (56 percent) indicated that they thought hacktivist groups such as Anonymous were a nuisance and nothing more. A result like this suggests that Anonymous has no serious social role to play.

At the same time, another majority of respondents (58 percent) indicated that Anonymous plays an important role in keeping people accountable. What is more, a slim majority (52 percent) *also* noted that hacktivist groups can play an important role in keeping people accountable if no one else will. Both of these majorities are basically saying that Anonymous does have a clear and important role to play as a source of accountability in the online ecosystem. In other words, respondents think that Anonymous is both a not really important nuisance *and* an important source of accountability. Not important and important — this is the confused world of online hacktivist groups.

Making matters even murkier, the size of the majority of people in favour of Anonymous functioning as an actor with a social role to play actually increases when people are asked about whether hacktivist groups play an important role in keeping specific actors accountable. People strongly think that Anonymous can play a good role in keeping private companies, governments and criminals accountable for their action (Figure 6.10), although they did not feel they had a major role to play as regards ordinary Internet users. Once again, these responses are inconsistent with the other expressed response that Anonymous is nothing but a nuisance.

All the confusion is understandable. The identity of Anonymous is not always clear even to itself. At times, elements of the organization have done some pretty destructive things. At other points, they have

Figure 6.10: Should Hacktivists Keep People Honest?

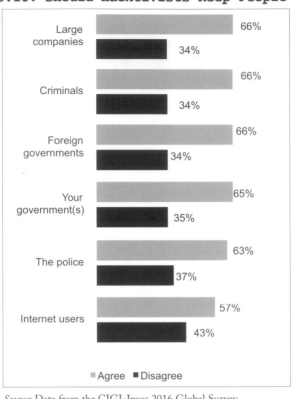

Source: Data from the CIGI-Ipsos 2016 Global Survey.

tried to help out those who are less fortunate, what Anons (members of Anonymous) might call "moral faggotry."[47]

User perceptions aside, there are some pretty good reasons why groups like Anonymous should not be allowed to simply run amok in the Internet ecosystem. One comes back to the Roman poet Decimus Juvenal's classic question: "Who watches the watchers?" (*Quis custodiet ipsos custodies?*) Anonymous might be able to wade into the midst of a political conflict or a criminal case to try to keep people honest, but Internet users are hard-pressed to keep the members of Anonymous accountable. A second, related problem is that sometimes Anonymous can get it wrong. Imagine that your name ended up on list of leaked pedophiles that Anonymous stole from some Dark Web server. Mistakes happen and there is no way to seek redress.

A third problem is that, like vigilantes in the real world, Anonymous can charge into a criminal case or political conflict with no knowledge of what other actors might be doing to try to improve the situation. Involvement in child abuse imagery criminal cases is a good example. The process that law enforcement undertakes when taking down a child abuse ring tends to follow a script. As a first step, law enforcement identifies the location of the servers that are hosting the illegal content. Then, they move to take administrative control of the servers. From there, they can begin to work to identify those who are producing, distributing or viewing child abuse imagery.

At any step in this process, the well-intentioned actions of a group such as Anonymous would severely jeopardize the success of the criminal case. Like all criminals, online pedophiles and child abusers are skittish. If Anonymous hacked a server and got a partial list of user names that they then published online, other users might bolt. If law enforcement actually had control of the server and was gradually compiling a list of all the users of the illegal websites, their work could be irrevocably damaged. Even a DDoS attack that took the websites off-line could be enough to send the criminals scuttling away from the closing net of law enforcement. Anonymous or other hacktivist groups might mean well, but they can easily do unintended harm.

Clearly, the role of non-state actors is a strange one. People distrust groups like Anonymous, but they also trust them to hold institutionally powerful groups accountable in a pinch. Cognitive dissonance like this is uncomfortable. The behaviour of Anonymous in the future will probably solidify people's opinions. If the group veers back to its early, prankish days, Internet users will lose all trust in the potential of hacktivists. If Anonymous stays on its current path of fighting for those who are disenfranchised, people might well come to the opinion that hacktivist groups have an important role to play in the Internet ecosystem.

The Effect of a Divided Physical World and the Single Global Internet

Policing the Dark Web and the Internet more generally requires that governments come up with solutions to the nagging problem of a world divided into discrete sovereign states with distinct legal rules and an Internet that is designed for technical efficiency and not politics or policing.

Savvy criminals have always taken advantage of the fact that the world is divided up into mutually exclusive jurisdictions. The difference now is that cybercriminals never need to leave a friendly jurisdiction to commit crime. The Internet allows criminals to spread their reach around the world from the comfort of their own homes. That makes for a dangerous mix in which combatting cybercrime is harder and committing cybercrime is more alluring because perpetrators are less likely to get caught.

Consider the cybercrimes emanating from Eastern Europe, particularly Russia and Ukraine. Many cybercrimes, ranging from spam, DDoS attacks and data theft, to ransomware and numerous others, originate in this region. Despite the high volume of criminal activity, cybercrimes in Eastern Europe are almost never followed by arrests or actual prosecutions. Accurately identifying the culprits certainly accounts for some of the lackadaisical effort in policing cybercrime.[48] The technological hurdles that result from the anonymity of the Dark Web loom large.

But, even when a culprit is plausibly identified, authorities in Russia and other Eastern European countries often don't move in on them. Adrian Culley, a cyber-security researcher at the IT security firm Damballa, describes the situation this way: "It has long been rumoured in the [cyber] security Industry that various Russian organized crime groups have been offered immunity from prosecution by Russian authorities and intelligence agencies as long as they do not [cyber] attack Russian citizens or interests. Many botnets and organized crime groups continue to operate from Russia and Eastern

Europe."[49] Since Western countries are often the target of malicious attacks from the region, this political cover offers yet another way for Russia to attack the United States and its allies over other geopolitical points of contention.

The extent to which Russia and other countries provide political cover for locally based cybercriminals as a matter of official policy is open to speculation. The issue, however, is really just a microcosm of the broader problem of a world where cybercrime can traverse borders with unparalleled freedom, while the law enforcement authority of governments cannot.

Right now, the bundle of processes on the books to help governments cooperate to fight crime across national borders are known as MLATs. The difficulty is that these processes are antiquated and in serious need of reform. They were designed for an earlier, pre-digital era. For countries to actually avail themselves of the MLAT process, they need to have a bilateral legal assistance treaty in place with other countries. Another problem, one which pertains more directly to the Russian example above, is that both countries have to agree the activity in question is actually a crime. And then, even if these conditions are satisfied, the MLAT form must be correctly filled out, which often requires knowledge of the laws and burdens of evidence in the country to which a request is being made.

Even if a country that has been a victim of a cybercrime successfully passes all of these hurdles, there is still no guarantee that the MLAT request will be acted upon in a timely manner. A final set of barriers, both technical and organizational, often militates against their success. The technical problem is that there is a mismatch between the time that it takes to process and fulfill an MLAT request and the period of time that most ISPs hold customer data. The MLAT approval process normally takes between six months and one year from start to finish, assuming there are no hiccups along the way. Most ISPs, on the other hand, only hold customer data for around six months. So, even with a successfully completed MLAT request, the digital evidence needed to arrest and prosecute a cybercriminal might be deleted before it can be retrieved.

The final organizational barrier is that law enforcement and prosecutors earn their stripes by dealing with crimes within their own jurisdictions. There is usually little professional reward for solving a crime in another country. Since criminals never sleep (in a borderless digital world, it is always crime time somewhere else), finding the time to help out foreign law enforcement agencies can easily be relegated to the bottom of the to-do list. Although some nations will be more responsive to requests than others, in many cases there is just not enough personal or professional reward at stake to incentivize the policing of cybercrime in other countries through the MLAT process.

These serious problems with the MLAT process need to be addressed if cybercrime is going to be dealt with effectively. Until such time, online criminals will continue to get away with their crimes, and ordinary users will trust the network less.

Conclusion

This chapter has explored some of the ways in which online crime can undermine the trust that people place in the Internet ecosystem. Crime in its various manifestations erodes people's perceptions of the security, reliability and real-world safety of the network.

As we see in example after example, when trust is eroded, people change their behaviour in ways that can be quite costly in both economic and broader political terms. A loss of trust results in a worse-functioning Internet ecosystem, limiting the ability of the network to generate innovation, economic growth and the free expression of ideas. Often, too, the steps proposed to build trust back up — such as shutting down the Dark Web or leashing hacktivist groups — can unintentionally feed back and undermine some of the other elements of trust.

Seven

Cyberwarfare in the Twenty-First Century

You could almost say that the Cold War never ended when it comes to the Internet. In the late 1990s, the US government discovered that a foreign source was conducting secret probes of its computer systems at the Pentagon, the National Aeronautics and Space Administration (NASA), the Energy Department and US universities and research labs. The incident, code-named Moonlight Maze, apparently originated in a mainframe computer in the former Soviet Union, but Russian authorities were quick to deny their involvement. Since then, there has been a long list of well-publicized cyber espionage attacks on governments around the world, many of them involving the old major players of the Cold War: the United States, China and Russia.

The attacks outlined in Box 7.1, along with other kinds of attacks on the personal data of private citizens and corporations described in earlier chapters, are undermining public trust in the Internet and contributing to the erosion of the Internet's digital social capital. Citizens around the world are worried about cyber attacks on their own governments as well as about attacks on their own personal data. The 2014 CIGI-Ipsos poll found that an overwhelming majority of citizens in most nations are concerned about important institutions in

Box 7.1: Major Cyber Espionage Attacks in the Twenty-First Century[1]

Early 2000s

- **Titan Rain (China vs. US).** Attacks by China (probably government/ military, could be corporate or others using Chinese computers) against US defence contractors at Lockheed Martin, Sandia National Laboratories, Redstone Arsenal and NASA. They also attacked British Defence departments and the FBI. Significant fallout and trust deficit between many countries and China resulted.

2006

- **Operation Olympic Games begins (US/Israel vs. Iran).** Covert US/ Israeli effort to gain access to Iranian nuclear facility computer controls and command centrifuges.

2007

- **Estonian Cyberwar (Russia vs. Estonia).** Russian pro-Kremlin group initiated DDoS attacks against Estonia, targeted parliament, banks, ministries and media. Followed Estonia's spat with Russia over removal of a war memorial.
- **US Secretary of Defense.** Unclassified email was hacked during a larger series of attacks probing the Pentagon's network.
- **Attacks in China (Tawain/US vs. China).** China claims foreign hackers from Taiwan and the US had spyware on classified and corporate computers.

2008

- **Cyber attack against US military computers (Unknown vs. US).** A foreign intelligence service left a USB key with malicious code in a US Department of Defense parking lot in the Middle East. Someone put the USB key into a computer and it took the US military 14 months to clean the downloaded malware from its networks.
- **Russia-Georgian War cyber attacks (Russia vs. Georgia).** DDoS attacks targeted Georgian websites, foreign ministry and media. A pipeline attack might have actually resulted from a sophisticated cyber attack on computerized control and safety features. Unique in that it was coordinated with Russian military actions.
- **Hack against Republican and Democratic presidential campaigns (China vs. US).** The attacks against the databases were probably launched by China or Russia.

2009

- **Cyber attack against Israel's Internet infrastructure (Russia/Hamas/ Hezbollah vs. Israel).** Occurred during January 2009 military offensive on Gaza. Focused on government websites. Israeli government blames Hamas or Hezbollah for paying a criminal organization in Russia to carry out the attacks.
- **July cyber attacks against South Korea/United States. (North Korea vs. South Korea/US).** DDoS type of attack that targeted government, intelligence, banks, media and financial sites. North Korea blamed for the attack.
- **GhostNet discovered (China vs. many).** Large-scale cyber espionage operation that infiltrated political, economic and media locations in 103 countries, to include embassies, foreign ministries and other government offices. Chinese government probably at fault but not conclusive.
- **Operation Aurora (China vs. US companies).** Cyber attacks against Google, originating in China with People's Liberation Army (PLA) links. Yahoo!, Morgan Stanley, Dow Chemical, Symantec, Adobe, Rackspace, Juniper Networks also targeted.

2010

- **Attack against Baidu search engine (Iran vs. China).** "Iranian Cyber Army" attacks the Chinese search engine and redirects users to a page showing Iranian political messages.
- **Stuxnet attack (US/Israel vs. Iran).** Cyber worm against Iran's Natanz nuclear facility, widely believed as combined effort of the United States and Israel. Destroyed nuclear centrifuges and set back Iran's nuclear program by years.
- **Burmese cyber attacks: (Burma[?] vs. Burma).** DDoS type of attack that disrupted most incoming and outgoing network traffic. Occurred before heavily rigged Burmese elections. Some suspect the Burmese government initiated the attack as an effort to silence dissent.
- **Japan-Korea cyberwar (Japan vs. Korea).** Cyberwar between Japanese and Korean Internet netizens corresponding with the one hundredth anniversary of the Japan-Korea treaty.
- **Shadow Network discovered (China vs. India/Dalai Lama).** China-based computer espionage operation stole classified documents and emails from Indian government, Dalai Lama office and other high-level government networks. Used social networking and cloud computing platforms to infect computers with malicious software.

2011

- **Attack against Canada.** Major cyber attack against Canadian government originating in China. Infiltrated three Canadian government departments and obtained classified information.
- **US Department of Defense hack.** The US reveals a Department of Defense contractor was hacked and 24,000 files were stolen (exact time of attack unknown).
- **Operation Tunisia (Anonymous vs. Tunisian regime).** The Anonymous hactivists targeted Tunisian government websites during the Tunisian revolution and also helped citizens evade government monitoring.
- **Paris G20 Summit cyber attack (unknown Asian country vs. France/ G20).** Email spam with malware attachment. Began with emails circulated by the French finance ministry; most of those infected worked on the G20. Targeted exfiltration of G20 documents. Reportedly led by an Asian country.
- **Operation Shady Rat discovered (China vs. many).** Started in mid-2006, actors attacked 72 organizations including the International Olympic Committee, the United Nations, business and defence contractors. Most assume China was responsible.

2012

- **Gauss Trojan. (? vs. Middle East).** Discovered in 2012; a state-sponsored computer espionage operation. Mostly targeted computers in the Middle East (primarily Lebanon, Israel and Palestine). Designed to steal banking information, browser passwords and other sensitive data. Very similar to Stuxnet and Flame (which were created by the US and Israel).
- **Shamoon (Iran vs. Saudi Aramco).** Cyber espionage virus in the energy sector. Group called "Cutting Sword of Justice" claimed responsibility for attack on 30,000 Saudi Aramco workstations. The US says Iran was probably responsible.
- **Flame malware discovered.** Cyber espionage attack that targeted government and educational institutions in the Middle East.
- **Red October cyber attack discovered.** Hackers used Word and Excel vulnerabilities to target government embassies, research firms, military installations, energy providers, and nuclear and other critical infrastructures in countries in Eastern Europe, former USSR and Central Asia, with some victims in Europe and North American. Had been in operation since 2007.
- **India hack.** Emails of 12,000 people penetrated, including high-level officials from Defence Research and Development Organisation, Indo-Tibetan Border Police, Ministry of Home Affairs and Ministry of External Affairs.

2013

- **South Korea cyber attacks (North Korea vs. South Korea).** Targeted financial institutions and Korean broadcaster YTN; North Korea probably responsible.

2014

- **Operation Newscaster (Iran vs. US, UK, Saudi Arabia, Iraq, Syria and Afghanistan).** Started as early as 2011. A cyber espionage covert operation allegedly conducted by Iran and directed at military and political figures; uses social networking websites to conduct spear phishing (email spoofing) attacks to infect computers with malware.
- **Operation Cleaver (Iran vs. US/Israel/China/Saudi/India/ Germany/France/Israel).** Covert cyberwarfare campaign targeting critical infrastructure organizations worldwide, allegedly conducted by Iran. Targets include US, Israel, China, Saudi Arabia, India, Germany, France and England.

2015

- **US Office of Personnel Management data breach (China vs. US).** Largest breach of government data in history of the US. US government blames Chinese hackers.

their nation being cyber attacked by a foreign government, terrorist organization or some other malicious actor.

But what is also interesting is that this concern is consistently a little higher in the developing world than it is in most developed countries. A statistically significant difference emerges between the two groups of countries in terms of public attitudes. This difference underscores the heightened sense of vulnerability, if not outright suspicion, regarding the Internet that citizens in emerging market and developing countries may feel. It also likely speaks to a perceived (and often real) capacity problem in developing countries, where citizens worry that their national institutions cannot handle being targeted in cyberspace.

Cyber attacks can take many different forms. They can be rudimentary DDoS attacks, or they can involve highly sophisticated attacks using malware that can disable the operating system of an entire

Figure 7.1: Concern over Important National Institutions Being Hacked

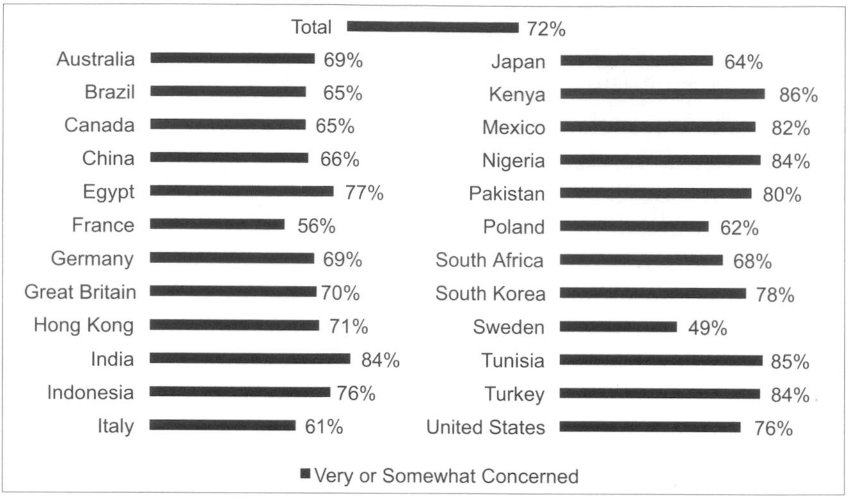

Total	72%			
Australia	69%	Japan	64%	
Brazil	65%	Kenya	86%	
Canada	65%	Mexico	82%	
China	66%	Nigeria	84%	
Egypt	77%	Pakistan	80%	
France	56%	Poland	62%	
Germany	69%	South Africa	68%	
Great Britain	70%	South Korea	78%	
Hong Kong	71%	Sweden	49%	
India	84%	Tunisia	85%	
Indonesia	76%	Turkey	84%	
Italy	61%	United States	76%	

■ Very or Somewhat Concerned

Source: Data from the CIGI-Ipsos 2014 Global Survey.

computer network. If the network is responsible for managing and storing sensitive financial data or for operating critical infrastructure (such as an oil or gas pipeline, a transportation system or a nuclear power plant), the damage from a well-planned cyber attack could be massive, leading to considerable economic damage and maybe even loss of life.*

Deleting data or taking systems off-line would obviously wreak havoc upon global communications and data flows, but the new tidal wave of malicious activity actually involves something even more insidious: data manipulation. With destroyed data, at least everyone involved knows where they stand. They need to start over, which is costly and annoying, but generally doable. Data manipulation is

---

* Even on a lower, more individualized scale, malware introduced into, say, the computer of a car could be lethal to its driver and occupants, as well as to anyone in the path of the out-of-control vehicle. A team of researchers at the University of Manchester demonstrated this possibility in 2015 when they got control of a car's brakes via a digital-radio signal.[2]

worse. It interferes with our fundamental understanding of what is true. Right now, we always trust, perhaps more than we should, what the data tells us. Without putting too metaphysical of a spin on it, data is truth. But increasingly, the integrity of that data can be altered. And altered data simply changes the nature of what is true, at least until we all know that it has been changed. Admiral Michael Rogers, director of the NSA, sums up the problem well: "Our system — whether it's in the private sector or for us in the military — is fundamentally founded on the idea of trust of the data we are looking at. What happens if the digital underpinning that we've all come to rely on is no longer believable?"[3]

The consequences at an individual level are, basically, personal ruin. If data on your financial, medical or legal position is altered, you will likely not be believed if you try to correct large, data-holding institutions. All you will have is your word, while the institution will have the data to show you are lying. Your bank, for example, will never believe you when you tell them that you actually had $100,000 in your savings account rather than $100,000 of debt, because, unlike in the case of fraud where there is a paper trail that the bank can follow, the paper trail in this case shows that you are in fact deeply in debt. Scaled up to a society-wide level, the consequences of manipulated or destroyed data are far worse. Chaos ensues. Our entire world is organized around records (increasingly digitized ones), and if those records cannot be trusted, the whole system is compromised.

Governments and IT security firms have not been caught completely flat-footed by the looming challenge of ensuring data integrity. The answer to maintaining integrity is publicity and decentralization. Estonia is at the forefront of maintaining integrity in its IT systems and Guardtime is one company at the vanguard of this process. Its CEO, Mike Gault, explains the problem of data integrity and a solution this way:

> For the last 40 years nobody has really figured out integrity, because they have tried to use the same tools: they have tried

to keep secrets in order to verify that their data is correct. And it just doesn't work. This was the insight from the Estonian side. Actually, confidentiality and integrity are opposite problems: the more people that witness a crime, the stronger the integrity of the evidence. But the less confidential the evidence becomes because more people know about it.

This insight led us to this technology [known as blockchain] and today this technology secures the Estonian IT systems. Government-held records, healthcare logs, financial transactions are registered into the blockchain, and can be independently verified for what happened to the data without having to go back to the administrators of the respective systems and trust them; in fact, without having to trust any party — the same principle as Bitcoin. This is widely deployed in Estonia now with great success.[4]

Blockchain works by allowing anyone to, should they wish to, possess part of the distributed ledger, and to watch and even approve any potential changes to the system on a constant real-time basis. Any piece of data can, at any point and time, be validated against the blockchain ledger to ensure that its time, authenticity and identity are correct. The blockchain ledger itself cannot be corrupted. The computational power needed to change even a single entry in the ledger would far surpass anything that any government could currently marshal because every ledger would need to be gamed at the same time. New technologies such as these can work to ensure that we trust the data that we see.

Security Through Resiliency

The whole problem of data integrity also underscores the importance of resilience in the digital age if we are to be secure. An example of resiliency and what can happen when it fails is the human body. Healthy people rarely get sick, but eventually we all catch a cold.

And, ultimately, the true hallmark of good health is not that a person never gets sick, but rather that if they do catch a cold they get well again.

Right now, most governments, firms and even individuals lack resilience, making the effects of cyber attacks that much worse. One basic measure of resilience — akin to a person's immune system — is whether a breach of a company's system is detected in-house or by some other external actor. It is a bit like asking if a person's immune system is able to identify a virus. Unfortunately, the proverbial immune system of most companies is pretty terrible at recognizing foreign invaders. One study from 2015 found, for instance, that upwards of 81 percent of network breaches were actually discovered by government, security companies or third parties (such as merchants), and then reported to the company in question.[5]

Additional data from Verizon's *2015 Data Breach Investigations Report* points to the same problem of limited resilience. Researchers at Verizon examined how many cyber attacks effectively breached a system in a matter of days (or less) and then gauged how many times the company's defenders (its immune system) were able to respond with similar alacrity. They found that from 2004 to 2014 there was, as they call it, a widening "defection deficit" — attackers were far more likely to breach a system quickly than the defender was to recognize that breach and respond effectively.[6] The lesson here is that many firms still lack one of the basic features of a resilient system, namely, the ability to identify an attack so that resources can be marshalled to fight back.

Another key element of a resilient system is its ability to repel invaders. Like the white blood cells in the human body, companies and governments need to develop better means to repel attacks after they occur. Distributed denial of service attacks provide an interesting glimpse of what happens when companies are targeted. As with the identification of a problem, the unfortunate reality is that many companies are again lacking in resilience against even this highly common form of cyber attack. A SANS Institute study from 2014, for example, points out that "almost 40% of enterprises are completely or mostly unprepared for DDoS attacks." What is more, 23 percent of respondents in the study actually indicated that they did not have a DDoS mitigation strategy in place.[7] This lack of preparedness is problematic to say the least, especially since DDoS attacks can continue relentlessly with little cost to the attacker, while costing the defender heavily. While coordinated mitigation strategies involving ISPs and other defenders do exist, many actors in the ecosystem remain fragile, making them easy prey for the many pathogens that exist online.

Malicious Cyber Activity

Already, some countries are starting to carry out cyber attacks as a kind of proxy warfare. For example, in 2007, Russia attacked the Internet infrastructure of the newly independent state of Estonia, disabling the country's communications and some of its major financial institutions. Russia did the same thing again a year later when it launched a cyber attack against the former Soviet Republic of Georgia, in tandem with the use of tanks and guns. The Stuxnet virus, which is widely believed to have been developed by the United States and Israel, severely damaged Iranian nuclear facilities at Natanz. In a widely publicized attack, North Korea hacked into the Sony Corporation's computer and email systems, destroying movie files and exposing private emails, many of them highly embarrassing to some of the company's top executives.

The attack on Sony was supposedly prompted by the company's impending release of a movie, *The Interview*, a comedy starring Seth Rogen and James Franco about an attempt to assassinate North Korea's leader Kim Jong-un. Although the North Koreans denied that they were the source of the attack, which was carried out by a proxy group calling itself the Guardians of the Peace, the US Director of National Intelligence, James Clapper, claimed that there was no doubt that North Korea was behind the intrusion. As Clapper publicly explained, "They [North Korean government officials] are deadly, deadly serious, no pun intended, about affronts to the supreme leader, whom they consider to be a deity."[8]

In retaliation for the hack, President Obama slapped sanctions on some of North Korea's top organizations and 10 of its senior leaders. Shortly after the United States' public declaration that North Korea was to blame for the intrusion into Sony's computer systems, the Internet in the repressive hermit kingdom went dark. The exact cause of the outage is unknown. But this could well have been a further warning shot by the United States that state-sponsored cyber attacks would not be tolerated.

Major US financial institutions such as JPMorgan Chase, Bank of America and Wells Fargo have also been knocked out by major cyber attacks purportedly carried out by the Islamic Republic of Iran and other Islamic extremist groups such as the Islamic State of Iraq and al-Sham (ISIS).* Perhaps the most serious attack to have taken place in recent years was the 2015 hack attack on the US Office of Personnel Management. Initially, officials thought that the hackers had taken around four million confidential personnel records of current and former employees of the US government. The actual number of breach records eventually grew to some 21.5 million records, and included very sensitive information, ranging from fingerprints and social security numbers to security clearance forms containing sensitive medical and family details. China was purportedly responsible for the cyber attack, done at arm's length.

There have been many other cyber attacks over the years, including a whole series of industrial espionage intrusions against major US companies led by the Chinese PLA. In frustration, the United States

---

*   When hackers broke into JPMorgan's network in 2014, they made off with the contact information of 83 million customers.[9]

has gone so far as to indict five prominent members of the PLA, which it believes are responsible for authorizing these attacks. In 2015, the administration also began to talk openly about the idea that economic sanctions could, and indeed would, be used as a response to ongoing state-backed cyber espionage.

Even with these sorts of countermeasures, the inconvenient truth is that these kinds of attacks could get a lot worse. Imagine a well-planned, highly sophisticated attack that permanently wiped out the databases of a major financial institution in the United States or Europe, wherein all of the company's financial records were destroyed, including any backup files. The resulting losses would be comparable to the collapse of Lehman Brothers or other major financial institutions during the US sub-prime mortgage crisis of 2008/09. Losses could potentially run into the trillions of dollars as the effects ricocheted through global financial markets.

All of this might sound implausible if you look only at the kinds of attacks that have taken place up until now. But many well-placed experts we have talked to say that this kind of scenario could happen and nobody is really ready for it, especially financial regulators, although central banks and private financial institutions are taking measures to strengthen their Internet firewalls and enhance data security, along with other defensive measures.

Or think of a scenario where the electrical power grid suffers a devastating cyber attack and the lights on the North American continent literally go out. Former ABC news anchor Ted Koppel, who explores such an eventuality in his book, *Lights Out*.[10] As he points out, "Deregulation of the electric power industry has resulted in a network of more than 3,000 companies, some of which are well protected, many of which are not, but all of which are interconnected."[11] He goes on to suggest that "[h]acking into the most vulnerable could lead to a domino-like penetration of even the most secure companies" because the "automated programs (known as supervisory control and data acquisition systems) that control the supply and demand of electricity…are, for the most part, standardized and therefore highly accessible. Multiple sources in the intelligence community and the military…[say] that Russia and China have already embedded cyber-capabilities within our electrical systems that would enable them to take down all or large parts of the grid. Iran's capabilities are close behind. North Korea is working toward such a goal."[12]

Not to be outdone, non-state actors such as ISIS are also trying to hack the US power grid in retaliation for US military engagement in Iraq and Syria. In October 2015, word broke that ISIS, heretofore a clearly growing but largely physical-world problem, had been trying to reach across the Atlantic Ocean and hack into the US power grid. The attacks failed, as the ISIS hackers were, fortunately, fairly unskilled at their job. As John Riggi, cyber division section chief at the FBI, characterized the attack: "Strong intent. Thankfully, low capability."[13] But the concern is that ISIS's burning motive to harm innocent people in the West might soon get coupled with heightened ability, perhaps, as we discussed in chapter six and in more detail below, through some shadowy Dark Web marketplace offering hacker expertise. As Koppel puts it, ISIS "may soon be able to hire capable experts and assemble the necessary equipment, which is available on the open market."[14]

With not only states but also malicious non-state groups taking aim, we should be worried about such disasters. But it is not simply the software of the Internet that is vulnerable. So, too, is the physical infrastructure over which the Internet operates, including telephone lines, switching stations, servers and the millions of miles of fibre optic cable which run overland and under the world's oceans to transmit terabytes of Internet data at lightning speed. For example, *The New York Times* reported in late October 2015 that Russian submarines and spy ships were carrying out operations near the underwater cables that carry the world's Internet communications.[15] The story ominously suggested that the Russians were quietly studying ways to slash these cables in a future crisis with special cutters outfitted on their submarines. Such an attack could easily bring the world's communications and global commerce to a crashing halt. As *The New York Times* reported, "The role of the cables is more important than ever before. They carry more than $10 trillion a day in global business, including from financial institutions that settle their transactions on them every second. Any significant disruption would cut the flow of capital. The cables also carry more than 95 percent of daily communications."[16]

If this sounds like pure science fiction, think again. Russia's relations with the West have severely deteriorated in recent years following Russia's invasion of Crimea and the projection of its military power in eastern Ukraine, Syria and the Trans-Caucasus region. Russian vessels now regularly conduct patrols near sensitive North Atlantic Treaty Organization (NATO) sites, including underwater fibre optic cables. Although undersea cables often get cut by ships dragging their anchors and are relatively easily repaired, that is not the case with a cable that is hundreds of metres below the surface at a remote location somewhere in the mid-Atlantic. The Norwegian government, in fact, has become so concerned about Russia's activities that it has asked its NATO partners to undertake a major new collective effort to track Russian submarine and naval movements in the North Atlantic. But it is not just Russia that is a threat. China's relations with the United States have deteriorated in recent years as China begins to flex its military muscles over its neighbours and extend its territorial claims into the South China Sea. Other regional powers, such as Iran and North Korea, are also getting into the cyberwarfare game in a major way.

A New War in Cyberspace?

Ordinary people can be forgiven for asking the seemingly naïve question, "Why do governments want to turn the Internet, which is now such a vital tool of global communications, economic growth and innovation, into an instrument of warfare?" Surely, it can't be in the long-term collective self-interest of nations to do so if it destroys the digital social capital — the trust — that allows the Internet to function. The response from the vast majority of the population would of course simply be, "You're absolutely right. Using the network for war collectively promises more harm than good." But, as we have seen before regarding the costs of crime and the preservation of user privacy, any particular country can use the network for nefarious purposes and come out ahead if everyone else acts with restraint. It is a classic prisoner's dilemma.

And so, with the prospect of personal gain at the expense of others, some governments use the Internet to spy on their citizens and do other unscrupulous things that include attacking the institutions of other countries via the Internet. Because of the way the Internet is designed, the short-term rewards for bad behaviour, at least for now, generally tend to outweigh the risks of getting caught or being called out. Until those costs change or new norms of cooperative behaviour emerge, governments will continue to sponsor cyber attacks or look the other way when attacks are carried out from their own soil.

One day, it may be possible to develop so-called "rules of the road" or "norms" to prevent these kinds of attacks from occurring or, at a minimum, to limit attacks against critical infrastructure such as communications networks, energy grids and financial institutions.[17] We are still probably a long way off from that day. However, governments around the world are eventually going to have realize that you can't have it both ways: you can't promote the Internet as a vital tool for communications and economic growth and innovation while also using it, to paraphrase the great military strategist Carl von Clausewitz, as a "virtual" extension of war by other means. If you turn the Internet into an online O.K. Corral of the Wild West where cyber renegades, like the outlaw cowboys who fought the Earps and Doc Holliday of a bygone era, duke it out, people may simply stop using the Internet altogether. What is certain, though, is that netizens are already changing their online behaviour, increasingly turning to restricted, privately secured networks — VPNs — to avoid prying eyes.[18]

Open but Vulnerable

It is ironic that the Internet, which was designed behind closed doors in the US Department of Defense to be an instrument to facilitate internal communications, is not secure. Vint Cerf, one of the original designers of the TCP/IP protocols that allow the Internet to work, summed up the thinking behind the early stages of the network in a series of interviews in the late 2000s. In one interview from 2009, when asked about the lack of thought about security when designing the system, Cerf candidly replied: "It's true that we didn't focus very heavily on the security side at the time that we were finalizing the current protocols that you're using. We were much more concerned about whether it worked at all, as opposed to, 'does it work securely?' If I had to do it all over again, I would go back and re-specify a requirement for strong authenticity of the devices on the Net, strong authenticity of the users and the applications that are running."[19]

In another interview a year earlier, Cerf cast the implications of a lack of security by design in the strongest possible terms, stating: "It's every man for himself. In the end, it seems every machine has to defend itself. The internet was designed that way."[20] What was true then, unfortunately, remains largely true today.

The problem of the open Internet designed with security as an afterthought has also been made more pronounced by the rapid proliferation of web-based programs and applications. The Internet's explosive growth and rapid commercialization, which is reflected in the proliferation of applications that operate on a large number of different mobile devices such as our cellphones and iPads, means that large amounts of old and dated software code still run many programs. Many of these recycled programs are actually vulnerable to being hacked, but they still get used. Companies are lackadaisical about security for the simple reason that it is a lot cheaper to build a new platform on code that is already written — even if it is inherently at risk of being hacked — than to start from scratch in order to design something more secure.

The problem is also exacerbated by government behaviour, where national spy agencies are buying up what are know as "zero-day vulnerabilities" or "exploits," which are essentially defects in the code of software that can be exploited by hackers and government intelligence and defence agencies and for which there are no defences. By adding zero days to their digital arsenals, governments are stoking a different kind of arms race and actually preventing efforts to make the Internet more secure.[21]

The market for zero-day vulnerabilities has evolved considerably in recent years. In the mid-2000s, companies were not usually willing to pay hackers and security researchers for the vulnerabilities they exposed in the companies' code. This left hackers with a choice of either giving the exploit to the company for free so that it could be patched, presenting it at a conference to gain academic notoriety or selling it to someone else, perhaps a government or a malicious hacker.

As more players have become involved in chasing zero days, and as a full-flung cottage industry has emerged, the price tag for these exploits of vulnerabilities has increased. In 2007, Charlie Miller, an early researcher who, to the chagrin of some, publicly declared that he sold exploits to governments, wrote an influential article that provided a list of estimated prices for zero-day exploits.[22] His list categorized items according to the type of vulnerability, and some of his categories, such as "some exploits," are somewhat unclear. In a few cases, however, his list of vulnerabilities points to the price tag that would come along with hacking a specific type of code. Some years later, in 2012, journalist Andy Greenberg assembled a similar list of prices attached to various zero-day exploits in different types of software.[23] Not all the types of software overlap between the two lists, but a side-by-side comparison gives a good sense of the fairly large price appreciation that has occurred between 2007 and 2012 (Table 7.1).

The price tag for vulnerabilities ranges considerably and is largely driven by supply and demand. On the supply side, unknown exploits that are highly effective (maybe even able to provide root access with a

Table 7.1: The Increasing Payday for Zero-Day Exploits

Type of Zero-Day Vulnerability 2007	Estimated Vulnerability Price in 2007	Software	Estimated Vulnerability Price in 2012 (US$)
Mozilla	$500	Adobe Reader	$5,000–$30,000
Microsoft Excel	>$1,200	Mac OSX	$20,000–$50,000
WMF exploit	$4,000	Android	$30,000–$60,000
ZDI, iDefence purchases	$2,000–$10,000	Flash or Java browsers plug-ins	$40,000–$100,000
"Weaponized exploit"	$20,000–$30,000	Microsoft Word	$50,000–$100,000
Vista exploit	$50,000	Windows	$60,000–$120,000
Internet Explorer	$60,000–$120,000	Firefox or Safari	$60,000–$150,000
Significant, reliable exploit	$125,000	Chrome or Internet Explorer	$80,000–$200,000
"Some exploits"	$200,000–$250,000	IOS	$100,000–$250,000

Source: Data from Miller, "Legitimate Vulnerability Market"; Greenberg, "Shopping for Zero-Days."

single stroke) are prized quite highly. On the demand side, prices tend to be conditioned by the number of potential buyers, which is itself a function of the number of users of a particular software in which a vulnerability has been discovered.

Making matters even worse, purchased zero-day exploits can also be combined with over-the-counter malware and other bits of malicious code. This lethal cocktail provides the purchaser with both the keys to the kingdom (the zero-day exploit for which there is no defence) and the guns to rule it (the malicious code that could do anything from steal information to, as in the case of Stuxnet, break centrifuges in a nuclear reactor).[24]

The whole ecosystem is a bit like the city of Venice, where elegant villas, shops and piazzas are built on old, wooden pylons that the early Venetians sunk into Venice's marshy lagoon. The pylons are now sinking, making the entire city vulnerable to severe flooding from tidal and storm surges from the Adriatic Sea. In the case of the Internet, those "surges" come from the hackers and cybercriminals who flood the Internet with their malware and botnets. Software firms with alarming regularity issue updates and patches to eliminate critical vulnerabilities, but users often ignore these updates, and there is always the risk that hackers will discover new vulnerabilities in the original code. Just as with those rotting, wooden pylons beneath the city of Venice, exposure to the ravages of the sea wreaks havoc.

The Rise of New Cyber Mercenaries

For Internet users, anonymity is a major source of both vulnerability and protection. If you want to hide on the Internet, you easily can. Sometimes being able to hide can protect people from the capricious whims of governments. Yet, although anonymity is important for political dissidents and those who fear for their own safety, it is proving to be something of a double-edged sword. The Internet's rapidly growing cast of bad characters can also disguise their identities. Using that concealment, hackers can undertake all sorts of nefarious acts via the Internet.

The Internet's anonymity is likewise proving a boon to some countries, which are turning to armies of so-called cyber mercenaries to do their dirty work for them. There are scores of freelance hackers and cybercriminals willing to sell their services to the highest bidder, like the buccaneers of a bygone era. As the *Financial Times* reported, "Just as England's Queen Elizabeth I officially licensed pirates to plunder the treasure ships of her rival Philip II of Spain in the 16th century, nations such as Russia and Iran are increasingly arming and encouraging criminal and activist groups with the cyber weaponry necessary to harm their adversaries, while keeping themselves at arm's length, say senior security and defence officials in the US and Europe."[25] However, there is nothing terribly romantic about someone sitting in a basement apartment or an Internet café in front of a computer screen as they tap and hack away. The problem is that we are living in an era of plausible deniability and this is proving to be an advantage to countries that want to outsource their attacks to hackers and criminals.

Countries and individuals alike can use the anonymity of the Dark Web to purchase services that can be used to harm others. And this notion returns us again to the reality that the Internet has bridged the gap between motive and ability like never before. With a few easy clicks, a person can download the Tor browser, access the Dark Web and find Dark Web sites where anonymous people around the world are offering up their services. From there, you can try to find a reputable service provider to hack any adversary or, as in some of the more blood-chilling examples, have an underaged family member raped for only $36,000 (Table 7.2).

Table 7.2 displays a price chart from a Dark Web site recovered from the Tor network. It shows plainly that for those with the motive to do harm, but who lack the skills to undertake such an act, there is now a readily available and anonymous market on the Dark Web connecting buyers and sellers, although, for obvious reasons, we certainly did not try to contact the operator of the site to confirm the validity of the services provided.

Similarly, Dark Web sites put sellers with hacking expertise in touch with those who want something nefarious done. As one "rent-a-hacker" from an actual Dark Web site puts it, "I'll do anything for money, i'm not a pussy :) if you want me to destroy some business or a persons [sic] life i'll do it." With services like these on offer, ordinary Internet users could hack a rival, an ex-lover or a public figure, just as non-state groups like ISIS could gain access to the hacking expertise that they would require to actually penetrate and shut down the US power grid. Once again, the real-world safety implications of the Dark Web weigh heavily upon the trust that users are willing to place in the digital ecosystem.

But what is sauce for the goose, is also sauce for the gander, and those who are in the business of trying to defend and thwart such attacks — intelligence and national security services around the world

Table 7.2: Fees — Dark Web Mercenary

	Regular Prices	Public Persons	1-2 Guards	3-4 Guards
Murder Types				
Regular	$45,000	$180,000	$360,000	$540,000
Missing in action	$60,000	$240,000	$480,000	$720,000
Death in accident	$75,000	$300,000	$600,000	$900,000
Cripple Types				
Regular	$12,000	$48,000	$120,000	$180,000
Uglify	$18,000	$72,000	$160,000	$240,000
Two hands	$24,000	$96,000	$200,000	$300,000
Paralyze	$30,000	$120,000	$240,000	$360,000

	Regular Prices	Public Persons	Family Members
Rape			
Regular	$8,000	$16,000	$32,000
Under age	$21,000	$32,000	$36,000
Bombing			
Simple	$7,000	$28,000	$32,000
Complex	$21,000	$32,000	$48,000
Beating			
Simple	$3,000	$12,000	$30,000

Source: Dark Web .onion site (URL redacted).

— are now investing billions of dollars to investigate the sources of malware and other cyber attacks through advanced forensic technical means. In some cases, if they are reasonably confident about the source, they will go public, as the US government did when it pointed the finger at North Korea for its attack on Sony Corporation. Sometimes states will also try to lay criminal charges against foreign governments, as the United States did with its indictment against several members of the Chinese PLA in 2014, who were, the government alleged, responsible for authorizing a series of major cyber attacks against the United States.

Under international law and article 51 of the United Nations Charter, states have the right to defend themselves. Many of those treaties were written before the cyber age, however, and international lawyers are still struggling to figure out how the "laws of war" apply to the cyber realm. There is a growing consensus that "kinetic" cyber attacks that threaten lives or lead to real physical damage, such as an attack on a country's electrical grid or nuclear power plants, should be construed no differently under international law than direct military attacks and that humanitarian norms about not doing harm to civilians should apply equally in cyberspace. Many believe that aggressor states should be subject to punitive sanctions if they sponsor or condone such attacks.

However, there is a large grey zone in cyberwarfare — industrial espionage, regular intelligence gathering and low-level cyber attacks — where the choices about what to do are more difficult. In extreme cases, governments may decide that they have no choice but to defend their national interests by retaliating, perhaps by resorting to sanctions or the use of force. But if the damage is relatively small or reputational, and there is no readily available international legal remedy, governments may be loath to resort to actions that could escalate a conflict with another country. There is also the risk, if governments decide to attribute culpability publicly, that they may get it wrong because of the difficulties of proving exactly where those attacks actually originated.

Will Deterrence and Arms Control Work in Cyberspace?

We now live in a world where states are increasingly attacking each other in cyberspace but where non-state actors are attackers too. It is a world that looks as if it is heading toward the precipice of full-blown cyberwar. We faced a similar situation during the Cold War. States stared eye to eye over their nuclear arsenals, even as they funnelled money, armaments and *matériel* to local proxies in the jungles of Vietnam and the mountains of Afghanistan. Given the parallels, it is reasonable to ask: do the lessons of deterrence and arms control from the Cold War apply to cyberspace?

Harvard University political scientist Joseph S. Nye, Jr., addresses this question directly. He concludes that that the lessons of deterrence, like most historical lessons, are imperfectly applied because of the Internet's anonymity, the speed of cyber attacks and because there are strong incentives for states and other non-state actors to try to game the system.[26] According to Nye, it will take a considerable period of time to change state behaviour and develop robust norms or rules that limit or proscribe cyberwarfare, but, as he also argues, rational self-interest is a powerful incentive for most political leaders to keep their fingers off the "Enter" key.

During the Cold War when the United States and the former Soviet Union stared at each other across the nuclear divide, nuclear strategists used the term "mutual assured destruction" (MAD) to describe the deterrence relationship between them. That is, if one side had actually tried to launch a nuclear attack there was a good chance it too would have been annihilated by its adversary's nuclear response. There was no real strategic advantage in conducting offensive nuclear warfare — where one side would be able to destroy the other side's nuclear arsenal in a pre-emptive nuclear attack. With the advent of satellites and other early warning systems, the victim of the attack would still have ample warning — minutes but not hours — to launch its own counterattack. Some of those missiles were (and still are) on submarines and thus relatively immune to a pre-emptive attack. In effect, deterrence "worked" because both sides accepted the risk of MAD.

However, a MAD world, as it was sometimes called, did not prevent nuclear brinksmanship in a succession of Cold War crises, the most famous of which was the Cuban Missile Crisis of October 1962. The superpowers eventually learned that they had to deal with each other extremely carefully, like two scorpions in a bottle. The ever-present risk of nuclear war also gave rise to a whole series of arms control agreements and confidence-building measures, such as the hotline agreement or strategic arms limitation treaties, that were intended respectively to promote effective communications in a crisis and stabilize the nuclear balance. The two superpowers did not invest heavily in building strategic defences against nuclear attack, not only because of the technical difficulties of shooting down a missile in full flight, but also because strategic defences were seen as eroding deterrence and altering the strategic balance in ways that could actually increase the incentives to launch a pre-emptive attack in a crisis. With robust strategic defences, the side launching a surprise attack might be able to fend off successfully the ensuing counterattack by the other side.

In the cyber world, given the present state of digital technology and defensive security systems, some believe that cyber attackers have a distinct advantage and deterrence is weak, although this is a matter of some contention. For example, computer networks, as defence analysts David Gompert and Martin Libicki point out, are growing increasingly important for military operations. This greater reliance upon digital technologies is likewise increasing the incentives for cyber attacks in the early stages of a conflict. "If each side is poised to strike early on, if not preemptively, for fear that waiting will endanger its forces," they note, "there could be an inclination to start with cyber operations. Thus cyber warfare could be perceived, rightly or wrongly, as a comparatively low-risk way to degrade an enemy's ability to maintain confidence in its systems, and hence the capabilities such systems provide. The threshold for cyber warfare could be low; the temptation high."[27]

Even though many governments and major private corporations are starting to invest heavily in securing their IT systems with a wide range of defensive security measures, there is still the human element, which can always be exploited. All it takes to breach a company's or government agency's defences is one employee inserting an infected key into a private network or failing to follow established security protocols.

The negative consequences of the human element are seen nowhere more clearly than in the Stuxnet virus, which was created by the United

States and Israel to attack nuclear facilities at Natanz in Iran in 2010. The Stuxnet virus used no less than four zero-day vulnerabilities for which there was no defence. Technologically, it was probably the most sophisticated piece of malware the world has ever seen. Yet, despite its technological sophistication, it was ultimately a human error that got it on the system at Natanz, setting the Iranian nuclear program back years.

What happened was that an engineer brought the virus across the "air gap" between the nuclear reactor's computers and the outside world. The virus took control of the computer system, causing centrifuges to spin wildly out of control until they broke apart, the computers all the while reporting to the Iranian nuclear scientists in the control room that everything was fine. The human element failed and the malware won.[28]

With both technical and human vulnerabilities plaguing Internet-based systems, it is also much cheaper to launch cyber attacks than it is to defend against them, just as it was in the nuclear realm. The same offence-versus-defence strategic logic still applies. Simple DDoS attacks can be launched relatively easily and cheaply by anyone who has the right software and know-how. More sophisticated, large-scale botnet attacks can be arranged as guns for hire over the Dark Web. Indeed, while one can launch a day-long attack for as little as $10, the cumulative damage of DDoS activity around the globe reaches as high as $920 million a day.[29]

Human weak points and offensive dominance already suggest that deterrence will be shaky in the cyber world. Another important difference with the nuclear realm, though, is the possibility of anonymity. Especially when it comes to the Dark Web, anonymity means that criminals and other cyber hackers can operate with relative impunity, with little fear of being caught. The key step in ensuring deterrence — the ability to retaliate — is effectively taken off the table if anonymity ensures that the culprit cannot be identified. Deterrence becomes weak or non-existent.

Despite the weaknesses of deterrence, the good news is that massive cyber attacks — defined as an attack on a major piece of critical infrastructure such as the electrical grid, a nuclear power plant or the global financial system — are still extraordinarily rare. One clear instance of such an attack was a cyber intrusion against the power grid of the Ivano-Frankivsk region in Ukraine on December 23, 2015. The attack, according to a later SANS Institute blog post, was highly coordinated and effective. As the SANS Institute put it:

> The cyber attack was comprised of multiple elements which included denial of view to system dispatchers and attempts to deny customer calls that would have reported the power out. We assess with high confidence that there were coordinated attacks against multiple regional distribution power companies. Some of these companies have been reported by media to include specifically named utilities such as Prykarpattyaoblenergo and Kyivoblenergo. The exact timeline for which utilities were affected and their ordering is still unclear and is currently being analyzed. What we do know is that Kyivoblenergo provided public updates to customers, shown below, indicating there was an unauthorized intrusion (from 15:30 — 16:30L) that disconnected 7 substations (110 kV) and 23 (35 kV) substations leading to an outage for 80,000 customers.[30]

Luckily, cyber attacks such as the one against Ukraine have yet to hit the mainstream and are still the exception rather than the rule, even though many countries, such as the United States, are investing heavily in developing both their offensive and defensive cyber-attack capabilities.[31] There are several reasons for this. The first is that it is still quite difficult given the current state of technology to mount a sustained cyberwarfare campaign. It would still take most countries years to acquire the detailed intelligence information and technical know-how to penetrate all of the different elements of the critical infrastructure of another country (how long this remains true is an open question).

And if they did carry out a massive cyber attack and were exposed as its source, they might well face physical, military retaliation. A second reason may be the fear of escalation if cyber aggression gets out of control. Cyber attacks on a major scale are still unknown territory for most countries, notwithstanding the investment some are making in it. Political leaders still have a lot to learn about the importance of the Internet and the consequences of a wired world, particularly where a nation's core vulnerabilities are increasing with the emerging IoT. Ironically, perhaps, countries that are not so heavily dependent on the Internet as the world's advanced industrial democracies may conclude that investing in cyberwarfare will place them at a strategic advantage because they are less vulnerable. That certainly appears to be the case with North Korea.

What Is to Be Done?

Governments do recognize that if cyberspace becomes truly the Wild West all might be lost. In the early 2000s, governments negotiated the Budapest Convention on Cybercrime with the aim of taking the first steps to harmonize laws so that Internet-enabled crime could be fought across borders. In 2009, in response to the growing number of cyber attacks, NATO countries convened a group of experts to clarify the application of international law to cyberwarfare. The end result was known as the Tallinn Manual. Despite these earlier efforts, cyberwarfare has remained a vexing problem.

But, to their credit, governments have not taken the lack of progress as a sign that progress should not be made. More recently, in June 2015, a group of government experts (GGE) at the United Nations, which had been quietly meeting for almost a year, submitted a major report to the UN Secretary-General on what countries should do to behave responsibly in the cyber realm.[32] The GGE report was noteworthy not only because of the group's widespread representation — its members come from Belarus, Brazil, China, Colombia, Egypt, Estonia, France, Germany, Ghana, Israel, Japan, Kenya, Malaysia, Mexico, Pakistan,

Russian Federation, Spain, United Kingdom and the United States — but also because it had actually been able to reach a consensus on the key norms, rules and principles to inform responsible behaviour in cyberspace. The report also addressed how international law should apply to the use of information and communications technologies. Some of its key recommendations were as follows:

> In their use of ICTs, States must observe, among other principles of international law, State sovereignty, the settlement of disputes by peaceful means, and non-intervention in the internal affairs of other States.

> Existing obligations under international law are applicable to State use of ICTs and States must comply with their obligations to respect and protect human rights and fundamental freedoms.

> States must not use proxies to commit internationally wrongful acts using ICTs and should seek to ensure non-state actors do not use their territory to commit such acts.

> The UN should play a leading role in promoting dialogue on the security of ICTs in their use by States, and in developing common understandings on the application of international law and norms, rules and principles for responsible state behavior.[33]

A growing number of countries, defence experts and even private companies such as the Microsoft Corporation believe that the way to eventually reduce the likelihood of cyberwar is to develop new norms of state behaviour or so-called "codes of conduct," much as the two superpowers did during the Cold War with a succession of confidence-building and arms control measures that were put in place after the Cuban Missile Crisis in 1962. The analogy, of course, is not perfect. Warheads and missile launchers are much easier to count (as well as much harder to build) than cyber weapons and the anonymity of the

Internet makes it extremely difficult to monitor what cybercriminals and other states are doing.

A promising beginning to the development of new cyber norms occurred at the September 25, 2015, summit between US President Barack Obama and President Xi Jinping of China. Both leaders agreed to a new agreement establishing new "rules of the road" to stop cybercrime.

The core of the memorandum of understanding was that both nations wanted to find ways to limit cyber attacks and, even more crucially, to stop any potential escalation of a cyber attack into something larger, something more damaging. These efforts might be too little to really stop the two cyber behemoths from going at each other in cyberspace, but talking almost never hurts.

The agreement also came with a surprisingly silvery lining. For the first time ever, China agreed with America on the concept that economic espionage was not a valid use of cyberspace, which had been and still is a large sticking point in US-China relations. The final output included language stipulating that "neither country's government will conduct or knowingly support cyber-enabled theft of intellectual property, including trade secrets or other confidential business information, with the intent of providing competitive advantages to companies or commercial sectors."[34]

Critics retort that such declarations are akin to throwing down a sandbag to stop a flood.[35] For example, the ink was barely dry on the US-China declaration before there were reports alleging that China had already violated the agreement. CrowdStrike, a company based in Irvine, California, said that it had documented a series of attacks against a number of US technology and pharmaceutical firms "where the primary benefit of the intrusions seems clearly aligned to facilitate theft of intellectual property and trade secrets, rather than to conduct traditional national security-related intelligence collection."[36]

It appears that codes of conduct might take some time for the message to sink in. They also require effective monitoring and compliance mechanisms, including enforceable sanctions for bad behaviour. As a senior Pakistani official noted at the 2015 meeting of the Internet Governance Forum in Brazil, for many governments, norms must be transformed into intergovernmental treaties in order to have real meaning. It may take a long time to develop agreed-upon norms and principles for cyberspace — let alone formal treaties, which may or may not even be a good idea, given the pace of technological change and the distributed nature of Internet governance. In any event, hopefully the day will come when states realize that it is in their own national interests to change their behaviour and abide by such norms.

It was fear of nuclear war during the Cuban Missile Crisis that brought the United States and the Soviet Union to the bargaining table and launched the beginning of arms control with the signing of the Limited Test Ban Treaty in 1963. But it doesn't necessarily have to take a crisis to change state behaviour. The changing attitudes of some countries toward piracy and the protection of intellectual property rights (IPR) are instructive. South Korea in the early 2000s was a hotbed of technology piracy. In fact, the problem was so widespread that the South Korean government became increasingly concerned about the impact of piracy on the country's international trade performance (and reputation), as well as its effect on the viability of its own developing software market.[37]

South Korea first appeared on the United States Trade Representative (USTR) Priority Watch List in 1989.[38] In response, South Korea introduced more robust intellectual property protections to help seek removal from the list.[39] Eventually, both the USTR and the UK Intellectual Property Office deemed South Korea's efforts to be successful. South Korea has not been on the list since 2009 and, in 2014, the USTR noted that South Korea had "transformed itself from a country in need of intellectual property rights enforcement into a country with a reputation for cutting-edge innovation as well as high-quality, high-tech manufacturing."[40]

But there were also internal, domestic reasons for the change in policy. In 2004, a director within the South Korean Ministry of Information and Communication noted, "This is not just a trade issue. We do need to promote our domestic software market."[41] The government in 2013 employed the slogan "Creative Economy" to describe its economic agenda, and it employed rhetoric about "cultural prosperity" in an effort to promote "a healthy ecosystem for the copyright industry."[42] As a report commissioned by the UK government noted, a two-pronged set of concerns, one domestic, one international, drove changes to South Korea's IPR policy regime.[43]

Similar pressures are evident in the slow transformation of Brazil's IPR regime. Brazil is infamous for pirated goods, ranging from physical goods (for example, pharmaceuticals and car parts) to media (such as music, movies and software). Some Brazilian politicians defend piracy, arguing it is the only way for the underprivileged classes to obtain content, products and technology that they otherwise would not have access to.[44] Piracy is also socially acceptable in Brazil. Many Brazilians do not consider illegal downloads at home to be piracy. Most believe piracy is defined as the action of *purchasing* an illegal copy of something — although even that remains widespread and socially accepted. Brazil actually has decent intellectual property laws, although there is little political will to enforce them.[45] Brazil has open-air markets where you can purchase pirated merchandise, ranging from compact disks to fake purses. The police are well aware of these spots and occasionally conduct raids, but the sellers always return. Some surmise there are agreements between police and sellers, and that the police receive kickbacks. Brazilian courts usually mete out punishment to software pirates according to their ability to pay. Profitable companies typically have higher indemnification rates, whereas smaller companies are fined at a lower rate. Ordinary citizens (for both general piracy and software piracy) are usually not punished at all unless they make big profits.

However, the Brazilian government's approach to piracy is changing because of lobbying from the Brazilian movie and music industries.

While it may be socially acceptable to steal from Hollywood because it is American, 50 percent of pirated movies in Brazil are produced domestically, and the film industry clearly wants this to change. For politicians passing tougher domestic laws against software piracy, new legislation is something of a double-edged sword. They understand that IPR reform will, in the long-term, result in a higher rate of economic growth. However, they also fear that enforcing IPR will hamper their re-election chances and diminish campaign contributions from lobbies representing local pirating industries. It is the classic issue of long-term benefits versus short-term political interests, and some politicians do not see sufficient incentive to support reform.

Some years ago, the *Harvard Business Review* ran an interesting article about the treatment of intellectual property in Japan. The author, American CEO Donald Spero, argued that the difference between Western and Japanese intellectual property protections (at the time) was more cultural than economic. "The goal of Western systems is to protect and reward individual entrepreneurs and innovative businesses," he asserted, whereas "the intent of the Japanese system is to share technology, not protect it. In fact, it serves a larger, national goal: the rapid spread of technological know-how among competitors in a manner that that avoids litigation, encourages broad-scale cooperation, and promotes Japanese industry as a whole."[46] Spero provided an example of his own company's experience in Japan after it entered the market in the mid-1970s. He described a nearly 15-year-long saga in which his company, Fusion, clashed with Mitsubishi after the Japanese rival stole its intellectual property and then tried to bully Fusion out of the Japanese market.[47]

Japan's approach to IPR eventually evolved for economic reasons. Hisamitsu Arai, who played a key role in formulating Japan's new approach to IPR, explains the shift: "When I took office as Commissioner of the Japan Patent Office (JPO) in 1996, the national IP [intellectual property] system was rigid and out-dated, and the country's IP law and policies needed reviewing in light of the new role for IP in Japan's new innovation policies. Urgent action was required, especially as Japan was struggling to recover from a long economic slump — the so-called 'lost decade' of the 1990s."[48]

Arai also directly connects IPR protection, innovation and economic growth. "Innovative activity would greatly increase, resulting in strong patents that would boost both the Japanese and the world economy. Japan's long recession at the time was blamed by many people on the financial system and banks; however, the weakness of industry and its lack of competitiveness was also responsible."[49] Arai argued further that "Japanese citizens should be encouraged to create new technologies, rather than purloining existing ones."[50] He concludes, "The vision from which Japan's [intellectual property] strategy grew is based on the belief that innovation and creativity should be rewarded; counterfeiting and piracy are a serious threat to realizing that vision."[51]

The relationship between IPR protection and development is tricky, because it is not direct. More IPR protection does not always result in more development. A study by the RAND corporation, for example, showed that stronger IPR seem to encourage innovation in emerging industrialized economies, but, interestingly, weak IPR seem to favour economic development in less developed countries.[52] However, that same study also showed that strong IPR may actually hamper innovation by incentivizing technology adoption through diffusion and absorption in lower-income developing countries.[53] But the overall lesson here is that the stronger and more mature a country's economy becomes, the more it will benefit from a stronger IPR regime and consider it to be in its own national self-interest to adhere to global norms. One day, the same could eventually happen with countries such as China, as economic self-interest trumps other considerations in the way they view and use the Internet.

Implications for China

In cyberspace, the United States and China are the two clashing titans. China, for its part, has something of a yin-yang approach to the

Internet. On the one hand, the Chinese government is actively pursuing an "Internet sovereignty" strategy. The idea that domestic government will be the ultimate arbiter of what goes on upon the Internet within a country's borders is a concern not only to the entire global community, but also to some members of the Chinese business community whose economic interests are at stake. This new policy thrust is consistent with the PLA's increasing attempts to use the Internet as a form of proxy warfare against the United States and other Western countries. It also complements the Chinese government's growing efforts to crack down on dissidents and control Internet content via the Great Firewall of China.

As noted by Marietje Schaake, a member of the European Parliament with the Alliance of Liberals and Democrats for Europe, China recently adopted "a wide-ranging national security law, which would increase China's control over foreign businesses and stifle crucial civil liberties of the population. The adoption of the law came days after the conclusion of the 17th EU-China summit in Brussels....A core component of the new Chinese law would make all key network infrastructure and information systems 'secure and controllable' in order to protect national security." She goes on to point out that "[t]he latter term is so broadly defined that it would even cover 'harmful cultural influences' as a national security threat. Foreign companies in China have argued that the law is too vague and fear it could force technology firms in particular to make products in China or use source code released to inspectors. This would force them to expose intellectual property."[54] Schaake also observes that "[h]uman rights experts have argued that the law includes elements that define criticism of the government as a form of subversion. A senior official at the National People's Congress (NPC) said that the new law provided a legal foundation for 'the management of internet activities on China's territory and the resisting of activities that undermine China's cyberspace security.' Details on the interpretation of the new law will emerge over time, but it remains to be seen whether this law is in line with WTO regulations."[55]

This law is no surprise, as it comes on the heels of a very similar anti-terrorism and bank technology regulation. Of concern to Schaake and other human rights advocates, though, is that "[t]he first law would force telecommunication services providers to provide Beijing with backdoors into their systems and install a form of forced data localization. The latter would have forced banks operating in China until 2019 to ensure that 70 per cent of their IT products qualify as 'secure and controllable' under Chinese law. Economic protectionism and restricting Internet freedom go hand in hand in China."[56]

On the other hand, there are countervailing economic and political pressures that point to a more open, multi-stakeholder approach to the Internet and Internet governance in China. China's Cyber Administration, its top Internet body, for example, is now engaging more with multi-stakeholder bodies, such as ICANN and the Brazilian-led NETmundial process (an open, global, bottom-up participatory process on the future governance of the Internet), and also looking to the Internet as a key instrument to promote economic development and innovation through its new "Internet Plus" strategy. It seems that Chinese Premier Li Keqiang, going by public comments, is trying to reduce reliance on old-time fiscal spending on physical infrastructure to rescue a deteriorating economic situation. "The favorable wind of Internet Plus is set to push the Chinese economy to a higher level," said Li.[57] The plan "aims to integrate mobile Internet, cloud computing, big data and the Internet of Things with modern manufacturing, to encourage the healthy development of e-commerce, industrial networks, and Internet banking, and to help Internet companies increase international presence."[58]

As one observer of the Chinese Internet economy notes:

Nowhere in the world are countries downloading applications as much as in China. In general Chinese people have around 90 applications on their smartphone, compared to an average of 30 worldwide. Very popular Chinese applications are WeChat (500 million active users, comparable to Whatsapp and Facebook); Dianping (200 million active users, comparable to Groupon and TripAdvisor; Didi Chuxing (200 million active users, comparable to Uber); and Youku Tudou (600 million active users, comparable to YouTube). Internet giants like Alibaba, Baidu and Tencent are focusing on further development of such 'platform applications,' providing more and more opportunities in just one application. Besides that, Chinese tech companies are looking abroad. Recently China's dominant car-hailing application Didi Chuxing announced an undisclosed investment into Uber's India rival Ola.[59]

Western security analysts are in something of a quandary when it comes to understanding Chinese interests and motivations in cyberspace. Jon Lindsay argues that:

[c]laims about Chinese cyber threats fall at the intersection of two different debates, one about the impact of information technology on international security and the other about the political and economic future of a rising power. The technology debate centers on whether ubiquitous networks create revolutionary or just the marginal evolutions of computer crime, signals intelligence, and electronic warfare. One side of this debate argues that interconnected infrastructure and easily accessible hacking tools make advanced industrial powers particularly vulnerable to serious disruption from weaker states or even nonstate actors. The other side argues that the defense industry and national security establishment greatly exaggerate the cyber threat. The political debate offers contrasting liberal and realist interpretations of China's meteoric growth. One side argues that China is increasingly integrated into the global community and international institutions and, furthermore, that the Communist government is committed to growth and stability to maintain its legitimacy. The other side argues that Chinese military modernization and the relative decline of the United States heighten the potential for opportunistic aggression, miscalculation in a crisis, or preventive war. The very

existence and magnitude of a shift in relative power is also a matter of debate.[60]

At some point, though, China is going to have to confront the merits of an open Internet as regards its own economic future versus a closed Internet that is based on the narrow principle of "Internet sovereignty." The path forward for engaging China and promoting new cyber norms will also require joining with Chinese partners to develop a better understanding of best practices to promote Internet affordability, accessibility, inclusivity, infrastructure and human digital capacities.

Conclusion

We could wake up someday soon to a changed world. We could wake up to a world without power, without clean water, without a working financial system. We could wake up to this world because someone somewhere decided to click "Enter." States are increasingly at each other's throats in cyberspace. Sometimes they attack each other directly; sometimes they do so using proxy cyber mercenaries and other non-state actors who hide in the recesses of the Dark Web.

As we have argued here, the Internet is the hidden wiring of the global economy and plays a critical underlying role in much of the world's infrastructure. Curbing great powers' appetites to turn the Internet into yet another battlefield will require practical initiatives, including fostering the development of new cyber norms between strategic rivals such as the United States and China, to reduce incentives to use the Internet as a tool of industrial espionage, exploitation and warfare. Ultimately, however, effective international cooperation will have to be driven by a different view of national interest — one that sees an open, comparatively secure Internet as the prerequisite to economic development, innovation and high-quality jobs, and not as a platform from which to attack others.

Eight

Internet Haves and Have-Nots

I n 2009, several students from MIT who were volunteering in Afghanistan helped the citizens of Jalalabad create a free, do-it-yourself Wi-Fi network for the city. Until then, satellite links had been prohibitively expensive for locals, and foreign organizations usually were the only ones able to afford regular access to the Internet.[1]

The project started in one of Afghanistan's most unique aid initiatives — the "Fab Labs." The Fab Labs were small-scale digital fabrication workshops set up across Afghanistan and largely staffed by young, tech-savvy expatriate volunteers. Their goal was to provide locals with the technology and business skills they needed to move on from basic projects and business ventures (such as printing T-shirts) to more complex ones.[2]

In the Jalalabad Fab Lab, Afghan students devised a way to share the lab's Wi-Fi across the city. At first, they combined cheap, off-the-shelf routers with laser-cut dishes fabricated in the lab itself. Then they realized that they could easily (and inexpensively) create functional dishes out of tin cans and other recycled rubbish.[3] This network, dubbed "JLink" or "FabFi," inspired a culture of ingenuity among its users. When the system went down, "the people [who] grew to be reliant on it — the kids, the students and so on — would climb on their roofs and fix it," observed Peretz Partensky, one of the Fab Lab expatriate volunteers.[4]

Partensky described the experience of bringing Jalalabad online: "They go on the internet and see people smiling and laughing, it transforms them...They see a video on the internet, they're blown away. For the amount of money it takes to sustain an individual soldier, you can provide internet for hundreds of thousands of Afghan students."[5]

The free Wi-Fi network in Jalalabad helped drive aid and local business. The city's public hospital, local elementary schools and even the dorms at Nangarhar University relied on JLink for Internet access. JLink helped doctors better communicate natal-health information to pregnant Afghan women. In another case, JLink connected Jalalabad's hospital to volunteer radiologists amid a shortage of local doctors who could read X-rays.[6]

Unfortunately, JLink did not have enough time to become self-supporting. By 2012, it had run through all the money in the initial National Science Foundation grant and was financed by the volunteers' own shrinking bank accounts.[7] The international community suffered from extreme donor fatigue in Afghanistan, and volunteers were unable to find traditional NGOs or international governments willing to financially support the project. Sadly, as noted by one aid worker in Afghanistan at that time, "the demise of the JLink is going to be a huge blow to Jalalabad's nascent community of tech entrepreneurs — creative, dedicated young people who are pushing innovation in their own communities and creating well-paying, skilled jobs for their peers."[8]

So far we have focused on the ways in which the trust of current Internet users is being eroded and looked at some of the ramifications of that loss of digital social capital, on everything from individual user behaviour to the economy as a whole. This chapter focuses on the multiple challenges that developing countries face in ICT and bringing their citizens online.

In a book on trust and the Internet, it may seem peculiar to also focus a chapter on a group of people who have yet to even use the technology. In some ways, it is indeed a bit strange. But, as the old saying goes, you never get another chance to make a first impression. As more and more people come online, their initial experience with the network is going to shape their general level of trust in the online ecosystem. Bringing the next billion or more users online so that they are able to fully engage with the system safely and in a meaningful way will determine everything from how much people use the network to the ways in which they do so.

In 2015, there were roughly three billion Internet users globally. Even with this many people online, there are billions more who have yet to experience the joy and occasional horrors of the World Wide Web. This gap between Internet users and those who do not yet use the network is commonly known as "the digital divide." As the next block of people gains access, their collective weight is going to determine much of what happens with the system, for good or ill. We need to make sure that these new users' engagement with the Internet contributes to the network's digital social capital so that the system can work to the advantage of all.

In unpacking how trust is going to be mediated by new users' first interaction with the system, let's start right at the beginning: physically connecting people to the network. Going from there, we can talk about issues of security, privacy, quality of access, inclusion and everything else.

The Internet Expansion S-curve: Bringing the Next Billion Online

The commercial Internet has expanded incredibly fast. According to World Bank statistics, in 1990, the world's entire Internet access rate was less than one half of one percent. By 2014, about 41 percent of the people in the world were online.[9] In absolute terms, that is basically a growth from around 260 million people online in 1990 to about three billion connected people in 2014. The growth is so large that precise quantifications of it are basically meaningless, other than to say that the Internet has spread probably faster, and is starting to reach further, than any other technology humanity has ever invented.

Even though the system has taken root in countries that vary along almost every possible social, political and economic dimension, there is a pretty consistent pattern in the way in which the Internet expands. All the countries that adopted the Internet early on, for example, have followed the same S-shaped adoption pattern. Internet expansion starts out slowly. At around five percent Internet adoption, the per-year rate of Internet expansion starts to speed up. Expanding year-over-year Internet access continues at this faster pace until around the point where 80 percent of the population is online. Beyond this level, the rate of expansion starts to slow down again. Figure 8.1 shows the Internet expansion S-curve for 14 early adopting countries that have moved from less than one percent access in 1990 to at or above 85 percent in 2014, which confirms the general shape of the pattern predicted early on by Theodore Modis.[10]

Figure 8.2 shows the same S-shaped pattern for an average of all 14 early adopting countries taken together. The average trend gives

Figure 8.1: The Internet's S-curve for 14 Early Adopter Countries

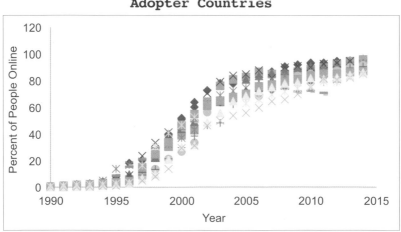

Source: Data from World Bank, n.d., "Data — Indicators," http://data.worldbank.org/indicator.

Figure 8.2: Average S-curve for All Early Adopters

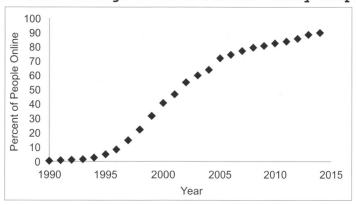

Source: Data from World Bank, "Data — Indicators."

us some insight into exactly how much the rate of expansion differs between the start, middle and end of the S-shaped pattern for early adopters. In general, countries gain access at an average rate of 0.57 percent per year until about five percent of the population is online. In the middle category (what could be called the expansion phase), between five and 80 percent overall penetration, Internet access expands at a much higher average rate of around 5.47 percent per year. Beyond 80 percent Internet diffusion, expanding access slows down again to around 1.74 percent per year.

The S-curve emerges due to something called network effects, in combination with the hard-nosed economics of expanding Internet access across physical distance.

Network Effects (Metcalfe's Law)

As Aristotle taught us, people are inherently social animals. We like being together. We find value in being connected to one another. The Internet's value — its underlying social capital — is in large part a derivative of the number of connected users of the system. The particular term for the systemic value of a system like the Internet is the "network effect," an idea devised by Robert Metcalfe. Metcalfe argued that the usefulness of a system is a function of the square of the number of connected users — or n^2. The systemic value of a networked system, such as the Internet, is a function of those connections: more connections equals more value.

Although the network effect was posited before there was a commercial Internet, this theoretical value of n^2 is also borne out by more recent empirical data. Years after Metcalfe devised this law, he returned to it and tested it with 10 years of data from Facebook. He found that Facebook's revenues for this period fit the predictions of his law remarkably closely.[11]

Consider these network effects on the benefit side of the equation that likely drive the rapid rate of expansion (beyond Facebook) of the Internet. The early Internet adopters are getting fairly few benefits from the network. Why use the Internet if there is no one else with whom you can communicate? At the same time, installing the physical infrastructure necessary to access the Internet is also expensive, meaning that only high-income earners can initially join the network in any given country. Especially in developing countries, this is a relatively small group, so access expands slowly though a narrow strata of society.

Beyond a certain point (five percent Internet adoption), however, just as with Metcalfe's law and Facebook's earnings, the gains that are generated by the growing number of connections surpass the costs, and people start to flood onto the network in droves. Companies, recognizing that people want to be online and will pay to be connected, invest to build the infrastructure needed to expand available connections because they can easily recoup their costs. Users, seeing that others are online and that they will gain from being online too, spend the money to get a personal or professional connection.

Empirically, the number where the rate of expansion really takes off is at around five percent in the 14 early adopting countries. From there, the relatively slow initial annual rate of expanding access of 0.57 percent jumps up to a rate of 5.47 percent, which amounts to almost a tenfold increase in how quickly new people were getting connected. After only a few years, a majority (around 80 percent) of the population was online in these early adopters. At that point, access expansion slows down again.

The Costs of the Last 20 Percent

Once roughly 80 percent of the population is online, the rate of expansion dramatically slows, from an average rate of 5.47 percent per year to only 1.74 percent per year. Once the "low-hanging fruit" has been gathered, getting the last 20 percent of people online is difficult, due to a combination of poor incentives, low income and less affordability, limited user capability and a lack of infrastructure.[12]

Incentives matter because people won't use the Internet if they don't think that it is worthwhile. The most salient incentive problem involves local content and content developed in local languages. In 2016, English was still by far the predominant language on the Web, coming in at around 53.6 percent of websites.[13] A user in Mali or Chad who does not speak English is going to find little of use in a large portion of the Internet and is unlikely to find any content hosted in his or her local language. The incentives to join the network are weak for people in this position. In Ghana, for example, roughly 21 percent of people reported not using the Internet because there was "no interesting content," while over 30 percent of respondents indicated that the "lack of local language content" kept them off-line.[14]

Poverty and the affordability of access to the system also matter. Most of the people who are not online are poor.[15] The reason is fairly straightforward. Despite what teenagers in the West might think — and the Internet meme of the "new" Maslow's Hierarchy of Needs in Figure 8.3 shows just how mainstream the idea has become that Internet access is the basis of life — getting online is not more important than basic necessities such as food or shelter, although it easily *could* be a crucial tool for finding food and shelter in the future.

A rough idea of how much income matters can be gleaned from the United States. A recent Pew Research Center study found that

Figure 8.3: Maslow's Hierarchy of Needs in 2014

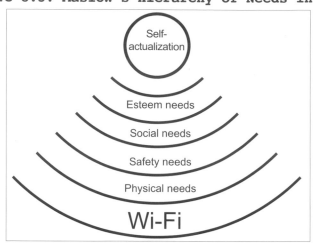

Source: The Web's take on A. H. Maslow, 1943, "A Theory of Human Motivation," *Psychological Review* 50: 370–96.

income level matters a lot for adoption rates, even in one of the richest countries in the world.[16] In families that earn above US$75,000 per year, Internet usage rates are at around 99 percent — basically, everyone who can practicably be online. Among US families that earn less than $30,000 a year, the level of Internet usage drops to 77 percent. This gap is significant.

The problem is far more acute in the world's poorest nations. In Ghana, for example, where only three percent of households have Internet access at home, a lack of income, exacerbated by the high price of access, is one of the largest inhibitors of Internet usage. In the 2011–2012 Research in ICT Africa survey, over 55 percent of Ghanaians indicated that they did not use the network because it was too "expensive to use."[17] Poverty inhibits the expansion of the network in all countries, both rich and poor.

There is also a supply-side problem to the access equation. Sometimes it simply costs too much to connect. The telephone network and the Internet are obviously quite different in many respects, but they are similar in that competition tends to be good for driving down prices. The OECD has done interesting work over the years to really explain what happens to prices with expanding competition in the mobile market. It finds that competition drives pricing-strategy innovation and also drives down costs. As the OECD's Alexia Gonzalez-Fanfalone, Sam Paltridge and Rudolf van der Berg put it, "It used to cost well over $2 a minute to call between OECD countries. The breakup of telecoms monopolies and the introduction of competition means callers now pay as little as $0.01 per minute, or may even have unlimited calls as part of a monthly bundle."[18] In the absence of competition, prices stay high, and the access to or use of networked systems is restricted to all but a rich few.

A third factor hindering adoption of the Internet is limited user capability. If you don't know how to work a computer or an iPad, let alone email, online banking or social media sites, adopting these technologies is extraordinarily difficult. Poll results from around the world show how human capacity matters with respect to network adoption. In India, for example, a 2013 study found that only 50 percent of people in urban centres are computer-literate.[19] In China, a study on the statistical basis of Internet usage in 2013 found that 58.1 percent of non-Internet users cited a lack of knowledge about computers and computer networks as the reason why they do not use the Internet. This number was up from 57.5 percent in 2012.[20] Finally, another McKinsey & Company study found that the primary reason that people in Africa do not connect to the Internet is that they just don't know how to do so.[21] In a world of ubiquitous computers, it is easy to forget how unintuitive the digital world actually is — using it is an acquired skill. Limited capacity due to low computer literacy will continue to keep people from accessing the Web, particularly across the developing world, but also among the elderly in more developed countries.

Finally, a lack of physical infrastructure is likely to severely inhibit people's ability to get online. Internet access tends to expand first in areas with high population concentrations — in other words, cities. Here, an investment in physical infrastructure connects several people simultaneously. After high urban concentrations, suburban areas are the next easiest to connect. But then, companies need to decide if they are going to expand deep into the countryside or into other remote areas to connect fewer people spread over a wider space. Often, the costs to expand access are prohibitively high and the network does not get built. For example, MTS Allstream Inc., a Winnipeg-based telecom provider, noted in 2010 that the cost of expanding access to rural Canada would cost an estimated CDN$7 billion, which is one of the reasons why remote areas even in a rich country such as Canada do not have Internet access.[22]

As Hernán Galperin puts it in a recent paper looking at survey results from a number of Latin American countries, "when households are sorted by geographical location, the evidence suggests that the urban/rural gap in service coverage remains significant, and is an important determinant of observed differences in residential adoption. Rural heads of households are between two and three times more likely to cite availability as the main reason for not subscribing to Internet services."[23] Indeed, the survey results go on to show that "on average, urban households are between seven and 33 percent (depending on the country) more likely to have residential connectivity, after controlling for income and other household characteristics."[24] The basic problem for rural areas is that there are simply too few people dispersed over too much territory to recoup the costs of building the physical infrastructure to connect people. New technologies can help (for instance, satellite or balloon-based Internet), but for now connecting people dispersed across an expanse of geography remains cost-prohibitive.

More broadly, the Internet cannot exist without a complex physical infrastructure of cables, spectrum and wireless signals. Developing and maintaining such a complex system "requires close collaboration between the private and public sectors. Government plays an important role; a supportive and predicable regulatory landscape helps investment in network infrastructure."[25]

In sum, the last 20 percent — and really all those who are not yet connected — are kept off-line by a variable combination of misaligned incentives, low income and poor affordability, limited user capability and a lack of infrastructure.

Internet Expansion in Lower-Middle-Income Countries

Most of those unconnected today are in the developing world. They also tend to be extremely poor, women, marginalized groups and the elderly.[26] In other words, the digital divide extends to different social groups within poorer countries (as it does to a lesser extent in richer countries).

Many of the world's poorest countries have yet to cross even the five percent threshold beyond which network adoption should really take off, although they are slowly edging in that direction, following the same pattern of rich countries. Lower-middle-income countries, on the other hand, have crossed this line, and the S-shaped pattern is taking shape, even though most of these countries have yet to reach Internet diffusion rates above 40 percent overall.

Figure 8.4 shows the average rate of expansion for all lower-middle-income countries, according to World Bank data. While overall the rate of expansion for these countries is slower than it was for the early adopting high income nations, the five percent threshold beyond which expansion speeds up is still there. Before that point, access expanded at a rate of 0.52 percent per year. After the five percent mark, the rate of expansion increased and the Internet started to touch new people at a rate of 2.11 percent of the population per year. Luckily for us all, the S-shaped pattern of the early adopters appears alive and well, which means that people will continue to come online faster than before for the foreseeable future in lower-middle-income countries.

Of course, the fact that access is expanding at an overall slower rate in lower-middle-income countries than in the rich early adopters

Figure 8.4: Internet Expansion in Lower- to Middle-Income Countries

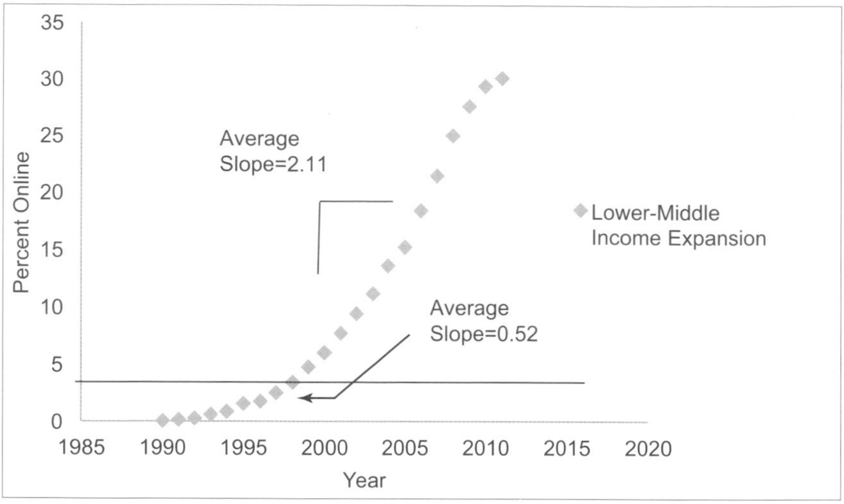

Source: Data from World Bank, "Data — Indicators."

is itself problematic. Considering just the very poorest nations of the world (those not represented in Figure 8.4), adoption rates are even negative in some years, meaning that many people are going off-line. This is likely due to a combination of reporting problems, economic turmoil and civil strife in those nations that are the worst off. Given that the technology to deliver the Internet to people's homes and hands has become both more effective and cheaper, it is doubly troubling that the rates of expansion in lower-middle-income countries (those in Figure 8.4) are slower for these new adopters than for the rich early adopters in the West.

The slower adoption rate for lower-middle-income countries comes back to the same factors that keep the last 20 percent off-line in the rich countries of the West: incentives, income and affordability, user capability and a lack of infrastructure.[27] Unfortunately, every one of these inhibitors of adoption tends to become more pronounced as the country in question moves down the ladder of economic and social development.

In one sense, bringing the next billion users online is taking care of itself, but it is happening more slowly than it could (or should) and is likely to affect user trust in a number of ways. This lag is a major challenge not only for public policy, but also for perceptions of trust and the creation of strong digital social capital in the developing world.

Breaking (or Building) the Trust of New Users

How new people come online will affect both their perceptions of the trustworthiness of the network and, by extension, their actual interaction with the Internet ecosystem.

People's views of the world are always conditioned by their own experiences.[28] Consistently, we tend to come to opinions about how things work early on in our encounters and these opinions are then quite difficult to change. Sometimes, especially for those who fall prey to what is known as the confirmation bias, people interpret otherwise neutral or ambiguous new information as supportive of their preconceived ideas.[29]

These first impressions, particularly when it comes to the Internet, can be formed remarkably fast, often in milliseconds. One study on the formation of first impressions of websites found that as few as 50 milliseconds are needed for users to form an impression of a website.[30] People's first impressions can then affect how they view later interactions with a particular website or product. The relationship is so strong that quickly formed assessments of aesthetics can actually be a better predictor of a system's perceived usability than the actual functionality of the system.[31] No wonder Apple does so well!

The point is that both how new users come online and their initial impressions of what they get to see are going to matter a great deal for the level of trust that they place in the Internet ecosystem and the way they will subsequently behave.

Although real events and unfolding processes help to inform our perceptions, how new users of the Internet in developing countries will react to coming online is still largely a matter of speculation. To get a picture of how trust might be negatively affected, we use a series of short vignettes. In each, we show why bridging the digital divide in the right way matters so much.

Vignette One: Free Facebook?

In August 2013, Facebook CEO Mark Zuckerberg launched what he called "Internet.org." The program was aimed at bringing people in the developing world online. Zuckerberg's rationale, as he described it in a report issued on Facebook at the launch of the program, was that "connectivity is a human right."[32]

The program was designed so that Facebook would partner with local telecom operators and technology companies around the world to provide people with free access to the Internet. Facebook is not alone in these efforts. Google, for its part, launched Project Loon, which aimed to transmit third-generation (3G) Internet to underserviced areas in the developing world from giant balloons. Twitter has also partnered with telecom companies to give people the ability to use the platform to share their ideas without having to pay for the data.

It all sounds great, but, as with many things in life, the devil is in the details. Shortly after the announcement, Facebook was met with a flurry of criticism about its Internet.org proposal. Many thought that the Internet.org program violated the net neutrality principle. A blog posting by Mozilla's chief legal and business officer, Denelle Dixon-Thayer, sums up the charge:

> Zero-rating does not at first pass invoke the prototypical net neutrality harms of throttling, blocking, or paid prioritization, all of which involve technical differentiation in traffic management. Instead, zero-rating makes some Internet content and services "free" by excluding them from data caps that apply to other uses of traffic (which can result in "blocking" of sorts if a user has no available data left in a billing period).

The impact of zero-rating may result in the same harms as throttling, blocking, or paid prioritization. By giving one company (or a handful) the ability to reach users at no cost to them, zero-rating could limit rather than expand a user's access to the Internet and ultimately chill competition and innovation. The promise of the Internet as a driver of innovation is that anyone can make anything and share it with anyone. Without a level playing field, the world won't benefit from the next Facebook, Google or Twitter.[33]

Facebook, ever attuned as it is to social trends and its reputation, as all publicly traded companies ought to be, recently repackaged their Internet.org program into something new called "Free Basics."[34] Free Basics is similar to zero-rating in that users don't have to pay for content or the use of applications. It is different because the playing field for free services has been opened up. As Zuckerberg puts it, what Facebook is "really trying to do is to use Free Basics as an open platform so that any developer who can give low bandwidth services for free can be zero-rated," so long as "they follow the basic rules."[35]

At first blush, the rules guiding inclusion in Free Basics all appear to make sense in a data-thin environment where developers are offering a free service to under-serviced areas. Free Basics' rules, as they are recounted in Russell,[36] are first, that services should encourage the exploration of the broader Internet wherever possible. Second, websites that require high bandwidth would not be included, and services should not use Voice over Internet Protocol (VoIP), video, file transfer, high-resolution photos or a high volume of photos. Third, Facebook expected its partner services to be optimized for smartphones and feature phones, and — finally — to be free from JavaScript or Secure Sockets Layer (SSL)/Transport Layer Security (TLS)/Hypertext Transfer Protocol Secure (HTTPS) elements.

The first three of the four rules make the program quite appropriate for free services for low-access areas. Wider access to the network (rule one) and no data-hogging video streaming (rule two) are probably appropriate rules when talking about free services provided to areas where chronic access problems abound. Rule three makes sense, again because most people coming online in developing countries are doing so on mobile platforms, and if the aim is to bring as many people as possible online, developers should target the largest possible number of people.

So far, so good — on the basis of these three rules, Facebook's new Free Basics platform appears to be more than just window-dressing. The generative potential of the Internet has always been the ability to innovate on top of the basic platform.[37] To the extent that Facebook's new Free Basics allows for that sort of open environment, the generative potential of the network should be secured and it will be combined with expanding access, making it an apparent win-win for both new users and companies.

However, the fourth rule is something of a wolf in sheep's clothing, with potentially large ramifications for user trust. The limitations placed upon the use of SSL/TLS/HTTPS in the development of the applications is problematic, because it means that these free services cannot encrypt data. Without getting into too many details, unencrypted data flows in plain text and is visible to all who want to look. When the data is encrypted, others are not able to peer into what is being sent or viewed. The function of SSL and HTTPS is to package the data, scramble it and then lock it with an encryption key. The intended recipient gets the key and is able to put everything back in its right order. However, while encrypted packets do cost more bandwidth than unencrypted services, the extra cost is only around two percent additional network capacity.[38] The added bandwidth is certainly not enough to crash the system and the added security is well worth the capacity cost.

User trust can be negatively affected by the lack of encrypted services. For example, lack of encrypted services precludes online banking or any other financial transaction via free services. Users cannot send their credit card or banking information over the network if it is unencrypted. The lack of encryption impinges upon the ability of people to use the network fully because it is *not secure*.

The other problem with the lack of encryption is that what users do online is *not private*. Without encryption, all the data generated by the users of zero-rated services will be freely available to the application designers and others. This is a Faustian bargain similar to the one we make when we use free email and free Facebook, and the companies sell our voluntarily turned over data to advertisers. In the developing world context, the bargain is even more lopsided. Those joining the network via services like zero-rated Free Basics do not even have the option to use encryption, so Facebook and every other application can gobble up every bit of information generated by these new users. Most likely, that is how Free Basics is going to pay for itself.

With no possibility of encryption, security and privacy are deeply compromised. Under the rules of Free Basics, user trust is compromised at the outset. In such a scenario, users might well opt for alternative means of getting online if markets are competitive, which they are generally not in these circumstances, or they might simply forego network access all together.

Vignette Two: Who Rules?

Another problem involves the trust-oriented notion of inclusiveness. Inclusion really boils down to a question of who decides. Everyone wants at least the possibility of being involved in decisions that directly affect them. You might not exercise your right to decide, but it is nice to know that if you wanted to become engaged, you could. People trust systems where engagement is possible.

New users are coming online at a time when there are numerous established Internet governance institutions. New users will enter into the Internet ecosystem and find themselves faced with these well-entrenched giants. This was not the pattern when the Internet began. John Postel, one of the inventors of the Internet, once said about the networking group that built the early Internet that "the first few meetings were quite tenuous. We had no official charter. Most of us were graduate students and we expected that a professional crew would show up eventually to take over the problems we were dealing with."[39] Vint Cerf had a similar point of view: "[W]e were just rank amateurs, and we were expecting that some authority finally would come along and say, 'Here's how we are going to do it.' And nobody ever came along."[40]

That was then and this is now. The early builders of the Internet got to design the system as they wanted. Now, Internet governance has become a truly arcane art and there are many practitioners, especially in the West, who jealously guard their right to shape and write the rules. This difference in inclusivity has already had some serious effects on user trust in the wider community and the network's level of digital social capital.

ICANN is one of the most well established and, in recent years, contentious Internet governance institutions. It basically coordinates the translation of the website address names that we type into a web browser — for example, www.cigionline.org — into the machine-readable numbers that computers use to communicate with each other. It ensures that these names and numbers are globally unique, thus preventing confusion and coordination breakdowns. In recent years, ICANN has also started to auction off new so-called generic top-level domains such as .wine, .amazon or .xxx. The sale of these domains has generated healthy revenues for ICANN and increasingly politicized the organization, as domain name addresses inherently involve issues of free speech, censorship, market access and control.[41]

On paper at least, ICANN is an open multi-stakeholder governance body. Anyone can attend an ICANN meeting. Anyone can speak, listen and contribute to the debate. But, after the talking, shouting and pontificating dies down, the course of action is effectively set by the ICANN board. And while election to the board is theoretically open to anyone with the experience and drive to do it, the background of most board members paints a picture of a much more exclusive and closed club.

Paul Twomey presented this point well at a 2015 conference at Columbia University. The numbers on ICANN's board membership from 2000 to 2015 are revealing.[42] An overwhelming plurality are from the United States. In contrast, China, which has the single largest block of Internet users in the world, has had only one board member at ICANN during this 15-year period. India, now also with a very large population using the Internet — around 240 million people in 2014 — has never been represented on the board (Table 8.1).

This same pattern holds across a number of the other core Internet governance institutions. For example, the Internet Society (ISOC), which engages with governments, the private sector and technologists to advocate for an open Internet, is overwhelmingly US-centric in its current board membership, with fully 46 percent of the body hailing from America. China, India and Brazil, all major Internet-using countries, are completely absent. The same story applies to the current makeup of the International Engineering Task Force (IETF), which sets the protocols that determine how the Internet works. In this case, 56 percent of their current board members are from the United States, and again most emerging Internet-using countries are conspicuously absent. Finally, the Internet Architecture Board (IAB), which looks after the main routing protocol of the Internet (TCP/IP), is even more well-populated by Americans, with fully 60 percent of the current board being from the United States. In other words, the West, and particularly the United States, has dominated the organizations that shape how the Internet works at a technical level. If we recall Lawrence Lessig's observation that code is law, then the dominance of the West and the exclusion of the rest puts most new Internet users in the position of being law takers rather than lawmakers (Table 8.2).

The point is that the persistent dominance of Westerners, particularly Americans, in core Internet governance institutions such as ICANN, ISOC, the IETF and the IAB shows how imbalanced the Internet governance ecosystem actually is in terms of its membership. Full blame cannot fall upon these organizations alone, as they are all

Table 8.1: ICANN Board Members Since 2000

Country	No. on Board		Years on Board	
United States	25	26.3%	109	32.6%
Germany	9	9.5%	20	6.0%
France	6	6.3%	14	4.2%
Australia	5	5.3%	21	6.3%
Canada	4	4.2%	11	3.3%
Brazil	4	4.2%	12	3.6%
Japan	3	3.2%	11	3.3%
Switzerland	3	3.2%	4	1.2%
United Kingdom	3	3.2%	9	2.7%
Spain	2	2.1%	6	1.8%
Hong Kong	2	2.1%	4	1.2%
Portugal	2	2.1%	7	2.1%
India	2	2.1%	13	3.9%
Finland	1	1.1%	3	0.9%
Chile	2	2.1%	12	3.6%
Italy	2	2.1%	9	2.7%
Malaysia	2	2.1%	4	1.2%
Netherlands	2	2.1%	7	2.1%
Philippines	1	1.1%	2	0.6%
New Zealand	1	1.1%	6	1.8%
Norway	1	1.1%	3	0.9%
Ireland	1	1.1%	3	0.9%
Latvia	1	1.1%	3	0.9%
Mexico	1	1.1%	6	1.8%
Senegal	1	1.1%	3	0.9%
Bulgaria	1	1.1%	3	0.9%
China	1	1.1%	3	0.9%
Ghana	1	1.1%	3	0.9%
South Korea	1	1.1%	2	0.6%
Taiwan	1	1.1%	5	1.5%
South Africa	1	1.1%	6	1.8%
Gambia	1	1.1%	3	0.9%
Kenya	1	1.1%	5	1.5%
Lebanon	1	1.1%	2	0.6%
	95	100.0%	334	100.0%

Source: Twomey, presentation on the "Plenary Panel 2: The Future of Multi-stakeholder Internet Governance." Reprinted with permission. Figures are current as of spring 2015. Percentages represent each country's share of total board membership and cumulative years on the board.

Table 8.2: Country Representation in Core Internet Governance Institutions

ISOC Current Country	Board Members	Share of Board Membership (%)
United States	6	46.2
Australia	1	7.7
New Zealand	1	7.7
Sri Lanka	1	7.7
Germany	1	7.7
Japan	1	7.7
Serbia	1	7.7
Belgium	1	7.7
Total	13	

IAB Current Country	Board Members	Share of Board Membership (%)
United States	9	60.0
Finland	2	13.3
Canada	2	13.3
Sweden	2	13.3
Total	15	

IETF Current Country	Board Members	Share of Board Membership (%)
United States	9	56.3
Finland	2	12.5
Costa Rica	1	6.3
Australia	1	6.3
Belgium	1	6.3
Ireland	1	6.3
Germany	1	6.3
Total	16	

Source: Twomey, presentation on the "Plenary Panel 2: The Future of Multi-stakeholder Internet Governance." Reprinted with permission. Figures are current as of spring 2015.

officially open to representation from around the world. And, in order to be involved in the actual day-to-day management of the technical side of the Internet, individuals need very specialized skills — skills in short supply in many countries, although that is now changing. All qualifiers and explanations for the lack of diversity in the Internet's governance bodies aside, the point remains that the institutions at the heart of Internet governance are not as open as they should be, given the rapidly shifting demographics of the Internet.

If left unaddressed, exclusion will result in a loss of trust. Indeed, new Internet entrants are already pushing back at their exclusion (be it actual or perceived) from Internet governance bodies. In 2012, for example, China, Russia and several new entrants to the Internet acted together to try to move ICANN's functions into a UN body — the International Telecommunications Union (ITU).

While the ITU has a history of being engaged in a coordination role for spectrum, telegraph code and all the rest, the proposed move was not suggested for functional reasons but for political ones. Had the move been successful, it would have meant a fundamental shift in how policy at the core of the Internet is made. The current governance model is multi-stakeholder, meaning that governments, private companies, technologists and civil society all have a role in making Internet policy. If governance moved to a UN body, only governments would have had standing to oversee the Internet's management of the top-level domain name system and other technical functions.

Such a move would have made the Internet ecosystem both more exclusive and tipped its current governance arrangements to governments, not all of which are democracies. Without formal standing, many actors — private companies, which own much of the Internet's infrastructure; technologists, who devise much of the network's protocols; and civil society, which acts as a moral compass for the ecosystem — would have been effectively barred from the governance process. At the same time, since the UN system is based upon a one-country, one-vote system (with the Permanent Five on the Security Council being the exception), non-Western nations (who are more numerous) would control the balance of power and the way in which the Internet's core names and numbers are administered.

Perhaps if the current Internet governance institutional arrangements were less well entrenched, new entrants would trust that the system would serve their interests more, and choose to join current arrangements. In any event, it is fair to say that the entrenched nature of the world's Internet governance institutions has already had implications for how much trust both developing and emerging market nations place in the online ecosystem and its governance structures.

Vignette Three: Private Gatekeepers

Some large private companies also dominate the Internet landscape and are creating potential trust problems at the individual user level. Across the world, data from the website-ranking company Alexa shows that American companies, such as Google, Facebook and YouTube (owned by Google), dominate the platform scene (Figure 8.5).

Across Latin and Central America, the Middle East and North Africa, Sub-Saharan Africa, and Asia, almost all of the top websites in each country are Western content platforms. In only six countries are the most widely used platforms not based in the United States.

In the case of China, for example, its huge domestic market of 640 million Internet users and a ban on Google has catapulted the local search engine, Baidu, to the top of the most popular website list. Compare that with Taiwan and Vietnam, where Google and Facebook are the second and third most-visited sites. Google and Amazon are the second and third most-popular sites in South Korea. In the Palestinian Territories, Facebook, Google and YouTube are the second, third and fourth most-visited sites. And, finally, in Kazakhstan, YouTube is the third most-visited site. So, while the dominance of Western companies is not complete, it is close to it, and almost all newer entrants are using services based in the United States.

The monopolistic global standing of the American Internet companies is not actually that surprising. The emergence of monopolies is actually an inherent product of networked systems.[43] In

Figure 8.5: The Dominance of the Few — Leading Websites by Country

Source: Data from Alexa.com.

technical terms, networks tend to form what are known as power-law distributions.

Power-law distributions are best understood relative to their most commonly known distant cousin: bell-shaped distributions. Many things in the world are distributed normally along the classic bell-shaped curve. Human height is a good example. The average height of men in North America is around five-foot-ten or five-foot-eleven. Because height is distributed normally, most people will be within striking distance of this average height. There will be outliers on both sides, but they will be fairly rare.

The power-law distributions formed by networks are different. Power-law distributions are marked by a few extremely large outliers and a long tail of cases at the smaller end of things. Cities are a good example. Most cities are fairly small, maybe a few hundred thousand people at most. But most countries also have one or two cities that have populations that number well into the millions. Academic citations are another example. Most works are never cited. Some works are cited thousands of times.

Networks form power laws where users (or site links) cluster disproportionately onto the same site. Recalling Metcalfe's law and the way in which network effects drove adoption of the network, the fact that clusters emerge is not too surprising. The value of networked systems is that they bring people together. The only reason to use Facebook is because everyone else does. Other social networking sites could certainly form for niche topics, but they won't have a lot of joiners because everyone wants to be networked to the same site as everyone else. Like a law of nature, networked structures such as the Internet create monopolies like the current American Internet giants.

The dominance of American companies has two implications. First, corporate dominance can interact with the newness of the Internet for later entrants, potentially distorting the picture that people have about what the Internet is and how it works. The potential confusion really comes to the fore when people are asked to say what they use online.

One study, for example, found that 11 percent of people in Indonesia and nine percent of people in Nigeria claimed on a survey that they use Facebook but do not use the Internet.[44] That these people believe that they are using the one without the other is pretty troubling. But, more troubling still is that many more of the respondents in a wider range of countries actually thought that Facebook and the Internet were the same thing.[45] A majority of respondents in Nigeria, Brazil, Indonesia and India agreed with the statement "Facebook is the Internet." In contrast, a still uncomfortably high number of American respondents — five percent — said the same (Figure 8.6).

These distorted perceptions are due to Facebook's dominant position in the social media marketplace. This dominance combines with new users' unfamiliarity with the technology. As a result, the scope of the Internet — what it can *really* do for people — is limited to its capacity as a source of photos, news stories and far-removed

Figure 8.6: Percentage of People Who Believe Facebook Is the Internet

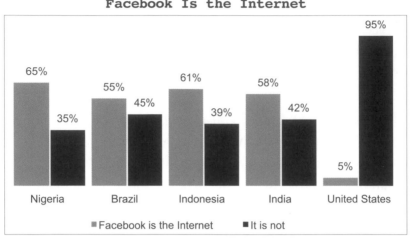

Source: Data from Leo Mirani, 2015, "Millions of Facebook users have no idea they're using the internet," Quartz, February 9, http://qz.com/333313/milliions-of-facebook-users-have-no-idea-theyre-using-the-internet/.

friend requests. The potential social capital that could be generated by bringing new people online is lost.

The other problem with large-scale corporate dominance in countries that are just now coming online, and in other countries as well, is that a few select corporations come to be the gatekeepers of information for all their users.

Twitter and Facebook are two interesting examples. Increasingly, rather than going directly to news sites, watching the news or reading a newspaper, Internet users in the United States are relying upon their Twitter feeds and Facebook walls as the primary sources of the news stories they read. One Pew Research Center study, for example, found that 52 percent of Twitter users in 2013 relied on their feed as a news source.[46] In 2015, the number of Twitterati using their feeds as their primary source of news jumped to 63 percent. The upward trend with Facebook is even more extreme. In 2013, only 47 percent of Facebook users turned to their wall as a primary source of news. By 2015, 63 percent of Facebookers now relied upon the site for their news. Presumably, as those who are just coming online become accustomed to the technology, their behaviour will likely mirror that of users in the United States.

Facebook and Twitter are now thrust into a new editorial role and are able to dictate the sort of content that is available on their platform. Jonathan Zittrain sums up the potential problem of what he calls "digital gerrymandering":

> Now consider a hypothetical, hotly contested future election. Suppose that Mark Zuckerberg personally favors whichever candidate you don't like. He arranges for a voting prompt to appear within the newsfeeds of tens of millions of active Facebook users — but …the group that will not receive the message is not chosen at random. Rather, Zuckerberg makes use of the fact that Facebook "likes" can predict political views and party affiliation, even beyond the many users who proudly advertise those affiliations directly. With that knowledge, our hypothetical Zuck chooses not to spice the feeds of users unsympathetic to his views. Such machinations then flip the outcome of our hypothetical election. Should the law constrain this kind of behavior?[47]

The gateway role that Facebook can play — and how it can potentially go wrong — took on an even more personal feel in 2014. To see what happens when people receive positive and negative content, researchers at the social media giant manipulated the newsfeeds of 689,003 randomly selected Facebook users. On some of the feeds, they reduced the amount of positive information that people received. They found that these people tended to write and post fewer positive things. On some of the other news feeds, the researchers did the opposite. They reduced the amount of negative content. People whose feeds became happier also started to post and upload more positive content.[48] The response to Facebook's experiment from Internet users was fairly negative to say the least, and people were rightly concerned about how a large company controlling so much of the content that we view on a daily basis might one day decide to run psychological experiments upon unsuspecting users. Manipulating people's feelings, while eroding people's trust that they are receiving the content that they want to view, can also have some all-too-real physical world ramifications. As privacy advocate Lauren Weinstein wrote via Twitter, "I wonder if Facebook KILLED anyone with their emotion manipulation stunt. At their scale and with depressed people out there, it's possible."[49]

While Facebook can increasingly use its control over content to affect the behaviour of online users, Google is a huge information gatekeeper in an even more hidden way. Billions of search queries are funnelled through Google each day. We rely more than ever before on this search engine as our gateway to research, news, weather and everything else.

The search results that Google produces are ranked. If they weren't, returned results would be a gigantic mess and we would be left trying to find the proverbial needle in a cyber haystack. Google's ranking algorithm is secret, but what it is basically supposed to do is provide a user with whatever Google thinks are the most pertinent search results based upon some combination of key word relevance, website external links and other indicators. The lack of transparency is needed so that people cannot game the system, but it also means that it is hard to say exactly what Google is doing and how it is subtly (or not so subtly) shaping the information to which we have access.

The ranking process can mess up in some funny ways, which really show the arbitrary way in which ranking algorithms work. They are certainly not neutral. In Egypt in 2015, for example, when you logged into Google from an Egyptian IP address and searched for "google" in the search bar, users got an unexpected result. Sitting at home or in an Internet café and searching for "google" on Google, you would expect to get a link to Google as the first returned result. Oddly, for a short stint in Egypt in 2015, that was not what happened. Instead, the number-one search result for the term "google" was actually a link to a website of an air conditioning repair guy named Mr. Saber.

One digital marketer named Eyad Nour came across this result and, after spending hours trying to figure out what was going on, decided to just call the air conditioning repairman. His account of their call is worth recounting in full for the humour value alone.

— *Hello, is this Mr. Saber?*

— Yes, who are you?

— *My name is Eyad Nour. I work in the field of Digital Marketing and I noticed that you're ranking #1 on Google. Did you know this?*

— Yes, a lot of people called me and told me that Google made a website about me.

— *No, I mean Google Search. When people search for the word "Google", you come first. Did you know that?*

— No. I just find people calling me and telling me they saw "my Google."

— *So, you never tried to do anything to promote your page?*

— What page?

— *Your page on Google Plus?*

— No, I just published it using my email which was created back in 2009, which is why I get a lot of people visiting my profile because of I have old email there.

— *Actually, I think it takes more than that. What happened with you is very rare. You are ranking #1 for the word "Google" on their own website, which I have never seen in my life. You are ranking above Google itself.*

— So people think I am the "mother company" of Google? *Laughing loud* This is great. I never thought about that. It all started a week ago when I noticed a lot of people calling me every day. Sometimes I even turn off my phone so I can sleep. Actually, most of them don't even know what I do, but maybe you can teach me how to get more people?

— *I teach you?! You're the master now! You teach me, master! I was calling you so you can tell me how you did it.*

— *He laughing for 10 seconds* You sound like a funny person. I think we could be friends. Look, you can come to my place at _____ St. and then [...] I will let you look into my computer to find out what I did. Maybe I clicked on something by mistake.

— *Me laughing* I wish it was that easy. We can't find the reason for your rankings on your computer files. Anyway, I do really appreciate your time and feel free to call me anytime if you need advice. I wish you the best.*

— Thank you, my friend. I will save your number right now and call you later.[50]

This particular story is amusing — Google messed up somewhere and an obscure air conditioning technician benefited from a ton of free marketing. But there is a definite downside to the combination of Google's dominance as a search engine and the opaque nature of its ranking algorithm. These issues directly impinge upon user trust because they affect the correctness of the content that people are likely to receive.

In his book *The Black Box Society*, Frank Pasquale details the effects that Google's ranking algorithm has on free expression and economic competition.[51] In one example, he outlines a compelling tale of a husband and wife team that ran a "vertical search" service called Foundem. Despite the impressive pedigree of the service owners and resoundingly positive reviews of the service by industry insiders, Google consistently ranked their service very, very low in its search results.

Google claimed the poor showing was because of the poor quality of the site, based upon their algorithm's ranking criteria. The owners of Foundem favoured "another explanation." As they put it, "If Google has no interest in an area, it will let an upstart be. But once it enters (or plans to enter) the market of a smaller finding service, it down ranks that service to assure the prominence of its own offering."[52] Eventually, after some public relations problems, Google relented and Foundem's search-result ranking was boosted.

Sometimes, Google also changes search results, not because of a potential corporate interest in the outcome, but because of political intervention by states. One example of this is the emergent RTBF policy in Europe. In May 2014, the European Court of Justice ruled in favour of a Spanish man named Mario Costeja-González, who had petitioned the court to compel Google to remove links to some 16-year-old news stories of his house foreclosure due to a failure to pay his debts (which he did eventually pay). The court ruled that Google had to remove the links from the European versions of the search platform. Doing so basically removes the signposts directing people to the information and does not actually affect whether the information is hosted on the Internet. Yet, since so many people use Google to find their basic information, this move is not without a very sizable effect in terms of what people are actually going to be able to access online. The ruling has essentially opened the floodgates on a series of requests to have similar factually true, yet potentially shameful, information removed from Google's search rankings.[53]

It is also but a small microcosm of what can happen when countries decide by fiat that Google (or other search engines) must modify its search results within their geographical borders. Before Google was banned from mainland China, it waffled back and forth between standing up to the regime on censorship and free speech issues and capitulating to the demands of the government. In 2013, for example, Google stopped a service that would inform users that their search query had triggered the Chinese Great Firewall.[54] Some sort of "horse trading" likely went on behind the scenes.

The point is that private companies are gatekeepers of the information that we have access to, both in the developed world and in countries that are only now starting to come online. The dominant positions of these companies can undermine the trust of users as their access to information is restricted, often in ways that the user can neither see nor understand. What is worse is that in a world of a few key giants, trust is really everything.

Vignette Four: "A Million Eyes" Watching You

Those who are coming online and those who are already online face a similar challenge. The headline of the June 2015 issue of that venerable consumer bible *Consumer Reports* grasped the significance of the IoT revolution: "The Brave New World of Smart Devices." Its lead story — "A Million Eyes" — offered a series of cautionary warnings about the risks of using smart devices. It told the story of the Dublin Women's Mini Marathon in Ireland. As thousands of runners streamed along the streets of Dublin, someone was scanning the activity trackers on their wrists and collecting digital data. In all, 563 runners inadvertently revealed their names, addresses and other kinds of personal information, including passwords, from the devices on their wrists.[55]

The person collecting the data was a Symantec researcher whose intent was to find ways of making these devices more secure, but if the scanning had been in the hands of someone else, the data collection could have been used for more nefarious purposes, even to do physical harm.

Consumer Reports cautions that smart devices "can also send a steady flood of personal data to corporate servers, where it's saved and shared, and can be used in ways you can't control. Websites and smart phone apps have been following our activities for a long time, tracking where we go; what we read, watch, and buy; what we write in our emails; and who we follow on Facebook and Twitter. But now connected devices gather data from some of the most private spaces in our lives — the bedside table, the kitchen counter, the baby's nursery."[56]

Internet users' perceptions of the IoT mirror the concerns expressed in the *Consumer Reports* article. The 2016 CIGI-Ipsos survey gives us some insight into how people feel about ubiquitous interconnected devices. While 58 percent of people indicate that they are not really bothered by the growing interconnection of devices, this number masks the very pronounced concerns they have expressed over the potential implications of Internet-enabled cars, houses, toothbrushes and more for people's privacy and security.

Privacy, in particular, looms large in people's minds when asked about the effects of ubiquitous interconnected devices. Fully 78 percent of people in the 2016 CIGI-Ipsos survey expressed concern that their information might be monitored as a result of growing Internet-enabled devices. Seventy-nine percent of people also worried that one consequence of the IoT would be the purchase and sale of their private data. And again, when asked bluntly if they were concerned about the privacy implications of the IoT, 79 percent of people confirmed that they are kept up at night by the privacy implications of the technology.

And people should be worried. Shodan, a web search service similar in some ways to Google, paints this picture plainly. Shodan bills itself as the first search engine for the IoT, and it lives up to the characterization. Shodan crawls the net looking for interconnected devices, ranging from webcams to building cameras, that use the Real Time Streaming Protocol and that employs either no password or the default password settings. From there, it accesses the device and provides a screenshot that any user with a Shodan account can access.[57] It gives the necessary tools to anyone who wants to become a digital peeping tom or sneaky spy, and is a perfect example of the potential privacy implications of the IoT. A cursory search of the term "port:554 has_screenshot:true" leads to pages upon pages of captured screenshots of people's bedrooms, children's nurseries, parking garages, computer server rooms and people's home security cameras.

People are also starting to realize the IoT has some very large security implications for users. One of the most common — and indeed creepy — examples is a hacked baby camera. Many parents now use Wi-Fi-enabled monitors with built-in audiovisual systems to watch their children. These technologies are useful because they allow parents to go about their day, while also allowing them to keep a watchful eye on their children via their smartphone. Unfortunately, most baby cameras are notoriously easy to hack (a weakness that plagues many IoT technologies, as the Shodan example illustrates). For the designers of these systems, state-of-the-art security protocols are just not worth the investment of time and resources. The technological innovations are too new (even if many of them are written upon significant blocks of old, often vulnerable recycled code) for companies to know if there is a market for their Internet-enabled products. Without a proven market, heavy investments in security measures and state-of-the-art code will likely not be foremost on the minds of designers.

But the consequences of this lack of security are very real, manifesting as anxiety, concern and even outright fear on the part of device users. In one illustrative case from the London area in Ontario, Canada, a father was in his son's room reading him a bedtime story.[58] He then heard sounds coming from the camera, which was mounted on the wall so that he could check in on his son via his smartphone. Holding his son in his arms, he moved toward the camera.

From there, the tale gets scary and bizarre. As the father recounted it, "I get up closer to the camera with my son in my arms and I hear eerie music." After that, a male's voice sounded through the two-way microphone, saying something like "as he rocks his son to sleep." As any parent would do, the father took his son and left the room. When he and his wife came back into the child's bedroom, the wall-mounted camera swivelled toward them. The father immediately unplugged it. This one example is but the tip of a very large iceberg of hacked IoT devices. Other parents have woken to people screaming at their children through their Internet-connected device in foreign languages.

Taken together, the very real privacy, security and safety concerns that follow from the IoT are impinging upon the trust that users are willing to place in the system, although there is still a sufficient bedrock of trust that if companies change their ways the IoT might still have a chance. The 2016 CIGI-Ipsos survey again sheds some illuminating light on users' current perceptions about the relative trade-offs between the convenience of interconnected devices and their privacy, security and safety concerns. When asked bluntly to draw up a tally of the balance in their minds about whether the IoT is really worth it, a majority of users (65 percent) still think that it is (Figure 8.7). But that balance is tenuous and hinges, more likely than not, on further developments in the technology being undertaken, so that the privacy, security and safety of users is maintained. If it is not, then user trust in the IoT will wane and the technology will not be used as widely as it might be otherwise. Some innovations might even not be adopted at all as people change their behaviour to protect themselves.

What is clear is that across the emerging IoT ecosystem, all countries need better safeguards to ensure that the public knows exactly what information these smart devices are gathering, and that information won't be gathered, shared or sold without public consent. The information also needs to be properly secured to reduce the risk of being compromised or stolen by unscrupulous marketers, criminals or even governments. The systems also need to be built with better access authorization protocols so that strangers cannot access domestic devices. As Vint Cerf put it at the 2015 Internet Governance Forum in João Pessoa, Brazil, "if I have an Internet-enabled refrigerator, I want there to be clear authentication protocols in place. I don't want the teenage kid next door to be able to access my fridge and order milk. That right has to be reserved for family members."[59]

The *Consumer Reports* story on the IoT has a telling prescription, urging manufacturers to come clean about what they are doing with the information they are collecting: "*Consumer Reports* thinks that manufacturers of Internet-connected devices should tell consumers in easy-to-understand language about the types of information being collected by those devices and how that information could potentially

Figure 8.7: The IoT Is (Currently) Worth the Risk

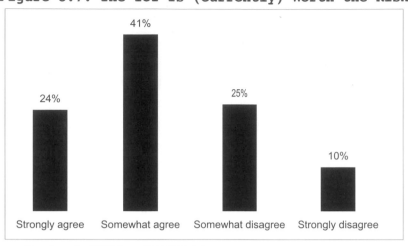

Source: Data from the CIGI-Ipsos 2016 Global Survey.

be shared, sold and used. Device manufacturers should also give consumers options to control the collection and use of their data."[60]

That is certainly a good place to begin. But we will need more than public appeals or self-enforcing, informal codes of conduct by device manufactures to ensure the privacy and safety of consumers. Legislatures and public authorities are going to have to raise the bar to ensure that proper standards and privacy regulations manage the IoT's space, particularly as more and more smart devices and the apps that run on them become available. New norms and rules about respecting privacy will also have to be developed for governments, which are major consumers of big data collection and analytics. It is not just the activities of federal intelligence-gathering and law enforcement agencies that require greater scrutiny and legislative oversight. As local governments and other public actors move into the IoT space, they too will require clearer norms and rules about the kinds of things they should or should not do in a networked world.

Why Bringing People Online Matters So Much

We end where we began. We need to bring new users online, because if we don't bridge the digital divide now, the divide between the haves and the have-nots will become even more pronounced. Already the Internet generates major economic benefits for those who use it.[61] Those who are currently off-line are missing out on the Internet's bounty.

In the future, the Internet will no longer be primarily a communications system as it is today. Emails, videos and other ways for people to send and receive content will become secondary to the Internet as a command and control system for the economy as a whole. As Carl Bildt puts it: "The Internet has already become the world's most important infrastructure. But this is only the beginning: soon it will be the infrastructure of all other infrastructures."[62]

Bildt's point is that the old analogue economy will be increasingly integrated with the digital one of the IoT. Everything from our toothbrushes to our stoves, fridges, cars, houses and even our cities will be integrated and connected via the Internet. The IoT promises tremendous efficiency gains. Experts vary in their estimates, but one research team places the economic potential of the IoT at as much as US$11.1 trillion by 2025.[63] Those who do not come online soon will miss out on these gains as well.

In short, the Internet is a global force multiplier. It will make people rich, but only if they trust it enough to use it, and only if the network's digital social capital is robust enough to allow the network to be used in generative ways for all. The stakes could hardly be higher. Bringing the next billion users online in the right way is clearly a key and vital goal.

Nine

A Web of Trust: Toward a Safe, Secure, Reliable and Open Internet

The Internet's ability to facilitate growth, innovation and the free expression of ideas could continue, even accelerate, if the trust that users place in the system can be maintained. But we stand on the edge. We could as easily fall in the other direction. To borrow astronomer Carl Sagan's words, "We have also arranged things so that almost no one understands science and technology. This is a prescription for disaster. We might get away with it for a while, but sooner or later this combustible mixture of ignorance and power is going to blow up in our faces."[1] As we teeter, there is still a chance for trust to be restored and for the Internet to continue to function well.

The Internet works because it is built on a foundation of digital social capital (that is, on its own brand of trust) that contains six basic elements, as outlined in chapter two: security, privacy, inclusion, reliability, correct content and safety. The network's digital social capital is a main source of the system's growth and innovation potential. When people lose their trust in the system, they use it differently or less or not at all, and the potential for society-wide gains vanishes.

The network's digital social capital is eroding at all levels. We increasingly fear for our safety and security online because of the proliferation of hackers and criminals who want to steal our identities, manipulate our data or cause real-world harm. Firms and governments increasingly violate our online privacy as they capture the digital footprints we leave behind us every time we switch on our mobile devices or go online. The threat to our privacy — and indeed our online security — is only going to grow as many of the ordinary objects of our daily lives go digital and the IoT engulfs the physical world, and as our cars, our refrigerators and even our toothbrushes are hooked up to the Internet. The Internet is generally reliable and provides us with the correct content, but this is not always the case as some users have found when they have been redirected to phony sites that masquerade as their destination. Governments in China, Russia, Iran and a troubling number of others also restrict what users can do and see online.

The world of the Internet is *not* "flat," to riff on the writings of *The New York Times'* Thomas Friedman.[2] Instead, its landscape is rocky, cratered with deep-walled canyons that are treacherous, if not impassable. In places it resembles a sun-baked desert, because there is limited or no access to the Internet because of content restrictions imposed by governments. Not everyone gets to enjoy the panoramic view on offer to those perched on the Internet's treetops in less restricted climes.

Throughout the book, we have pointed to the numerous ways in which criminals, governments, companies and other users have taken actions that have undermined the trust that users place in the network. It leaves us in a pessimistic spot. And raises the final question that we need to tackle in this book: how we can make the Internet safer, more private and secure, open and inclusive?

There is no simple or easy answer to this question. There are myriad interests involved and many ongoing trends that will be hard to reverse. But the answer depends upon measures that will strengthen the Internet's stock of digital social capital. One aspect of the restoration of the network's digital social capital will be technological.

Another will be political, arising from innovative changes made to the Internet's complex systems of governance.

Technology and Trust

The *MIT Technology Review* called 2014 "The Year of Encryption," because following Edward Snowden's sensational revelations that the US government had hacked into the servers of major US Internet companies such as Microsoft and Google there was a major push "to encrypt everything."[3] The magazine reported that "Yahoo [had] encrypted its e-mail service and Google extended encryption to every search term that users enter." Microsoft was also in the process of ensuring that by year's end "all the data traveling to and from its networks" would be locked away from prying eyes. And it went on to point out that according to tech experts, "within a few years, every file crossing the Internet could be protected with encryption, which uses mathematics to scramble and unscramble messages."[4] Encryption is certainly an improved form of defence, but it is by no means perfect. It does not "guarantee complete privacy" because, as the *MIT Technology Review* pointed out, "cyphers can be broken or compromised."[5]

Encryption keys on our cellphone may make us feel that our text messages and emails are secure and not being read by someone else, but they can also make the work of criminals and terrorists easier by thwarting the efforts of security and intelligence agencies to intercept their communications. For example, TechCrunch reported in early 2016 that "terrorists are communicating over a new secure Android app after getting kicked off WhatsApp, Telegram and other messengers. Called 'Alrawi,' the encrypted chat app makes it harder for governments and security agencies to spy on terrorist plans. Though supposedly not as advanced in its security as WhatsApp or Telegram, it still shields users from having their texts intercepted."[6] It went on to point out that "without a reputable company behind Alrawi, there's no one to ban ISIS from using it."

Encryption is also no guarantee against human failures and the foibles of those who have access to sensitive data and information in any organization. The theft of 80 million personal files and social security numbers from the health insurance provider Anthem would not have been stopped by encryption because the cybercriminals who launched that attack had stolen the credentials of least five administrator-level employees in the organization.[7] Anthem's experience is just one more example of the fact that humans are the weakest link in IT security systems.

Because encryption is somewhat of a double-edged sword, and therefore not really very different from most other technological innovations, governments want the private sector to provide back doors to encrypted communications so they can gain access to the content of messages. A steady parade of senior law enforcement and intelligence officials in the US government, such as FBI Director James Comey, and President Obama's Secretary of Homeland Security, Jeh Charles Johnson, have publicly expressed their growing concerns about the stampede to encryption. The governments' ideal solution, which is not actually technologically feasible, is to modify the terms on which such technologies are made available by companies so that they (and ideally not criminals) can gain access to data on the Internet.[8] In other words, they want a back door into encrypted data and services. A succession of terrorist attacks in 2015 and 2016 have given credence to their claims, but also stoked a major debate among intelligence and law enforcement officials, technologists and champions of the right to privacy and free speech.

Following the ISIS-led or ISIS-inspired terrorist attacks in early December 2015 in San Bernardino, California, ABC News reported that the young couple who were responsible for the attacks had devices — presumably cellphones or computers — which used encrypted communications that made it difficult for authorities to conduct their investigation into the origins of the attack.[9] The same story pointed out that an earlier attack in May 2015 in Garland, Texas, by two

ISIS followers targeting an event showing cartoons of the Prophet Mohammed had been preceded by a flurry of encrypted messages between the attackers and terrorists overseas. Locked behind the walls of encryption, these messages could not be deciphered by government officials.

Earlier, a series of high-profile stories in major news outlets blamed the November 2015 terrorist attacks in Paris on encrypted tools like WhatsApp, alleging that these tools had allowed the terrorists to secretly plan and successfully carry out their attacks. Subsequent evidence proved to be inclusive and the sensationalist claims were retracted.[10] However, what is undeniable is that the debate about encryption has become a highly charged one following terrorist attacks on both sides of the Atlantic.

Critics of those against ubiquitous encryption argue that ordering companies such as Apple and Google to hand over encryption keys to government officials so that they have a back door to private communications won't solve anything. Terrorists will simply be able to buy encrypted devices and software in countries where national laws do not proscribe encryption back doors. Governments, especially the US government, are also not very good at securing confidential data, as a spate of highly publicized cyber attacks, which have compromised the personnel and security clearance records of literally millions of federal employees, reveal. There is no assurance that even if governments had the keys they would be able to secure them properly or prevent them from falling into the wrong hands. As journalist Bob Sullivan contends,

> For starters, U.S. firms that sell products using encryption would create backdoors, if forced by law. But products created outside the U.S.? They'd create backdoors only if their governments required it. You see where I'm going. There will be no global master key law that all corporations adhere to. By now I'm sure you've realized that such laws would only work to the extent that they are obeyed. Plenty of companies

would create rogue encryption products, now that the market for them would explode. And of course, terrorists are hard at work creating their own encryption schemes.

There's also the problem of existing products, created before such a law. These have no backdoors and could still be used. You might think of this as the genie out of the bottle problem, which is real. It's very, very hard to undo a technological advance.

Meanwhile, creation of backdoors would make us all less safe. Would you trust governments to store and protect such a master key? Managing defense of such a universal secret-killer is the stuff of movie plots. No, the master key would most likely get out, or the backdoor would be hacked. That would mean illegal actors would still have encryption that worked, but the rest of us would not. We would be fighting with one hand behind [our] backs.

In the end, it's a familiar argument: disabling encryption would only stop people from using it legally. Criminals and terrorists would still use it illegally.[11]

One of Sullivan's most telling observations is about the interaction of potential policies and their loop back onto the trust that users place in the system. Governments are calling for back doors in encryption because they want to compensate for a problem where parts of the network are being used by terrorists and criminals to cause real-world harm. In the terms we have employed in this book, governments are compelled to act because the network is less trustworthy. On the one hand, a policy like having back doors in encryption might reduce the real-world safety implications of the network, but on the other hand it makes *all* of our online data less secure — meaning that users will lose trust in the system because it is less secure and less private.

Many governments have recognized that this trade-off exists and have come out publicly against the idea that back doors in encryption are worth the risks to network security and user privacy. Two notable examples are France (itself the target of a number of terrorist attacks involving the use of Internet messaging apps to coordinate attacks) and the Netherlands. In early 2016, France's Minister for Digital Affairs Axelle Lemaire publicly declared his government's position on back doors into encryption, stating: "What you are proposing is a vulnerability by design.[...]While the intention is commendable, it opens the door to actors whose intentions are less than commendable."[12] These sentiments echo the position of the government of the Netherlands. In this case, the position against back doors came from the Dutch Ministry of Security and Justice. Ard van der Steur, the head of the ministry, stated that back doors in encryption would make networks and digital systems "vulnerable to criminals, terrorists and foreign intelligence services."[13]

Is there a technical fix to the privacy problem so that enforceable limits can be imposed on intelligence agencies when they gather data? Some members of the technical community have suggested that new cryptography tools could be used by intelligence agencies so that data searches of telephone records, for example, would not unduly compromise privacy because cryptographic protocols would keep databases encrypted while also ensuring that there are proper controls on how data is accessed and used when actual searches take place.[14] But even with cryptography there is potential for abuse if those who have access to private data overstep their bounds and protocols are breached because of human malfeasance or error.

There is another problem, though. When existing technology is readily available to enhance Internet security and reliability, it doesn't always get used, sometimes because it is costly. Sometimes, it is not used simply because the private companies responsible for operating the Internet's core infrastructure don't take the problem seriously. Tom Simonite describes the problem: "It is disturbingly easy to attack the backbone of the Internet to block access to a major online service like YouTube, or to intercept online communications at vast scale. So say security researchers trying to rouse the industry into doing something about long-standing weaknesses in the protocol that works out how to route data across different networks making up the Internet. Almost all the infrastructure running that protocol does not even use a basic security technology that would make it harder to block of intercept data."[15]

One concrete example of this sort of process in action involves a technology known as DNSSEC. The DNS translates the website names that humans write into the alphanumeric domain addresses that computers read. DNSSEC is a security protocol that signs off on the domain that a user is trying to access, validating that the page you are viewing is the one that you mean to access. The technology promises to prevent DNS spoofing, misdirection and other forms of malicious cyber attacks that can compromise people's data. Using this technology helps make the network more secure and may even restore trust in the Internet ecosystem, but it is not widely adopted.[16] The Asia Pacific Network Information Centre estimates, for example, that only around 14 percent of domain queries globally are validated through a DNSSEC process.[17]

Another example is the adoption of distributed ledgers based upon the blockchain technology, which we referred to in chapter seven. The technology was first developed in 2008 as the underlying authentication system for the cryptocurrency bitcoin. Its broader applications as a way to maintain the integrity of data are only now being realized. One recent report by the UK Government Office of Science illustrates this point well.[18] They show that blockchain could help to restore trust across the Internet ecosystem by ensuring the reliability and correctness of the content to which people have access. In the future, with the right investment and foresight, businesses, governments and even individuals could all rely on blockchain or distributed ledger technology to reduce corruption, improve service delivery and allow for better innovation on top of the technology of the Internet. It is already generating enthusiasm in the financial community as a way to instantaneously settle financial transactions and to transform current settlement and payment methods by reducing transactions and operational costs.[19] Distributed ledgers, and other technology of this sort, will be the source of the frictionless universe discussed in chapter three.

Beyond the failure to rapidly adopt technologies that could help maintain and even restore user trust, there is also the problem of companies producing digital products that fail to deal with security and privacy concerns at the development stage. New apps are particularly plagued by this process, as they often include accidentally built-in vulnerabilities. The cause is that app developers are in a highly competitive marketplace and that dealing with security and privacy upfront are costly propositions, especially when developers don't even know if the app will get users. Just as it took car manufacturers in an earlier age many years to make automobiles safer with seat belts and airbags, the tech sector is contending with similar market pressures while exploiting consumer ignorance.

For example, Lorenzo-Franceschi Bicchierai pointed out on *Motherboard* that even in a highly sensitive sector such as online banking, where security matters a great deal, key vulnerabilities remain, despite some notable improvements: "The main improvement since 2013 is that most apps now encrypt data as it travels from the app to the bank servers, using the standard web encryption known as SSL or TLS, which is slowly becoming the standard on the web. In 2013, 90 percent of apps had some traffic unencrypted; now, it's just 35 percent. While this is good news, there's still a considerable amount of apps through which a hacker could intercept the traffic and trick users into giving out their credentials on a spoofed login page."[20]

In addition to problems of design and adoption, there is also a constant battle between those who wish to secure the network — thereby enhancing trust — and those who wish to do harm by stealing our personal information. For example, an encryption algorithm, probably completely unknown outside of the tech world, is used to secure over one-quarter of the world's Internet traffic. Its simple and unassuming name is SHA-1. The trouble is that criminal groups are getting close to breaking the encryption algorithm in a cost-effective way, which would leave web traffic using this security method as vulnerable as if it were sent openly and in public. The major web-searching companies, such as Google, Yahoo! and Microsoft, now plan to phase out connections that are secured by older methods and replace them with new ones.[21] Each time a method to secure web traffic is compromised, companies are forced to respond to make the network more secure, but there is no magic bullet. It is a perennial struggle. Action begets reaction *ad infinitum*.

This and other examples suggest that technological fixes alone won't solve the Internet's mounting trust deficit when it comes to online privacy, security, reliability, content or safety. But they can help to decelerate the process.

Toward a Strategy of Prevention: Hygiene and Cyber Resilience

Many breaches of security are preventable. As discussed in chapter six, 80 percent or more of cyber attacks could be prevented if Internet users improved their digital hygiene by configuring their systems properly, using antivirus software and updating their programs and applications with the most current software patches, and exercising discretion online.

Beyond these measures of improved digital hygiene, companies and governments must come to the realization that a healthy organization is not one that never gets ill, but one where occasional illness may occur but is recoverable. In other words, companies should focus on investing in their organizational resilience so that when attacks occur, they can be dealt with expeditiously.

Insurance markets can help promote both better digital hygiene and a practical shift in behaviours toward activities that improve corporate and governmental resilience.* For example, among the firms that participated in a 2015 Financial Industry Regulatory Authority (FINRA) study, only "61 percent purchased standalone cybersecurity insurance; 11 percent purchased a cybersecurity rider with their fidelity bond; and 28 percent did not rely on any type of cybersecurity insurance."[22]

These numbers are a bit grim, especially the fact that over a quarter of firms surveyed do not even have any sort of insurance against the possibility of a data breach or DDoS attack. Moreover, given the FINRA survey is likely not representative of the economy as a whole, it is quite likely that smaller firms, especially those outside of the financial industry, have an even worse track record on the purchase of insurance. In other words, individuals, companies and governments fail to adequately protect themselves because the cost of doing so is higher than the cost of rolling the dice and hoping they never get attacked.

As matters now stand, insurance markets are more a part of the problem than of the solution. As Benjamin Dean points out, several companies that have experienced massive data breaches have had large portions of their ensuing costs covered by insurance.[23] All this does is reduce the incentive for these companies to adequately invest in cyber defences that could actually improve their organizational resiliency. But it does not need to be this way.

Instead, insurance companies — as well as other risk-pricing markets — could actually help the situation by gauging premiums relative to the defensive steps that companies take. Companies that purchase equipment from reputable suppliers, employ accredited cyber security expertise — either in-house or through an external company — and who properly train their employees would pay less on their cyber premiums than companies that fail to properly develop their organizational resiliency. Employing risk-pricing mechanisms, insurers

---

* We are grateful to Joseph S. Nye Jr. for pointing us in the direction of insurance as a tool to produce better behaviour.

and underwriters who assess the risks of software and security defences could become important catalysts in the creation of a more secure and resilient cyberspace and one that users will trust.

Governance and Trust

There is widespread recognition that the Internet also requires improved, if not new, governance arrangements to enhance its stock of eroding digital capital. The discussion is analogous to the debate political scientists are having about the breakdown of trust in democracies and the important role that institutions and their reform have to play in restoring trust and effective governance.

Proposals for reforming the governance structures of the Internet vary widely and there remain deep divisions as to the direction such reforms should take. Some countries — China and Russia, to name two — would like to see governments exercise greater sovereign control over the Internet's basic infrastructure, which today is largely managed by the not-for-profit and private sectors. But it is not just authoritarian regimes that are seeking greater control. As discussed in chapter four, many democratic countries are looking to exercise greater sovereign jurisdiction over the Internet and data flows in the name of privacy, human rights, security, IPR protection, economic prosperity and competitiveness.

When it comes to developing new governance arrangements, some countries want to put the Internet under the control of the United Nations. Some say that the status quo is fine and management of the Internet should be left in the hands of the technical community and the private sector. Others in civil society want to strengthen multi-stakeholder governance arrangements so that everyone who believes they have a vested interest in the operations of the Internet has a voice in how it is managed and run.

Each of these suggested ways forward runs into the idea that user trust is contingent upon the perceived inclusiveness of the governance arrangements that make decisions affecting the billions of current and future Internet users. A good place to start is to look again at the trend we pointed out in chapter one. The 2014 CIGI-Ipsos poll is illustrative. When asked who should run the Internet, a majority of people — 57 percent — chose the multi-stakeholder option: a "combined body of technology companies, engineers, non-governmental organizations and institutions that represent the interests and will of ordinary citizens, and governments." Fifty-four percent said they would trust an international body of engineers and technical experts, which was a little higher than the 50 percent favouring the United Nations alone. National governments and the United States had lower levels of trust, at 47 and 36 percent respectively (Figure 9.1).

This initial finding that Internet users want everyone to work together is supported further by some related results from the 2016 CIGI-Ipsos poll. Asked this time about who should be involved in the development and enforcement of new rules about how user data gets used, a majority of respondents thought that every actor, ranging from technical bodies to ordinary citizens, should have a hand on the helm (Figure 9.2).

Figure 9.1: The Public's Preference for Multi-stakeholder Governance

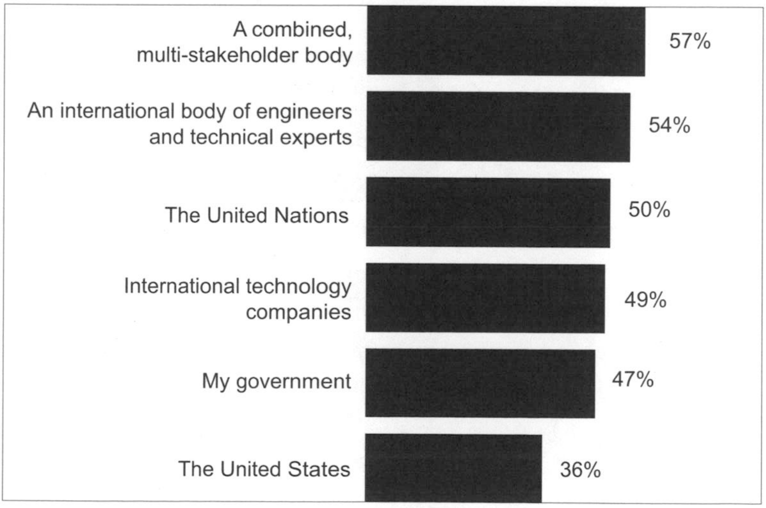

A combined, multi-stakeholder body	57%
An international body of engineers and technical experts	54%
The United Nations	50%
International technology companies	49%
My government	47%
The United States	36%

Source: Data from the CIGI-Ipsos 2014 Global Survey.

People also think that everyone shares the responsibility to make the Internet ecosystem safe. When asked if governments should work with private companies, civil society, technologists and academics to address cyber threats, an overwhelming majority — 85 percent — indicated that an all-hands-on-deck scenario is best.

The 2016 survey also highlights concerns over the privacy of user-generated data. Eighty-three percent of respondents felt that new rules were needed for how companies and governments deal with user-generated data. This finding suggests that the concerns noted in chapter eight about the coming challenges of the IoT are likely to

Figure 9.2: Who Should Make and Enforce Rules on User Data?

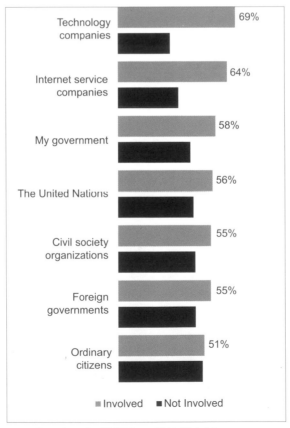

Source: Data from the CIGI-Ipsos 2016 Global Survey.

grow more pronounced. It also suggests that governments — and of course private companies — need to get a handle on their snooping into what users do, lest they lose the trust of people the world over.

A large majority of respondents (84 percent) are also firmly of the view that governments, private companies and users all need to be much better at implementing and enforcing existing rules to ensure that our data is protected from prying eyes. Clearly, ensuring the privacy of user data is going to be a priority for all in the coming years.

The responses also suggest that no one actor can go it alone. One clear message that Internet users are trying to get across to the governments and private companies that shape so much of the Internet ecosystem and its activities is that they do not do enough to protect users. The 2016 survey asked if governments and private companies were doing enough to protect ordinary users from dangers from criminals, companies and governments. The answer was a resounding no.

Users feel that companies, for example, are doing a poor job keeping them safe (Figure 9.3). Concerns over other users, the respondent's government, foreign governments and other companies are all fairly similar, with 69 percent of people responding that the companies that

Figure 9.3: Are Companies Doing Enough to Protect Your Data from...

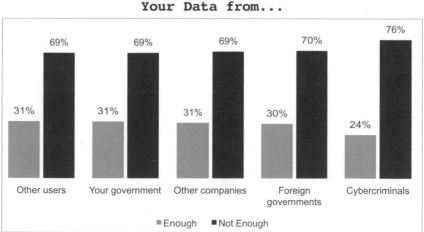

Source: Data from the CIGI-Ipsos 2016 Global Survey.

they use are not doing enough. The protections provided by companies against online criminals is even more pronounced, with 76 percent of respondents disparaging corporate protections. In the wake of so many data breaches that lead to the compromise of user data, it is no wonder that people think better protections should be forthcoming.

Users also think that governments are falling down on the job (Figure 9.4). In fact, they are generally seen as doing even less at protecting ordinary people than are companies. When asked to pinpoint whether governments did enough to protect people from other Internet users, private companies or foreign governments, around 71 percent of people indicated that the protections provided were inadequate. Users express even more dissatisfaction with governments' efforts to protect against cybercrime than they do with private companies' efforts. At least part of the reason why governments are more on the hook is likely because providing protection has been their historical role.

One of the conundrums when trying to restore trust as regards the security of operating systems or platforms is that such efforts, by necessity of design, may lead to further intrusions on individual privacy. For example, in the 2015 rollout of the Windows 10

Figure 9.4: Are Governments Doing Enough to Protect Your Data from...

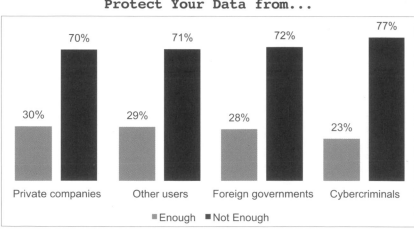

Source: Data from the CIGI-Ipsos 2016 Global Survey.

operating system, Microsoft baked into the new system much higher levels of security (which users clearly want). Confronted with ever-evolving cybercrime, Microsoft rejected their old way of doing things and now pushes out security updates on a regular basis that patch vulnerabilities to help keep users safe. As the Windows team blogged, "Windows 10 has more built-in security protections to help safeguard you against viruses, phishing, and malware, it's the most secure Windows ever. New features are now delivered through automatic updates, helping you to stay current and your system to feel fresh, so you're free to do."[24]

These additional security features also come with a largely unavoidable loss of user privacy. Microsoft has to access, by default, a pile of information, including location data, usage of applications and browser history in order to monitor security breaches[25] — a compromise that many users are apparently prepared to accept.

Getting Internet Governance Right

The obvious danger of not getting governance "right" is that the Internet as we know it will become so damaged or such a dulled instrument of global communications that it no longer spurs economic growth, innovation and the free expression and dissemination of ideas. As Vint Cerf explains, "The secret to the Internet's success has been its loosely coupled character. In other words, no [one] was coerced to join or use it or implement it. Interconnection of the networks of the Internet was accomplished under bilateral or multilateral agreements among the implementing entities. The freedom to choose the equipment, software, services, and business models has been the key to the widespread investment in Internet infrastructure."[26] Cerf goes on to argue that "one of the most interesting aspects of the Internet's development and evolution is the creation of a variety of bottom-up institutions dedicated to maintaining and evolving the Internet's functionality and capacity."[27] His overall point is that "bottom-up, multi-stakeholder models are far better suited to Internet policy development than purely intergovernmental processes such as those typical of international treaty organizations." He also acknowledges that governments too "should be involved" because they have "important responsibilities to their citizens,"[28] but they should not be charged with running it. In other words, don't throw the baby out with the bathwater in the rush to address the Internet's real or perceived deficiencies.

A Layered Approach to Internet Governance

Getting governance right begins with the recognition that there is no one-size-fits-all approach to the Internet's governance challenges. Michael Chertoff and Paul Rosenzweig offer the idea of "layered Internet governance" to capture the notion that a combination of new norms, new rules and new kinds of collaborative institutional arrangements will be required to manage the evolution of the Internet.[29] That is a good place to begin. For example, the multi-stakeholder model can certainly be strengthened with respect to institutions such as ICANN, which assigns the top-level domain names and manages the overall addressing system of the Internet. There is also a strong argument to be made for strengthened multi-stakeholder governance arrangements at the national level, as some countries have done — such as Brazil, with its Marco Civil legislation — so that no single interest can dominate key decision making and legislation on vital matters of Internet policy.

The private sector also needs better norms and rules to guide its own behaviour, especially when it comes to collecting, storing and handling private information when citizens download an app or new software. Governments also need to be far more circumspect and restrained when they surreptitiously collect online data and monitor the online behaviour of citizens in the interests of national security. As pressure mounts to regulate the Internet, countries are going to have to weigh the benefits of greater regulation and controls in the name of privacy or security against the potential costs of stifling innovation, prosperity and the free flow of global commerce and ideas. Many of these ideas are being taken up in the work of the GCIG. There are also other groups studying the Internet's governance challenges, such as the United Nations' GGE or the members of the Freedom Online Coalition, a group of 29 countries dedicated to promoting Internet freedom and the principles of free expression, association, assembly and privacy online on a worldwide basis.

As Table 9.1 summarizes, each component of trust must be enhanced via technological innovation, the development of and adherence to new norms, and through the actions of national governments and international institutions.

Strengthening and Developing New Norms

Norms are ingrained habits of behaviour or, as Alexis de Tocqueville once observed, "the habits of the heart" that guide and shape human interactions in the physical world and in the twenty-first century in cyberspace. There is a clear need, as we have argued in this book, to strengthen the habits of the heart among Internet providers, developers and users, especially the private sector which is responsible for managing more than 85 percent of the Internet infrastructure and the Internet's own network of networks. Industry norms clearly need to be strengthened when it comes to making clear to consumers how their online personal data is going to be stored, shared or used for commercial purposes. Public concern on this issue is high (see Figure 9.5).

Further, as the GCIG "Social Compact" statement notes, ignorance is also a widespread problem because "[n]ot all individuals understand the full scope of what they have placed online deliberately or what information has been captured and stored by others as they go about their daily activities. Nor do most individuals know to what commercial use their data are deployed."[30] The statement continues, to point out that "companies exceed governments in their capacity to collect, store in centralized repositories, integrate, analyze and make use of personal data. These companies are increasingly attractive

Table 9.1: Measures to Strengthen Digital Social Capital

Components of Digital Social Capital	Technology	Norms/Rules	Institutions
Security	• Encryption • Blockchain • DNSSEC	• Budapest Convention on Cybercrime • Insurance regulation	• MLAT reform
Privacy	• Encryption • Tor • Privacy by design	• No back doors • No bans of anonymity • RTBF	• Privacy commissioners • Legislative oversight • Courts
Reliability	• IPv6 • Expansion of infrastructure	• Net neutrality	• Regulatory enforcement of norms
Correct content	• VPNs • Tor	• Restrictions on censorship • Free flow of information • Right to be forgotten	• Courts • Governments • ISPs
Inclusivity	• Distributed technologies such as blockchain	• Adherence to multi-stakeholder models • Collaborative security	• ICANN, IETF, IAB, etc., reform
Safety	• Access authentication technologies • Isolation technologies for the IoT	• Changing passwords • System redundancy	• Critical infrastructure board • Law enforcement

Source: Authors.

targets for cyber intrusion, and susceptible to efforts to jeopardize the confidentiality, availability and integrity of these large data pools." For that reason, "these companies have to demonstrate to their users a high level of respect for, and protection of, the security and privacy of their information."[31]

Major corporations in the Internet space could, in fact, go a step further by voluntarily establishing and adhering to corporate codes of conduct similar to the guiding principles of the UN Social Compact that

Figure 9.5: Internet Users' Concern Over Private Company Company Monitoring of Online Activity and Sale of User-generated Data

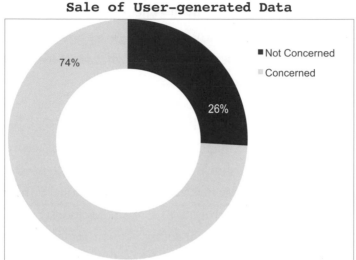

Source: Data from the CIGI-Ipsos 2016 Global Survey.

were developed by John Ruggie, the UN Secretary-General's Special Representative on Human Rights and Transnational Corporations and Other Business Enterprises.[32] The UN Social Compact is directed at helping to integrate the management of human rights risks into contract negotiations on investment projects between host state entities and foreign business investors. It was the product of four years (2007–2011) of research and multi-stakeholder negotiations. Though not without controversy, because it lacks strong and effective oversight and enforcement mechanisms, it is slowly gaining widespread acceptance, and its regular gatherings cast a spotlight on whether Compact members are adhering to their commitments. More than 1,000 corporations have signed on to its 10 guiding principles, as have more than 160 countries. It has also been endorsed by 80 member cities, and many countries are now also actively pursuing Compact principles nationally.

New norms and codes of conduct are also desirable in transactions between private corporations and governments. The GCIG proposed a social compact among citizens, private corporations and governments, which explicitly states that "[t]he obligation of states to protect and promote rights to privacy and freedom of expression are not optional." The GCIG urges governments to "guarantee the same human rights protection [off-line and online] to all individuals within their borders." Additionally, "any interference with the right to privacy should not be arbitrary or unlawful, bearing in mind what is reasonable to the pursuance of legitimate aims."[33]

The GCIG also recommends widespread acceptance of the OECD's privacy guidelines, which "state that exceptions to its principles, including those relating to national sovereignty, national security and public policy (*ordre public*), should be as few as possible, and made known to the public." It also suggests that the "2013 International Principles on the Application of Human Rights to Communications Surveillance, developed at the initiative of civil society, are an important reference regarding how international human rights law should apply in the current digital environment" and calls on states "to comply with the following principles: legality, legitimate aim, necessity, adequacy, proportionality, competent judicial authority, due process, user notification, transparency, public oversight, integrity of communications and systems, safeguards for international cooperation, safeguards against illegitimate access and the right to effective remedy."[34] On the thorny matter of encryption, the GCIG is unambiguous in its recommendations: "Governments should not create or require third parties to create 'back doors' to access data that would have the effect of weakening the security of the Internet. Efforts by the Internet technical community to incorporate privacy-enhancing solutions in the standards and protocols of the Internet, including end-to-end encryption of data in transit and at rest, should be encouraged."[35]

Although we are clearly a long way from developing a new social compact for the digital age, formal and informal recommendations such as these are useful markers for pointing the way to stronger norms of behaviour in cyberspace that can help to restore trust in the system as a whole.

As discussed at greater length in chapters six and seven, interstate relations will also benefit from negotiation of new norms, especially regarding offensive strategic cyberwarfare and cybercrime. Such norms should be focused on developing commitments to avoid attacking critical infrastructure, facilitating cross-border law enforcement on cybercrime, helping to secure global supply chains and also increasing transparency and reporting of critical vulnerabilities in a responsible manner. The agreement between China and the United States to cooperate on cybercrime, including industrial espionage, represents a promising beginning in interstate relations between strategic rivals, and there is no reason why this agreement should not be extended by encouraging other states to adopt the same set of core commitments and principles.

Harmonizing Rules

The Internet doesn't just need new and stronger norms to guide the behaviour of private and government actors — it also requires the harmonization of regulatory standards across national boundaries. As discussed in chapter five, the Internet is fragmenting as different countries develop new regulatory regimes regarding the storage and use of data, routing requirements, net neutrality and content restrictions. Regulations that promote privacy and security will invariably differ from country to country and be shaped by different national cultural and historical interests and traditions. That is political reality. What is important is that legislatures and courts understand the broader economic consequences of their decisions. Governments must also pursue negotiations with other states to harmonize new rules in order to reduce transaction costs for corporations that operate in different national jurisdictions and are integrated into global value chains.

In their *Primer on Globally Harmonizing Internet Jurisdiction and Regulations*, Michael Chertoff and Paul Rosenzweig argue that "data localization and sovereign unilateralism will come with significant costs — both economic and social ones. Global companies will be subject to competing and inconsistent legal demands, with the inevitable result that consumers will suffer diminished access to the network overall. Among other things, decisions about the location of servers and hardware will be driven by legal gamesmanship rather than technological or infrastructure considerations."[36] Accordingly, they assert, "The current free-for-all of competing nations needs to be replaced with an agreed-upon international system for a choice-of-law rule. What is needed is the harmonization of existing rules within an agreed-upon framework of law." Certainly, as they note, the choice of which rules to abide by is not an easy one and will be the subject of intensive negotiations between states. But, at the end of the day, it will be important to secure international agreement on clear norms to promote cooperation on cybercrime and limits on the use of cyber weapons, especially if we are to avoid chaos and economic upheaval. Further, greater international cooperation is required to avoid arbitrary seizure of domain names, content and to clarify rules about cross border data requests in the efforts of law enforcement officials to go after cybercriminals.[37]

Strengthening Institutions through Multi-stakeholder Engagement and Better Coordination

Stronger multi-stakeholder engagement in the oversight and management of the Internet has become somewhat of a rallying cry for those who are deeply involved in Internet governance issues. It is also an increasingly accepted principle of governance that echoes through many reports and recommendations on the future of Internet governance, such as the landmark NETmundial declaration in Brazil in April 2014, which endorsed the principle that Internet governance should be built on democratic, multi-stakeholder processes, ensuring the meaningful and accountable participation of all stakeholders, including governments, the private sector, civil society, the technical community, the academic community and users.[38]

But the bigger, unanswered questions are how and where should the model actually be applied and developed? A vast array of institutions are currently responsible for managing the Internet — some are public, but many are private or not-for-profit. They all have their own unique governance structures with varying degrees of openness and inclusivity. Joseph Nye Jr. characterizes the Internet's distributed governance system as a "regime complex."[39] He points out that there are non-governmental bodies — for example, the Internet Engineering Task Force, the World Wide Web Consortium and the ISOC — that help to set technical standards and protocols for the Internet. Their governance procedures are informal and based on what he describes as "rough consensus and running code."[40] There is also ICANN, which assigns the top-level domain names of the Internet and top-level numeric addresses. National governments currently serve on a governmental committee to advise ICANN, but are looking for a stronger voice, if not an outright vote, over its operations.

There have been numerous proposals directed at giving ICANN's "shareholders" — the technical community and civil society — greater control over ICANN's board and its decisions. A raft of UN agencies ranging from the ITU, the WTO, the UN Conference on Trade and Development, and the World Intellectual Property Organization have also had a major hand in setting Internet-related standards and regulations on copyright and intellectual property. At the national level, computer emergency or security incident response teams deal with Internet disruptions and other transborder management problems. And the list of institutions goes on.

Nick Ashton-Hart is a close observer of the international machinery of Internet governance from his base of operations in Geneva. He says that global Internet-related policy discussions are being carried out independently in many different global forums, by governments and stakeholders, generally with only ad hoc interprocess coordination, thereby contributing to the confusion. He notes that there are now more than 200 mechanisms to address online security issues, including literally dozens of international and UN-based processes, and dozens more regional initiatives are developing policies that impact all Internet users. Ashton-Hart is the leading champion of a holistic "light touch" approach to the institutional coordination problem, one that does not disturb or disrupt ongoing work, but instead leverages the strength of different international bodies at the governmental and non-governmental level to ensure results are sustainable. He has proposed a potential solution that is based upon elements of global coordination systems used in the humanitarian community to handle complex humanitarian emergencies.[41]

Conclusion

As the world is engulfed by the IoT, the Internet's governance challenges at both the national and international level are going to grow by leaps and bounds. Developing countries and emerging market economies will vote with their feet if they are not better represented in the existing governance architecture of the Internet, as discussed in chapter eight. As Joseph Schumpeter captures in his elegant phrase "the gale of creative destruction," technological change has always both sparked new ideas and eliminated old ways of doing things.[42] Earlier technological revolutions spurred by inventions such as the flying shuttle and the cotton gin led to massive economic and social changes. The difference between century-old examples and today is not related to the process of change itself, but rather to the timing of the transitions and their impact on society and its institutions. The changes wrought by the flying shuttle probably seemed precipitous back in the 1700s, but in fact they took place over decades and were relatively well paced. Society and institutions adapted accordingly. The problem now is that transitions can occur in months rather than years. Individuals can adapt to change on their own, but institutions tend to fall behind the curve and take longer to reform and change. Unless there is a concerted, inclusive global effort to address the Internet's looming trust deficit with technological and governance innovations, the world will not be able to harness the full potential of the eighth wonder of the world. But if we are to keep it safe, we need to recognize that there is no monopoly on trust and really no immunity from responsibility.

Notes

One: Sex, Spies and the Internet

1. Brian Krebs, 2015, "Online Cheating Site Ashley Madison Hacked," *Krebs on Security* (blog), July 15, http://krebsonsecurity.com/2015/07/online-cheating-site-ashleymadison-hacked/.

2. Kim Zetter, 2015, "Hackers Finally Post Stolen Ashley Madison Data," *Wired*, August 18, www.wired.com/2015/08/happened-hackers-posted-stolen-ashley-madison-data/.

3. Katie Bo Williams, 2015, "Head of Louisiana GOP among those in Ashley Madison data dump," *The Hill*, August 20, http://thehill.com/business-a-lobbying/top-gop-official-in-ashley-madison-data-dump-hack.

4. David Gilbert, 2016, "Ashley Madison Web Traffic Drops By Over 80% Since Hack, Vietnam Replaces US As Top User," *International Business Times*, January 18, www.ibtimes.com/ashley-madison-web-traffic-drops-over-80-hack-vietnam-replaces-us-top-user-2269465.

5. Julie Hirschfeld Davis, 2015, "Hacking of Government Computers Exposed 21.5 Million People," *The New York Times*, July 9, www.nytimes.com/2015/07/10/us/office-of-personnel-management-hackers-got-data-of-millions.html?_r=0.

6. Jai Vijayan, 2014, "4 Worst Government Data Breaches Of 2014," *Information Week*, December 11, www.informationweek.com/government/cybersecurity/4-worst-government-data-breaches-of-2014/d/d-id/1318061.

7.   Fibernet, 2012, "Utah Department of Health Hacked, Thousands of Records Compromised," September 18, www.fiber.net/utah-department-of-health-hacked-thousands-of-records-compromised/.

8.   Robert D. Putnam, 2000, *Bowling Alone: The Collapse and Revival of American Community*, New York, NY: Simon & Schuster, 19.

9.   Alexis de Tocqueville, 1969, *Democracy in America*, New York, NY: Doubleday, 287.

10. Francis Fukuyama, 1996, *Trust: The Social Virtues and the Creation of Prosperity*, New York, NY: Free Press Paperbacks.

11. Paul Resnick, Richard Zeckhauser, Eric Friedman and Ko Kuwabara, 2000, "Reputation Systems," *Communications of the ACM* 43 (12): 46.

12. Fred B. Schneider, ed., 1999, *Trust in Cyberspace*, Washington, DC: National Academy Press.

13. GCIG, 2015, *Toward a Social Compact for Digital Privacy and Security*, https://ourinternet.org/.

14. Pamela Paxton, 2002, "Social Capital and Democracy: An Interdependent Relationship," *American Sociological Review* 67 (2): 254–77.

15. Cited in Eoghan McNeill, 2015, "How many Fortune 500 accounts are hacked right now? It's 6 Code Summit highlights," *WebSummit* (blog), November 13, https://blog.websummit.net/how-many-fortune-500-accounts-are-hacked-right-now-its-6-code-summit-highlights/.

Two: An Ecosystem Based on Trust

1.   Bill Woodcock and Vijay Adhikari, 2011, "Survey of Characteristics of Internet Carrier Interconnection Agreements," San Francisco, CA: Packet Clearing House, www.pch.net/resources/papers/peering-survey/PCH-Peering-Survey-2011.pdf.

2.   Cisco, 2010, "Cisco Visual Networking Index: Forecast and Methodology, 2009–2014," White Paper, June 2, 7, http://large.stanford.edu/courses/2010/ph240/abdul-kafi1/docs/white_paper_c11-481360.pdf.

3.   Brian McKenna, 2013, "What does a petabyte look like?" ComputerWeekly.com, www.computerweekly.com/feature/What-does-a-petabyte-look-like.

4.   Internet Live Stats, 2015, "Total Number of Websites," www.internetlivestats.com/total-number-of-websites/#trend.

5.	Jamie Bartlett, 2014, *The Dark Net: Inside the Digital Underworld*, London, UK: William Heinemann.

6.	Gareth Owen and Nick Savage, 2015, *The Tor Dark Net*, GCIG Paper Series No. 20, Waterloo, ON: CIGI, 6. https://ourinternet-files. s3.amazonaws.com/publications/no20_0.pdf.

7.	Eric Jardine, 2015, *The Dark Web Dilemma: Tor, Anonymity and Online Policing*, GCIG Paper Series No. 21, Waterloo, ON: CIGI, www. cigionline.org/sites/default/files/no.21_1.pdf; Eric Jardine, 2016, "Tor, What is it Good For? Political Repression and the Use of Online Anonymity-Granting Technologies," *New Media & Society* (March, online first): 1–18.

8.	Harold D. Lasswell, 1972, *Politics: Who Gets What, When, How*, New York, NY: Meridian Books.

9.	Adam Smith, (1776) 2003, *An Inquiry in the Nature and Causes of the Wealth of Nations*, New York, NY: Bantam Books, 572.

10.	Lawrence Lessig, 1999, *Code and Other Laws of Cyberspace*, New York, NY: Basic Books; Mark Raymond and Laura DeNardis, 2015, "Multistakeholderism: Anatomy of an Inchoate Global Institution," *International Theory* 7 (3): 572–616.

11.	Joe Miller, 2014, "Google and Apple to introduce default encryption," BBC.com, September 19, www.bbc.com/news/technology-29276955.

12.	TechCrunch, 2016, "Apple vs. FBI," http://techcrunch.com/tag/apple-vs-fbi/.

13.	Fred B. Schneider, ed., 1999, *Trust in Cyberspace*, Washington, DC: National Academy Press, 14.

14.	Dave Evans, 2011, "The Internet of Things: How the Next Evolution of the Internet Is Changing Everything," White Paper, April, San José, CA: Cisco, www.cisco.com/web/about/ac79/docs/innov/IoT_IBSG_0411FINAL.pdf.

15.	Dan York, 2014, "IPv4 Exhaustion Gets Real — Microsoft Runs Out Of U.S. Addresses For Azure Cloud — Time To Move To IPv6!" Internet Society, June 13, www.internetsociety.org/deploy360/blog/2014/06/ipv4-exhaustion-gets-real-microsoft-runs-out-of-u-s-addresses-for-azure-cloud-time-to-move-to-ipv6/.

16.	CBC News, 2013, "Rogers cellphone outage caused by software problem," October 9, www.cbc.ca/news/business/rogers-cellphone-outage-caused-by-software-problem-1.1932019.

17. Lauren O'Neil, 2013, "Brooklyn man with @rogers Twitter handle feels the 'wrath of 1,000 Canadians' during service outage," CBC News (*Your Community* blog), October 10, www.cbc.ca/newsblogs/yourcommunity/2013/10/brooklyn-man-with-rogers-twitter-handle-feels-the-wrath-of-1000-canadians-during-service-outage-1.html.

18. Quoted in ibid.

19. Statista, 2015, "Number of eBay's total active buyers from 1st quarter 2010 to 1st quarter 2015 (in millions)," www.statista.com/statistics/242235/number-of-ebays-total-active-users/.

20. Zach Epstein, 2014, "eBay thought user data was safe, but 145 million accounts were compromised in massive hack," BGR Media, May 27, http://bgr.com/2014/05/27/ebay-hack-145-million-accounts-compromised/.

21. Elizabeth Weise and Jessica Guynn, 2014, "24% of Americans stopped buying online because of breaches," *USA Today*, June 3, www.usatoday.com/story/tech/2014/06/03/internet-security-survey/9907947/?sf26903754=1.

22. Glenn Greenwald, Ewen MacAskill and Laura Poitras, 2013, "Edward Snowden: the whistleblower behind the NSA surveillance revelations," *The Guardian*, June 11, www.theguardian.com/world/2013/jun/09/edward-snowden-nsa-whistleblower-surveillance.

23. BBC News, 2011, "Germany: Nuclear power plants to close by 2022," BBC News, May 30, www.bbc.com/news/world-europe-13592208.

24. Jason Rabinowitz, 2014, "Survey Shows Growing Number of Airline Passengers Demand Faster In-Flight WiFi," *Forbes*, July 22, www.forbes.com/sites/jasonrabinowitz/2014/07/22/survey-shows-growing-number-of-airline-passengers-demand-faster-in-flight-wifi/.

25. Alex Hern, 2015, "Wi-Fi on planes opens door to in-flight hacking, warns US watchdog," *The Guardian*, April 15, www.theguardian.com/technology/2015/apr/15/wi-fi-on-planes-in-flight-hacking-us-government.

26. Matthew Hoye and Rene Marsh, 2015, "GAO: Newer aircraft vulnerable to hacking," *CNN*, April 14, www.cnn.com/2015/04/14/politics/gao-newer-aircraft-vulnerable-to-hacking/.

27. Lawrence Lessig, 1999, *Code and Other Laws of Cyberspace*, New York, NY: Basic Books.

28. Albert O. Hirschman, 1970, *Exit, Voice, and Loyalty: Responses to Decline in Firms, Organizations and States*, Cambridge, MA: Harvard University Press.

29.   *Wall Street Journal,* 2015, "China's Xi Jinping Calls for Internet Sovereignty," *The Wall Street Journal Video,* December 16, www.wsj.com/video/china-xi-jinping-calls-for-internet-sovereignty/F4262F56-279A-47D4-95A1-9E750C428758.html.

Three: A World Online — Economics, Innovation and the Internet of Things

1.   Taylor Clark, 2014, "How Palmer Luckey Created Oculus Rift," *Smithsonian Magazine,* November, www.smithsonianmag.com/innovation/how-palmer-luckey-created-oculus-rift-180953049/?noist=&amp=&amp=&preview=&page=1.

2.   Ibid.; Robert Purchese, 2013, "Happy Go Luckey: Meet the 20-year-old creator of Oculus Rift," Eurogamer.net, November 7, www.eurogamer.net/articles/2013-07-11-happy-go-luckey-meet-the-20-year-old-creator-of-oculus-rift.

3.   Clark, "How Palmer Luckey Created Oculus Rift"; Peter Rubin, 2014, "The Inside Story of Oculus Rift and How Virtual Reality Became Reality," *Wired Magazine,* May 20, www.wired.com/2014/05/oculus-rift-4/.

4.   Purchese, "Happy Go Luckey…"; Palmer Luckey, 2012, "@ Palmer Tech posts — Oculus 'rift': An open-source HMD for Kickstarter," MTBS3D Oculus Rift DK1/2 Forum, April 15, www.mtbs3d.com/phpbb/viewtopic.php?f=140&t=14777%20-%20p72507.

5.   Luckey, "@PalmerTech posts…"

6.   Purchese, "Happy Go Luckey…"

7.   Clark, "How Palmer Luckey Created Oculus Rift"; Purchese, "Happy Go Luckey…"

8.   Clark, "How Palmer Luckey Created Oculus Rift"; Purchese, "Happy Go Luckey…"

9.   Luckey, "@PalmerTech posts…"

10. Clark, "How Palmer Luckey Created Oculus Rift"; Purchese, "Happy Go Luckey…"

11. Clark, "How Palmer Luckey Created Oculus Rift."

12. Mark Zuckerberg, 2014, "I'm excited to announce that we've agreed to acquire Oculus VR, the leader in virtual reality technology….," Facebook post, March 25, www.facebook.com/zuck/posts/10101319050523971.

13. Dixon is quoted in Peter Rubin, 2014, "The Inside Story of Oculus Rift and How Virtual Reality Became Reality," *Wired Magazine*, May 20, www.wired.com/2014/05/oculus-rift-4/.

14. Jessica Leber, 2014, "35 Innovators under 35 2013: In the jobless economic recovery, an online labor marketplace thrives," *MIT Technology Review*, www.technologyreview.com/lists/innovators-under-35/2013/entrepreneur/leah-busque/.

15. Alexia Tsotsis, 2011, "TaskRabbit Turns Grunt Work into a Game," *Wired Magazine*, July 15, www.wired.com/2011/07/mf_taskrabbit/.

16. Leber, "35 Innovators under 35 2013…"

17. Tsotsis, "TaskRabbit Turns Grunt Work into a Game."

18. Busque is quoted in Leber, "35 Innovators under 35 2013…"

19. Casey Newton, 2013, "Temping fate: can TaskRabbit go from side gigs to real jobs?" *The Verge*, May 23, www.theverge.com/2013/5/23/4352116/taskrabbit-temp-agency-gig-economy; Tsotsis, "TaskRabbit Turns Grunt Work into a Game."

20. Quoted in Tsotsis, "TaskRabbit Turns Grunt Work into a Game."

21. Ted Greenwald, 2014, "35 Innovators Under 35: A novel way to get data off paper records and into the digital age," *MIT Technology Review*, www.technologyreview.com/lists/innovators-under-35/2014/humanitarian/kuang-chen/; Alex Howard, 2012, "A startup takes on 'the paper problem' with crowdsourcing and machine learning," *Radar*, October 5, http://radar.oreilly.com/2012/10/captricity-digitizing-documents-crowdsource.html.

22. Howard, "A startup takes on 'the paper problem' with crowdsourcing and machine learning."

23. Greenwald, "35 Innovators Under 35…."

24. Ibid., Howard, "A startup takes on 'the paper problem' with crowdsourcing and machine learning."

25. Natala@AWS, 2011, "Re: MTurk CENSUS: About how many workers were on Mechanical Turk in 2010?" Amazon Web Services: Amazon Mechanical Turk (Beta) Forum, January 26, https://forums.aws.amazon.com/thread.jspa?threadID=58891.

26. Greenwald, "35 Innovators Under 35: A novel way to get data off paper records and into the digital age."

27. Howard, "A startup takes on 'the paper problem' with crowdsourcing and machine learning."

28. Quentin Hardy, 2012, "How Big Data Gets Real," *The New York Times* (*Bits* blog), June 4, http://bits.blogs.nytimes.com/2012/06/04/how-big-data-gets-real/?_r=0.

29. Greenwald, "35 Innovators Under 35: A novel way to get data off paper records and into the digital age."

30. Ibid.

31. Robert D. Atkinson, Stephen J. Ezell, Scott M. Andes, Daniel D. Castro and Richard Bennett, 2010, *The Internet Economy 25 Years After. Com: Transforming Science and Life*, March, Washington, DC: The Information Technology & Innovation Foundation, 8.

32. Atkinson et al., *The Internet Economy 25 Years After.Com*, 9.

33. Matthieu du Rausas, James Manyika, Eric Hazan, Jacques Bughin, Michael Chui and Rémi Said, 2011, *Internet matters: The Net's sweeping impact on growth, jobs, and prosperity*, McKinsey Global Institute, May, mckinsey.com/insights/high_tech_telecoms_internet/internet_matters.

34. James Manyika, Jacques Bughin, Susan Lund, Olivia Nottebohm, David Poulter, Sebastian Jauch and Sree Ramaswamy, 2014, *Global flows in a digital age: How trade, finance, people, and data connect the world economy*, April, San Francisco, CA: McKinsey Global Institute, www.mckinsey.com/insights/globalization/global_flows_in_a_digital_age.

35. Ibid.

36. Ibid., 2.

37. OECD, 2015, *OECD Digital Economy Outlook 2015*, Paris, France: OECD Publishing, www.oecd.org/publications/oecd-digital-economy-outlook-2015-9789264232440-en.htm.

38. James Manyika, Michael Chui, Jacques Bughin, Richard Dobbs, Peter Bisson and Alex Marrs, 2013, *Disruptive technologies: Advances that will transform life, business, and the global economy*, McKinsey Global Institute, May, www.mckinsey.com/insights/business_technology/disruptive_technologies.

39. Chartered Accountants of Australia & New Zealand and PricewaterhouseCoopers, 2015, *Digital Currencies: Where to from Here?* White Paper, 6, www.charteredaccountants.com.au/~/media/FutureINC/publications/1214-13%20PM_FutureInc_Digital%20Currencies%20paper.ashx.

40. Ibid.

41. Melanie Hicken, 2013, "Someone bought a $100,000 Tesla with Bitcoins," CNN Money, December 12, http://money.cnn.com/2013/12/06/autos/tesla-bitcoin/.

42. Julie Campbell, 2015, "University accepts mobile wallets payments with Bitcoin," Mobile Commerce Press, June 3, www.mobilecommercepress.com/university-accepts-mobile-wallets-payments-with-bitcoin/8516865/.

43. Fen Hampson, personal notes taken from the meeting.

44. David Dean, Sebastian DiGrande, Dominic Field, Andreas Lundmark, James O'Day, John Pineda and Paul Zwillenberg, 2012, *The Internet Economy in the G-20: The $4.2 Trillion Growth Opportunity*, The Connected World Series, March, Boston, MA: Boston Consulting Group, www.bcg.com/documents/file100409.pdf.

45. Ibid., 6–9.

46. Ibid., 10-11.

47. Cited in Mario Berrios and Markus Pilgrim, 2013, "SMEs and job creation: Is small still beautiful?" International Labor Organization, July 26, www.ilo.org/global/about-the-ilo/newsroom/comment-analysis/WCMS_218252/lang--en/index.htm.

48. James Manyika et al., *Global flows in a digital age*, 3.

49. OECD, *OECD Digital Economy Outlook 2015*, 84.

50. Ibid., 91.

51. Dave Evans, 2011, "The Internet of Things: How the Next Evolution of the Internet Is Changing Everything," White Paper, April, San José, CA: Cisco Internet Business Solutions Group, 3, www.cisco.com/web/about/ac79/docs/innov/IoT_IBSG_0411FINAL.pdf.

52. Ibid.

53. Joseph Bradley, Christopher Reberger, Amitabh Dixit and Vishal Gupta, 2013, *Internet of Everything: A $4.6 Trillion Public-Sector Opportunity*, White Paper, San José, CA: Cisco, 1, http://internetofeverything.cisco.com/sites/default/files/docs/en/ioe_public_sector_vas_white%20paper_121913final.pdf; Joseph Bradley, Christopher Reberger, Amitabh Dixit, Vishal Gupta and James Macaulay, 2013, *Internet of Everything (IoE):Top 10 Insights from Cisco's IoE Value at Stake Analysis for the Public Sector*, Economic Analysis, San José, CA: Cisco, www.cisco.com/web/about/ac79/docs/IoE/IoE-VAS_Public-Sector_Top-10-Insights.pdf.

54. Shane Mitchell, Nicola Villa, Martin Stewart-Weeks and Anne Lang, 2013, *The Internet of Everything for Cities: Connecting People, Process, Data, and Things To Improve the 'Livability' of Cities and Communities*, San José, CA: Cisco Systems, 6-9, www.cisco.com/c/dam/en_us/solutions/industries/docs/gov/everything-for-cities.pdf.

55. Ibid.

56. Manyika et al., *The Internet of Things: Mapping the Value Beyond the Hype*.

57. UK Government Office for Science, 2016, *Distributed Ledger Technology: Beyond Blockchain*, January 19, www.gov.uk/government/publications/distributed-ledger-technology-blackett-review.

58. Brian Voo, n.d., "20 Amazing Creations You Can Make With 3D Printing," Honkkiat.com, www.hongkiat.com/blog/3d-printings/.

59. Cartridge World, 2015, "Top 5 Coolest Things That Have Been 3D Printed," www.cartridgeworld.com/top-5-coolest-things-that-have-been-3d-printed/.

60. Joseph Schumpeter, (1942) 1994, *Capitalism, Socialism and Democracy*, London, UK: Routledge, 82-83.

61. World Bank, 2016, *World Development Report 2016: Digital Dividends*, Washington, DC: World Bank, 2, doi.10.1596/978-1-4648-0671-1, www-wds.worldbank.org/external/default/WDSContentServer/WDSP/IB/2016/01/13/090224b08405ca05/2_0/Rendered/PDF/World0developm0000digital0dividends.pdf.

62. Statistics Canada, 2015, "Employment by major industry group, seasonally adjusted, by province (monthly) (Canada)," www.statcan.gc.ca/tables-tableaux/sum-som/l01/cst01/labr67a-eng.htm.

63. Natasha Lomas, 2015, "Driverless Car Accident Reports Make Unhappy Reading For Humans," TechCrunch, October 9, http://techcrunch.com/2015/10/09/dont-blame-the-robot-drivers/#.nsaemnr:TFpO.

64. Camille von Kaenel, 2016, "Driverless Cars May Slow Pollution," *Scientific America*, January 19, www.scientificamerican.com/ article/driverless-cars-may-slow-pollution/.

Four: Big Brother in the Internet Age

1. George Orwell, (1949) 2008, *Nineteen Eighty-Four*, New York, NY: Penguin Books, 3.

2. Laura DeNardis, 2012, "Hidden Levers of Internet Control: An Infrastructure-Based Theory of Internet Governance," *Information, Communication and Society* 15 (5): 720–38.

3. Cited in Emma Barnett, 2010, "Facebook's Mark Zuckerberg says privacy is no longer a 'social norm,'" *The Telegraph*, January 11, www.telegraph.co.uk/technology/facebook/6966628/Facebooks-Mark-Zuckerberg-says-privacy-is-no-longer-a-social-norm.html.

4. Glenn Greenwald, 2014, *No Place to Hide: Edward Snowden, The NSA, and the U.S. Surveillance State*, New York, NY: Metropolitan Books, 171.

5. Cited in Ryan Tate, 2009, "Google CEO: Secrets Are for Filthy People," Gawker Media, December 4, http://gawker.com/5419271/google-ceo-secrets-are-for-filthy-people.

6. Jennifer Westhoven, 2005, "CNET: We've been blackballed by Google," *CNN Money*, August 5, http://money.cnn.com/2005/08/05/technology/google_cnet/.

7. Christopher Williams, 2011, "How Egypt shut down the internet," *The Telegraph*, January 28, www.telegraph.co.uk/news/worldnews/africaandindianocean/egypt/8288163/How-Egypt-shut-down-the-internet.html.

8. Jon Boone, 2015, "Dissenting voices silenced in Pakistan's war of the web," *The Guardian*, February 18, www.theguardian.com/world/2015/feb/18/pakistan-war-of-the-web-youtube-facebook-twitter.

9. James Bamford, 2016, "The Espionage Economy: US firms are making billions selling spyware to dictators," *Foreign Policy*, January 22, http://foreignpolicy.com/2016/01/22/the-espionage-economy/.

10. David Omand, 2015, *Understanding Digital Intelligence and the Norms that Might Govern It*, GCIG Paper Series No. 8, Waterloo, ON: CIGI, https://ourinternet.org/publication/understanding-digital-intelligence-and-the-norms-that-might-govern-it/.

11. Greenwald, *No Place to Hide*.

12. Glenn Greenwald and Ewen MacAskill, 2013, "NSA Prism program taps in to user data of Apple, Google and others," *The Guardian*, June 7, www.theguardian.com/world/2013/jun/06/us-tech-giants-nsa-data.

13. Statista, 2015, "Worldwide market share of leading search engines from January 2010 to April 2015," www.statista.com/statistics/216573/worldwide-market-share-of-search-engines/.

14. Statista, 2015, "Statistics and facts about Social Networks," www.statista.com/topics/1164/social-networks/.

15. Litmus, 2015, "Email Client Market Share." Calculated from 1.01 billion opens tracked by Litmus Email Analytics in April 2015. https://emailclientmarketshare.com/.

16. Adam Segal, 2016, *The Hacked World Order: How Nations Fight, Trade, Maneuver, and Manipulate in the Digital Age*. New York, NY: Council on Foreign Relations Books, 120-21.

17. Omand, *Understanding Digital Intelligence and the Norms that Might Govern It*.

18. Statista, 2012, "Average number of search queries per user in European countries in December 2012," www.statista.com/statistics/254710/average-number-of-search-queries-per-user-in-european-countries/.

19. Eurostat, 2015, "Hourly Labour Costs," http://ec.europa.eu/eurostat/statistics-explained/index.php/Hourly_labour_costs.

20. Eric Jardine, 2016, "Tor, What is it Good For? Political Repression and the Use of Online Anonymity-Granting Technologies," *New Media & Society* (March, online first): 1–18.

21. Tor Project, n.d., "Tor Metrics," https://mctrics.torprojcct.org/userstats-relay-country.html.

22. Glenn Greenwald, 2013, "XKeyscore: NSA tool collects 'nearly everything a user does on the internet,'" *The Guardian*, July 31, www.theguardian.com/world/2013/jul/31/nsa-top-secret-program-online-data.

23. Cited in ibid.

24. Eric Jardine, 2015, *The Dark Web Dilemma: Tor, Anonymity and Online Policing*, GCIG Paper Series No. 21, Waterloo, ON: CIGI, https://ourinternet-files.s3.amazonaws.com/publications/n21.pdf; Gareth Owen and Nick Savage, 2015, *The Tor Dark Net*, GCIG Paper Series No. 20, Waterloo, ON: CIGI, https://ourinternet.org/publication/the-tor-dark-net/; Michael Chertoff and Tobby Simon, 2015, *The Impact of the Dark Web on Internet Governance and Cyber Security*, GCIG Paper Series No. 6, Waterloo, ON: CIGI, https://ourinternet-files.s3.amazonaws.com/publications/GCIG_Paper_No6.pdf.

25. Catherine Treyz, 2015, "NSA ends bulk phone data collection," CNN, November 28, www.cnn.com/2015/11/28/us/nsa-ends-bulk-phone-surveillance/.

26. Jeff John Roberts, 2014, "'Brightest Flashlight' Android app disclosed location of 50 million people, but FTC imposes no fine," Gigaom Research, April 9, https://gigaom.com/2014/04/09/brightest-flashlight-android-app-disclosed-location-of-50-million-people-but-ftc-imposes-no-fine/.

27. Lookout, n.d, "App Genome Report," www.lookout.com/resources/reports/appgenome.

28. Cited in Kashmir Hill, 2012, "How Target Figured Out A Teen Girl Was Pregnant Before Her Father Did," *Forbes*, February 16, www.forbes.com/sites/kashmirhill/2012/02/16/how-target-figured-out-a-teen-girl-was-pregnant-before-her-father-did/.

29. Ibid.

30. Frank Pasquale, 2015, *The Black Box Society: The Secret Algorithms That Control Money and Information*, Cambridge, MA: Harvard University Press, 29.

31. Cited in John Brownlee, 2010, "GameStation EULA collects 7,500 souls from unsuspecting customers," Geek.com, April 16, www.geek.com/games/gamestation-eula-collects-7500-souls-from-unsuspecting-customers-1194091/.

32. Ibid.

33. Stefan Stieger, Christoph Burger, Manuel Bohn and Martin Voracek, 2013, "Who Commits Virtual Identity Suicide? Differences in Privacy Concerns, Internet Addiction, and Personality Between Facebook Users and Quitters," *Cyberpsychology, Behavior, and Social Networking* 16 (9): 629–34, doi:10.1089/cyber.2012.0323.

34. Brooke Torres, n.d., "Job Seekers: Social Media is Even More Important Than You Thought," *The Muse*, www.themuse.com/advice/job-seekers-social-media-is-even-more-important-than-you-thought.

35. Jonathan Dame, 2014, "Will employers still ask for Facebook passwords in 2014?" *USA Today*, January 10, www.usatoday.com/story/money/business/2014/01/10/facebook-passwords-employers/4327739/.

36. World Bank, n.d., "Data — Indicators," http://data.worldbank.org/indicator.

37. Vindu Goel, 2015, "Survey Finds Americans Don't Trust Government and Companies to Protect Privacy," *The New York Times* (*Bits* blog), May 20, http://bits.blogs.nytimes.com/2015/05/20/survey-finds-americans-dont-trust-government-and-companies-to-protect-privacy/?smprod=nytcore-ipad&smid=nytcore-ipad-share&_r=1.

38. Ali al-Halawani, cited in Helmi Noman, 2011, "In the Name of God: Faith-Based Internet Censorship in Majority Muslim Countries," Open Net Initiative, August 1, https://opennet.net/sites/opennet.net/files/ONI_NameofGod_1_08_2011.pdf.

39. Open Net Initiative, 2009, "Internet Filtering in Iran," https://opennet.net/sites/opennet.net/files/ONI_Iran_2009.pdf.

40. Cited in Golnaz Esfandiari, 2012, "Iran's National Internet Gets Late Spring Launch Date," Radio Free Europe (*Persian Letters* blog), February 21, www.rferl.org/content/irans_national_internet_gets_late_spring_launch_date/24491847.html.

41. Open Net Initiative, "Internet Filtering in Iran."

42. Cited in Reporters Without Borders, 2008, "YouTube Access Unblocked After Offending Videos Removed," Reporters Without Borders, February 27, http://en.rsf.org/pakistan-youtube-access-unblocked-after-27-02-2008,25889.html.

43. Declan Walsh, 2010, "Pakistan blocks YouTube access over Muhammad depictions," *The Guardian*, May 20, www.theguardian.com/world/2010/may/20/pakistan-blocks-youtube-sacrilegious.

44. Palash Ghosh, 2012, "Pakistan Shuts Down YouTube To Block Access To 'Innocence Of Muslims' Film," *International Business Times*, September 17, www.ibtimes.com/pakistan-shuts-down-youtube-block-access-innocence-muslims-film-789860.

45. Ali Sethi, 2013, "Banistan: Why Is YouTube Still Blocked in Pakistan?" *The New Yorker*, August 7, www.newyorker.com/tech/elements/banistan-why-is-youtube-still-blocked-in-pakistan.

46. Open Net Initative, 2010, "Turkey," https://opennet.net/sites/opennet.net/files/ONI_Turkey_2010.pdf.

47. Quoted in Eliana Dockterman, 2014, "Turkey Bans Twitter," *Time*, March 20, http://time.com/32864/turkey-bans-twitter/.

48. Ibid.

49. Open Net Initiative, 2012, "China," http://access.opennet.net/wp-content/uploads/2011/12/accesscontested-china.pdf.

50. Ibid.

51. Andrew Griffin, 2015, "Reddit blocked in China, as country's 'Great Firewall' gets ever wider," *The Independent*, June 26, www.independent.co.uk/life-style/gadgets-and-tech/news/reddit-blocked-in-china-as-countrys-great-firewall-gets-ever-wider-10347357.html.

52. Gary King, Jennifer Pan and Margaret E. Roberts, 2013, "How Censorship in China Allows Government Criticism but Silences Collective Expression," *American Review of Political Science* (May), 1, http://gking.harvard.edu/files/gking/files/censored.pdf.

53. Open Net Initiative, "China."

54. King et al., "How Censorship in China Allows Government Criticism but Silences Collective Expression."

55. Open Net Initiative, "China."

56. Jane Perlez, 2015, "Chinese Rights Lawyer, Pu Zhiqiang, Is Given Suspended Prison Sentence," *The New York Times*, December 21, www.nytimes.com/2015/12/22/world/asia/china-pu-zhiqiang-sentence.html.

57. Ronald Deibert, 2013, *Black Code: Surveillance, Privacy, and The Dark Side of the Internet*, Toronto, ON: McClelland & Stewart.

58. *BBC News Magazine*, 2013, "Trending: the story behind No woman, No Drive," *BBC News Magazine*, October 28, www.bbc.com/news/magazine-24711649.

59. Alaa Wardi and Hisham Fageeh, 2013, "No Woman, No Drive" (video recording), *YouTube*, Alaa Wardi Channel, October 26, www.youtube.com/watch?v=aZMbTFNp4wI.

60. *The Guardian*, 2013, "Dozens of Saudi Arabian women drive cars on day of protest against ban," October 26, www.theguardian.com/world/2013/oct/26/saudi-arabia-woman-driving-car-ban.

61. Nahlah Ayed, 2013, "Why Saudi Arabia is the world's top YouTube Nation," CBC News, April 1, www.cbc.ca/news/world/nahlah-ayed-why-saudi-arabia-is-the-world-s-top-youtube-nation-1.1359187.

62. Ibid.; Matt Smith, 2013, "Young Saudis getting creative on YouTube," Reuters, November 18, www.reuters.com/article/2013/11/18/us-saudi-youtube-idUSBRE9AH0GY20131118.

63. Rory Jones and Ahmed al Omran, 2014, "Saudi Arabia Plans to Regulate Local YouTube Content," *The Wall Street Journal*, April 24, www.wsj.com/articles/SB10001424052702304518704579521463293165726.

64. Ibid.

65. Freedom House, 2014, "Freedom on the Net: Saudi Arabia," https://freedomhouse.org/report/freedom-net/2014/saudi-arabia.

66. Reporters Without Borders, 2014, "Saudi Arabia: prime centre of content blocking," Reporters Without Borders Enemies of the Internet, http://12mars.rsf.org/2014-en/2014/03/11/saudi-arabia/.

67. Melissa Etehad, 2014, "Why are Twitter and Facebook still blocked in Iran?" Al Jazeera America, April 19, http://america.aljazeera.com/opinions/2014/4/iran-twitter-rouhaniinternetcensorship.html.

68. Vasudevan Sridharan, 2015, "Iran launches own search engine Yooz to beat internet-related sanctions," International Business Times, February 16, www.ibtimes.co.uk/iran-launches-own-search-engine-yooz-beat-internet-related-sanctions-1488112.

69. Doug Bernard, 2015, "Iran's Next Step in Building a 'Halal' Internet," Voice of America, March 9, www.voanews.com/content/irans-next-step-in-building-a-halal-internet/2672948.html.

70. Reporters Without Borders, 2015, "Iran: Cyberspace ayatollahs," http://12mars.rsf.org/2014-en/2014/03/11/iran-the-revolutionary-guards-the-supreme-council-for-cyberspace-and-the-working-group-for-identifying-criminal-content/.

71. Patrick Howell O'Neill, 2015, "The big money behind Iran's Internet censorship," The Daily Dot, February 22, www.dailydot.com/politics/iran-censorship-circumvention-tech/; Open Net Initiative, "Internet Filtering in Iran."

72. Nicole Perlroth, 2014, "Big Web Crash in China: Experts Suspect Great Firewall," The New York Times (Bits blog), January 22, http://bits.blogs.nytimes.com/2014/01/22/big-web-crash-in-china-experts-suspect-great-firewall/?_r=0; Melissa Block, 2014, "China Sends 500 Million Users on An Internet Detour" (radio recording), National Public Radio, January 23, www.npr.org/2014/01/23/265358234/china-sends-500-million-users-on-an-internet-detour.

73. Block, "China Sends 500 Million Users on An Internet Detour"; Matthew Hilburn, 2014, "More Questions than Answers About China Internet Outage," Voice of America, January 22, www.voanews.com/content/more-questions-than-answers-about-china-internet-outage/1835525.html; Perlroth, "Big Web Crash in China"; Randell Suba, 2014, "China witnesses massive Internet outage: What really happened and why?" TechTimes, January 23, www.techtimes.com/articles/2899/20140123/china-witnesses-massive-internet-outage-what-really-happened-and-why.htm.

74.   Perlroth, "Big Web Crash in China."

75.   Hilburn, "More Questions than Answers About China Internet Outage"; Suba, "China witnesses massive Internet outage."

76.   Anthony Zurcher, 2014, "China's 'Great Firewall' could be culprit in massive internet outage," BBC News (*Echo Chambers* blog), January 23, www.bbc.com/news/blogs-echochambers-25868297.

77.   *Global Times*, 2014, "Alarm bells should ring for Internet security," *Global Times*, January 23, www.globaltimes.cn/content/838921.shtml#. UuACQT8o6Uk.

78.   Cited in Zurcher, "China's 'Great Firewall' could be culprit in massive internet outage."

79.   Cited in Suba, "China witnesses massive Internet outage."

80.   Charles Clover, 2015, "Chinese internet: Commerce and control," *Financial Times*, March 13, www.ft.com/cms/s/0/2622e476-c89e-11e4-b43b-00144feab7de.html#axzz3inq4nmIv.

81.   Ibid.

82.   Cited in ibid.

83.   Dalberg Global Development Advisory Group, 2014, *Open for Business? The Economic Impact of Internet Openness*, March, www.dalberg.com/documents/Open_for_Business_Dalberg.pdf.

84.   Ibid.

85.   Vikki Chowney, 2011, "SOPA: an introduction, update and review," Econsultancy.com, December 20, https://econsultancy.com/blog/8550-sopa-an-introduction-update-and-review.

86.   David Moth, 2012, "SOPA debate looks set to rage despite blackout protests," Econsultancy.com, January 20, https://econsultancy.com/blog/8756-sopa-debate-looks-set-to-rage-despite-blackout-protests.

87.   Declan McCullagh, 2012, "Wikipedia, Google blackout sites to protest SOPA," CNN, January 17, www.cnet.com/news/wikipedia-google-blackout-sites-to-protest-sopa/.

88.   Chowney, "SOPA"; Kym McNicholas, 2012, "Mark Zuckerberg Speaks Out On SOPA and PIPA," *Forbes*, January 18, www.forbes.com/sites/kymmcnicholas/2012/01/18/mark-zuckerberg-speaks-out-on-sopa-and-pipa/.

89.   Chowney, "SOPA."

90.   McCullagh, "Wikipedia, Google blackout sites to protest SOPA."

91.   McNicholas, "Mark Zuckerberg Speaks Out On SOPA and PIPA."

92.   Peter Eckersley and Parker Higgins, 2011, "An Open Letter From Internet Engineers to the U.S. Congress," Electronic Frontier Foundation, December 15, www.eff.org/deeplinks/2011/12/internet-inventors-warn-against-sopa-and-pipa.

93.   Scott Steinberg, 2012, "The SOPA and PIPA War: An Analysis," *Rolling Stone*, January 20, www.rollingstone.com/culture/news/the-sopa-and-pipa-war-an-analysis-20120120.

94.   Evan Greer, 2015, "The Trans-Pacific Partnership suggests Obama has no sense of irony," *The Guardian*, May 8, www.theguardian.com/media-network/2015/may/08/trans-pacific-partnership-obama-irony.

95.   OECD, 2011, *The Role of Internet Intermediaries in Advancing Public Policy Objectives*, Paris, France: OECD.

96.   Google, n.d., "Enabling Trade in the Era of Information Technologies: Breaking Down Barriers to the Free Flow of Information," http://static.googleusercontent.com/media/www.google.com/en//googleblogs/pdfs/trade_free_flow_of_information.pdf.

97.   Ibid.

Five: One or Many, Internet or Fragnet?

1.   *The Wall Street Journal*, 2015. "China's Xi Jinping Calls for Internet Sovereignty," video, December 16, www.wsj.com/video/china-xi-jinping-calls for internet sovereignty/F4262F56-279A-47D4-95A1-9E750C428758.html.

2.   William J. Drake, Vinton G. Cerf and Wolfgang Kleinwächter, 2016, "Internet Fragmentation: An Overview," Future of the Internet Initiative White Paper, January, Geneva, Switzerland: World Economic Forum.

3.   Rolf H. Weber, 2014, *Legal Interoperability as a Tool for Combatting Fragmentation*, GCIG Paper Series No. 4, Waterloo, ON: CIGI, https://ourinternet-files.s3.amazonaws.com/publications/gcig_paper_no4.pdf.

4.   Larry Downes, 2014, "How Netflix Poisoned the Net Neutrality Debate," *Forbes*, November 25, www.forbes.com/sites/larrydownes/2014/11/25/how-netflix-poisoned-the-net-neutrality-debate/; Dan Rayburn, 2014, "New Study for M-Labs Sheds light on Widespread Harm Caused by Netflix's Routing Decisions," StreamingMediaBlog.com, October 29, http://blog.streamingmedia.com/2014/10/mlab-netflix-routing-decisions.html.

5.   Ben Scott, Stefan Heumann and Jan-Peter Kleinhans, 2015, *Landmark EU and US Net Neutrality Decisions: How Might Pending Decisions Impact Internet Fragmentation?* GCIG Paper Series No. 18, Waterloo, ON: CIGI, https://www.cigionline.org/sites/default/files/no18.pdf.

6.   Matt Ford, 2014, "Will Europe Censor This Article?" *The Atlantic*, May 13, www.theatlantic.com/international/archive/2014/05/europes-troubling-new-right-to-be-forgotten/370796/; Jeffrey Toobin, 2014, "The Solace of Oblivion," *The New Yorker*, September 29, www.newyorker.com/magazine/2014/09/29/solace-oblivion.

7.   Ibid.; Ford, "Will Europe Censor This Article?"

8.   Ford, "Will Europe Censor This Article?"

9.   Ibid.; Toobin, "The Solace of Oblivion."

10.   Cited in Ford, "Will Europe Censor This Article?"

11.   House of Lords, 2014, "EU Data Protection law: a 'right to be forgotten'?" House of Lords, European Union Committee, 2nd Report of Session 2014–2015, July 30, www.publications.parliament.uk/pa/ld201415/ldselect/ldeucom/40/40.pdf.

12.   Ford, "Will Europe Censor This Article?"

13.   Toobin, "The Solace of Oblivion."

14.   Ford, "Will Europe Censor This Article?"

15.   *Vanity Fair*, 2014, "Cover Exclusive: Jennifer Lawrence Calls Photo Hacking a 'Sex Crime,'" *Vanity Fair*, November, www.vanityfair.com/hollywood/2014/10/jennifer-lawrence-cover.

16.   Samuel Gibbs, 2014, "Google removes results linking to stolen photos of Jennifer Lawrence nude," *The Guardian*, October 20, www.theguardian.com/technology/2014/oct/20/google-search-results-linking-stolen-nude-photos-jennifer-lawrence. See also Jessica Contrera, 2015, "A reminder that your Instagram photos aren't really yours: Someone else can sell them for $90,000," *The Washington Post*, May 25, www.washingtonpost.com/news/arts-and-entertainment/wp/2015/05/25/a-reminder-that-your-instagram-photos-arent-really-yours-someone-else-can-sell-them-for-90000/.

17.   Toobin, "The Solace of Oblivion."

18.   Ibid.

19.   Cited in ibid.

20. Neil Ray, 2014, "Prepare for Changes to the US-EU Safe Harbor Agreement," *National Law Review*, May 1, www.natlawreview.com/ article/prepare-changes-to-us-eu-safe-harbor.

21. David Meyer, 2016, "Looks Like Data Will Keep Flowing From the EU to the US After All," *Fortune*, February 2, http://fortune. com/2016/02/02/looks-like-data-will-keep-flowing-from-the-eu-to-the-u-s-after-all/.

22. Will Marshall, 2014, "European Regulators Take Aim at US Tech Companies: The digital protectionism being contemplated isn't the answer to the 'data gap' or to sluggish economic growth," *The Wall Street Journal*, May 12, http://online.wsj.com/news/articles/SB10001 424052702304831304579542203474599422.

23. Carl Bildt, 2015, "Brussels should resist the urge to rig the rules of cyber space," *Financial Times*, May 4.

24. Ibid.

25. Jonah Force Hill, 2002, "Internet Fragmentation: Highlighting the Major Technical, Governance and Diplomatic Challenges for U.S. Policy Makers," Spring, Cambridge, MA: Belfer Center, Harvard University, 6.

26. Computer Desktop Dictionary, n.d., "Data Localization — Computer Definition," www.yourdictionary.com/data-localization.

27. James Kinsella, 2015, "Should US cloud domination matter to Europeans?" *Zettabox.com* (blog), June 10, https://blog.zettabox.com/ should-US-cloud-domination-matter-to-Europeans.

28. Techworld, 2015, "Zettabox gambles on EU privacy laws to take on Google, Amazon and Microsoft in cloud storage battle," Techworld.com, June 11, www.techworld.com/news/cloud/cloud-startup-zettabox-touts-privacy-and-local-storage-to-appeal-to-eu-customers-3615326/.

29. European Commission, 2015, "The EU Data Protection Reform and Big Data Factsheet," April, http://ec.europa.eu/justice/data-protection/files/data-protection-big-data_factsheet_web_en.pdf.

30. Mark Scott, 2015, "European Cloud Companies Play Up Privacy Credentials," *The New York Times* (*Bits* blog), June 9, http://bits. blogs.nytimes.com/2015/06/09/european-firms-play-up-privacy-credentials/.

31. Ibid.

32. Loretta Chao and Paulo Trevisani, 2013, "Brazil Legislators Bear Down on Internet Bill. Push for Data Localization Follows Espionage Revelations; Measure Could Cost U.S. Companies," *The Wall Street Journal*, November 13, www.wsj.com/articles/SB1000142405270230 4868404579194290325348688.

33. Danielle Kehl, Kevin Bankston, Robyn Greene and Robert Morgus, 2014, "Surveillance Costs: The NSA's Impact on the Economy, Internet Freedom and Cyberspace," New America's Open Technology Institute Policy Paper, July, Washington, DC: New America's Open Technology Institute, 8, www.newamerica.org/downloads/ Surveilance_Costs_Final.pdf.

34. Frederik Obermaier and Benedikt Strunz, 2014, "Germany Plans To Ban Tech Companies That Play Ball With NSA," *Süddeutsche Zeitung*, May 16, http://international.sueddeutsche.de/post/85917094540/ germany-plans-to-ban-tech-companies-that-play-ball.

35. Kehl et al., "Surveillance Costs," 10.

36. Matthias Bauer, Hosuk Lee-Makiyama, Erik van der Marel and Bert Verschelde, 2014, "The Costs of Data Localisation: Friendly Fire on Economic Recovery," ECIPE Occasional Paper No. 3, Brussels, Belgium: European Centre for International Political Economy, www.ecipe.org/app/uploads/2014/12/OCC32014__1.pdf.

37. James M. Kaplan and Kayvaun Rowshankish, *Addressing the Impact of Data Location Regulation in Financial Services*, GCIG Paper Series No. 14, Waterloo, ON: CIGI, 1. https://ourinternet-files.s3.amazonaws. com/publications/no14_web.pdf.

38. Ibid.

39. *The Economist*, 2014, "Brazil's internet law: The net closes," March 29, www.economist.com/news/americas/21599781-brazils-magna-carta-web-net-closes.

40. IXmaps, 2015, "Canadian Network Sovereignty: Boomerang Routes," http://ixmaps.ca/sovereignty.

41. Ibid.

42. Quoted in Mitch Potter and Michelle Shephard, 2013, "Canadians not safe from U.S. online surveillance, expert says," *The Toronto Star*, June 7, www.thestar.com/news/world/2013/06/07/canadians_not_ safe_from_us_online_surveillance_expert_says.html.

43. Kathleen Hennessey and Vincent Bevins, 2013, "Brazil's president, angry about spying, cancels state visit to U.S.," *The Los Angeles Times*, September 17, http://articles.latimes.com/2013/sep/17/world/la-fg-snowden-fallout-20130918.

44. Ibid.

45. Kathleen Caulderwood, 2014, "Brazil Builds Internet Cable To Portugal To Avoid NSA Surveillance," *International Business Times*, November 1, www.ibtimes.com/brazil-builds-internet-cable-portugal-avoid-nsa-surveillance-1717417; Anna Edgerton and Jordan Robertson, 2014, "Brazil-to-Portugal Cable Shapes Up as Anti-NSA Case Study," *Bloomberg Business*, October 30, www.bloomberg.com/news/articles/2014-10-30/brazil-to-portugal-cable-shapes-up-as-anti-nsa-case-study.

46. Jonathan Zittrain, 2008, *The Future of the Internet and How to Stop It*, New Haven, CT: Yale University Press.

47. Walter Isaacson, 2013, *Steve Jobs*, New York, NY: Simon and Schuster, 514-15.

48. Stephen Shankland, 2010, "Jobs: Why Apple banned Flash from the iPhone," CNET, April 29, www.cnet.com/news/jobs-why-apple-banned-flash-from-the-iphone/.

49. Steve Jobs, 2010, "Thoughts on Flash," Apple.com, April, www.apple.com/ca/hotnews/thoughts-on-flash/.

50. Shankland, "Jobs"; John Sullivan, 2010, "Pot, meet kettle: a response to Steve Jobs' letter on Flash," Ars Technica, April 30, http://arstechnica.com/apple/2010/04/pot-meet-kettle-a-response-to-steve-jobs-letter-on-flash/.

51. Sullivan, "Pot, meet kettle."

52. Doug Gross, 2011, "Did Steve Jobs kill Adobe Flash?" CNN, November 9, www.cnn.com/2011/11/09/tech/mobile/flash-steve-jobs/.

53. Ibid.

54. Michael Chertoff and Paul Rosenzweig, 2015, *A Primer on Globally Harmonizing Internet Jurisdiction and Regulations*, GCIG Paper Series No. 10, Waterloo, ON: CIGI, 2, https://ourinternet-files.s3.amazonaws.com/publications/gcig_paper_no10_0.pdf.

Six: Crime, Punishment and the Deep Dark Web

1. Eric Jardine, 2015, *The Dark Web Dilemma: Tor, Anonymity and Online Policing*. GCIG Paper Series No. 21, Waterloo, ON: CIGI, www.cigionline.org/sites/default/files/no.21_1.pdf.
2. Jamie Bartlett, 2014, *The Dark Net: Inside the Digital Underworld*, London, UK: William Heinemann.
3. Larry Seltzer, 2013, "The Morris Worm: Internet malware turns 25," ZDNet, November 2, www.zdnet.com/article/the-morris-worm-internet-malware-turns-25/.
4. Eric Jardine, 2015, *Global Cyberspace Is Safer than You Think: Real Trends in Cybercrime*, GCIG Paper Series No. 16, Waterloo, ON: CIGI, www.cigionline.org/sites/default/files/no16_web_3.pdf.
5. Jardine, *Global Cyberspace Is Safer than You Think*.
6. Godwin J. Uro, 2001, "Privacy and Security Concerns as Major Barriers for E-Commerce: A Survey Study," *Information Management & Computer Security* 9 (4): 165–74; Bomil Suh and Ingoo Han, 2002, "Effect of Trust on Customer Acceptance of Internet Banking," *Electronic Commerce Research and Applications* 1 (3–4), 247–63; Bomil Suh and Ingoo Han, 2003, "The Impact of Customer Trust and Perception on Security Control on the Acceptance of Electronic Commerce," *International Journal of Electronic Commerce* 7 (3): 135–61; Audun Josang, Roslan Ismail and Colin A. Boyd, 2007, "A Survey of Trust and Reputation Systems for Online Service Provision," *Decision Support Systems* 43 (2): 618–44.
7. Privacy Rights Clearinghouse, n.d., "Chronology of Data Breaches," www.privacyrights.org/data-breach/new.
8. Center for Strategic and International Studies, 2013, "The Economic Impact of Cybercrime and Cyber Espionage," July, Washington, DC: Center for Strategic and International Studies, www.mcafee.com/ca/resources/reports/rp-economic-impact-cybercrime.pdf.
9. World Economic Forum, 2016, *The Global Risks Report 2016, 11th Edition*, Geneva, Switzerland: World Economic Forum, www3.weforum.org/docs/GRR/WEF_GRR16.pdf.
10. Juniper Research, 2015, "Cybercrime and the Internet of Threats," http://106.186.118.91/201504/Cybercrime-and-the-Internet-of-Threats.pdf.

11. Andrea Ipolyi, 2014, "84% of IT security risks are a result of human elements while only half of budgets are spent to defend against them," *Balabit*, https://andrea.blogs.balabit.com/2014/03/84-of-it-security-risks-are-a-result-of-human-elements/.

12. Kim Zetter, 2009, "Senate Panel: 80 Percent of Cyber Attacks Preventable," *Wired*, http://www.wired.com/2009/11/cyber-attacks-preventable/.

13. Verizon, 2015, *2015 Verizon Data Breach Investigations Report*, www.verizonenterprise.com/DBIR/2015/.

14. Benjamin Dean, 2015, "Why companies have little incentive to invest in cybersecurity," The Conversation, March 4, http://theconversation.com/why-companies-have-little-incentive-to-invest-in-cybersecurity-37570.

15. Ingrid Lunden, 2015, "Target Says Credit Card Data Breach Cost It $162M In 2013-14," TechCrunch, February 25, http://techcrunch.com/2015/02/25/target-says-credit-card-data-breach-cost-it-162m-in-2013-14/.

16. Maya Rajamani, 2015, "Data Breach Cost Home Depot $7M In 1st Quarter Of 2015," Law 360, May 20, www.law360.com/articles/657893/data-breach-cost-home-depot-7m-in-1st-quarter-of-2015.

17. Katie Dvorak, 2015, "Anthem may face costs of more than $100M following hack," FierceHealthIT, February 13, www.fiercehealthit.com/story/anthem-may-face-costs-more-100m-following-hack/2015-02-13.

18. Semafone, 2014, "86% of customers would shun brands following a data breach," Semafone, March 27, www.semafone.com/86-customers-shun-brands-following-data-breach/.

19. SafeNet, 2014, "Global Survey Reveals Impact of Data Breaches on Customer Loyalty," www.safenet-inc.com/news/2014/data-breaches-impact-on-customer-loyalty-survey/.

20. John Leyden, 2015, "Anonymous loose cannon admits DDoSing social services and housing websites," The Register, February 10, www.theregister.co.uk/2015/02/10/anonymous_hacktivist_ian_sullivan_admits_ddos_attacks/.

21. Kaspersky Lab, 2014, "Global IT Security Risks Survey 2014 — Distributed Denial of Service (DDoS) Attacks," 5, http://media.kaspersky.com/en/B2B-International-2014-Survey-DDoS-Summary-Report.pdf.

22. Cited in Leyden, "Anonymous loose cannon admits DDoSing social services and housing websites."

23. John Pescatore, 2014, "DDoS Attacks Advancing and Enduring: A SANS Survey," SANS Institute, February, www.sans.org/reading-room/whitepapers/analyst/ddos-attacks-advancing-enduring-survey-34700.

24. M. Van Eeten, J. Bauer, H. Asghari, S. Tabatabaie and D. Rand, 2010, "The Role of Internet Service Providers in Botnet Mitigation: An Empirical Analysis Based on Spam Data," www.econinfosec.org/archive/weis2010/papers/session4/weis2010_vaneeten.pdf.

25. Ibid., 9.

26. Eric Jardine, forthcoming, "A Continuum of Internet-Based Crime: How the Effectiveness of Cybersecurity Policies Varies across Cybercrime Types," in *Research Handbook on Digital Transformations*, edited by F. Xavier Olleros and Majlinda Zhegu, Northampton, MA: Edward Elgar.

27. Kaspersky Lab, "Global IT Security Risks Survey 2014."

28. Jardine, *The Dark Web Dilemma*.

29. Nicholas Christin, 2012, "Traveling the Silk Road: A measurement analysis of a large anonymous online marketplace," Working paper, November 30, 8, http://arxiv.org/pdf/1207.7139.pdf.

30. Jason Koebler, 2012, "Online Black Market Drug Haven Sees Growth Double," US News & World Report, August 7, www.usnews.com/news/articles/2012/08/07/online-black-market-drug-haven-sees-growth-double; Andy Greenberg, 2013, "End Of The Silk Road: FBI Says It's Busted The Web's Biggest Anonymous Drug Black Market," *Forbes*, October 2, www.forbes.com/sites/andygreenberg/2013/10/02/end-of-the-silk-road-fbi-busts-the-webs-biggest-anonymous-drug-black-market/#1c68ec6347d2.

31. Andy Greenberg, 2014, "The FBI Finally Says How It 'Legally' Pinpointed Silk Road's Server," *Wired*, September 5, www.wired.com/2014/09/the-fbi-finally-says-how-it-legally-pinpointed-silk-roads-server/; Andy Greenberg, 2014, "FBI's Story of Finding Silk Road's Server Sounds a Lot Like Hacking," *Wired*, September 8, www.wired.com/2014/09/fbi-silk-road-hacking-question/.

32. Gareth Owen and Nick Savage, 2015, *The Tor Dark Net*, GCIG Paper Series No. 20, Waterloo, ON: CIGI, https://ourinternet-files.s3.amazonaws.com/publications/no20_0.pdf.

33. Europol, 2011, "Operation Rescue," www.europol.europa. eu/content/operation-rescue.

34. BBC, 2014, "Child abuse image investigation leads to 660 arrests," BBC News, July 16, www.bbc.com/news/uk-28326128.

35. BBC, 2015, "50 arrests in NI online abuse images probe in past year, say police," BBC News, March 15, www.bbc.com/news/uk-northern-ireland-31896685.

36. Cited in Laurie Segall, 2015, "Pastor outed on Ashley Madison commits suicide," CNN Money, September 8, http://money.cnn.com/2015/09/08/technology/ashley-madison-suicide/index.html.

37. Cited in Koebler, "Online Black Market Drug Haven Sees Growth Double."

38. Elizabeth Nolan Brown, 2014, "You Can't Stop the Dark Net (Yet Everyone Keeps Trying)," *Hit & Run* (blog), August 1, https://reason.com/blog/2014/08/01/dark-net-drugs-sales-more-than-double.

39. ASN, "Some Statistics about Onions," Tor Project blog, https://blog.torproject.org/blog/some-statistics-about-onions.

40. Jardine, *The Dark Web Dilemma*; Eric Jardine, 2016, "Tor, What is it Good For? Political Repression and the Use of Online Anonymity-Granting Technologies," *New Media & Society* (March, online first), 1–18.

41. Cited in Sean Gallagher, 2011, "Anonymous takes down darknet child porn site on Tor network," Ars Technica, October 23, http://arstechnica.com/business/2011/10/anonymous-takes-down-darknet-child-porn-site-on-tor-network/.

42. *Daily Mail*, 2011, "Hacker group Anonymous publishes internet addresses of 190 paedophiles in hi-tech 'sting,'" *Daily Mail*, November 3, www.dailymail.co.uk/sciencetech/article-2057068/Hacker-group-Anonymous-publishes-internet-addresses-190-paedophiles-hi-tech-sting.html.

43. Kevin Morris, 2013, "Anonymous has finally released the names of Rehtaeh Parsons's alleged rapists," The Daily Dot, July 24, www.dailydot.com/news/rehtaeh-parsons-rapists-names-identity-revealed-anonymous/.

44. Cited in ibid.

45. Geordon Omand, 2015, "Rehtaeh Parsons's father credits Anonymous for reopening investigation," CBC News, August 3, www.cbc.ca/news/canada/nova-scotia/rehtaeh-parsons-s-father-credits-anonymous-for-reopening-investigation-1.3177605.

46. Cited in ibid.

47. Gabriella Coleman, 2014, *Hacker, Hoaxer, Whistleblower, Spy: The Many Faces of Anonymous*, London, UK: Verso.

48. Samantha Bradshaw, Mark Raymond and Aaron Shull, 2015, "Rule Making for State Conduct in the Attribution of Cyber Attacks," in *Mutual Security in the Asia-Pacific: Roles for Australia, Canada and South Korea*, edited by Kang Choi, James Manicom and Simon Palamar: 153–72, Waterloo, ON: CIGI.

49. Tim Ring, 2014, "East European cyber criminals 'protected from prosecution,'" SC Magazine, February 4, www.scmagazineuk. com/east-european-cyber-criminals-protected-from-prosecution/ article/332548/.

Seven: Cyberwarfare in the Twenty-First Century

1. Dmitri Alperovitch, 2011, *Revealed: Operation Shady RAT*, McAfee White Paper, www.mcafee.com/us/resources/white-papers/wp-operation-shady-rat.pdf; BBC News, 2011, "Cyber Attack on France Targeted Paris G20 Files," BBC News, March 7, www.bbc. com/news/business-12662596; Dan Glaister, 2009, "China Accused Over Global Computer Spy Ring," *The Guardian*, March 30, www. theguardian.com/world/2009/mar/30/china-dalai-lama-spying-computers; Lee Glendinning, 2008, "Obama, McCain Computers 'Hacked' During Election Campaign," *The Guardian*, November 7, www.theguardian.com/global/2008/nov/07/obama-white-house-usa; Siobhan Gorman, 2008, "Georgia States Computers Hit by Cyberattack," *The Wall Street Journal*, August 12, www.wsj.com/ articles/SB121850756472932159; Bradley Graham, 2005, "Hackers Attack Via Chinese Web Sites," *The Washington Post*, August 25, www.washingtonpost.com/wp-dyn/content/article/2005/08/24/ AR2005082402318.html; Jennifer Griffin, 2007, "Pentagon Source Says China Hacked Defense Department Computers," FOX News, September 4, www.foxnews.com/story/2007/09/04/pentagon-source-says-china-hacked-defense-department-computers.html; Michael Joseph Gross, 2011, "Exclusive: Operation Shady Rat — Unprecedented Cyber-Espionage Campaign and Intellectual-Property Bonanza," *Vanity Fair*, September, www.vanityfair.com/

news/2011/09/operation-shady-rat-201109; Phil Muncaster, 2012, "10,000 Indian Government and Military Emails Hacked," *The Register*, December 21, www.theregister.co.uk/2012/12/21/indian_ government_email_hacked/; Ellen Nakashima, 2011, "Cyber-intruder Sparks Response, Debate," *The Washington Post*, December 8, www. washingtonpost.com/national/national-security/cyber-intruder-sparks-response-debate/2011/12/06/gIQAxLuFgO_story.html; NATO Review, "The History of Cyber Attacks — A Timeline," *NATO Review Magazine*, www.nato.int/docu/review/2013/cyber/ timeline/EN/index.htm; David E. Sanger, 2012, "Obama Order Sped Up Wave of Cyberattacks Against Iran," *The New York Times*, June 1, www.nytimes.com/2012/06/01/world/middleeast/obama-ordered-wave-of-cyberattacks-against-iran.html?pagewanted=all&_r=1; Jeff Williams, 2014, "The New Target for State-Sponsored Cyber Attacks: Applications," DARKReading, December 17, www.darkreading. com/attacks-breaches/the-new-target-for-state-sponsored-cyber-attacks-applications-/a/d-id/1318215; Grace Wyler, 2011, "Pentagon Admits 24,000 Files Were Hacked, Declares Cyberspace A Theater of War," *Business Insider*, July 14, www.businessinsider.com/pentagon-admits-24000-files-were-hacked-declares-cyberspace-a-theater-of-war-2011-7; Kim Zetter, 2012, "Meet 'Flame,' The Massive Spy Malware Infiltration Iranian Computers," *Wired*, May 28, www.wired. com/2012/05/flame/; Kim Zetter, 2012, "Flame and Stuxnet Cousin Targets Lebanese Bank Customers, Carries Mysterious Payload," *Wired*, August 9, www.wired.com/2012/08/gauss-espionage-tool/; Kim Zetter, 2013, "Cybersleuths Uncover 5-Year Spy Operation Targeting Governments, Others," *Wired*, January 14, www.wired. com/2013/01/red-october-spy-campaign/.

2.   Cited in Chris Vallance, 2015, "Car hack uses digital-radio broadcasts to seize control," BBC News, July 22, www.bbc.com/news/ technology-33622298.

3.   Cited in Elias Groll, 2015, "Cyber Spying is Out, Cyber Lying Is In," *Foreign Policy*, November 20, http://foreignpolicy.com/2015/11/20/u-s-fears-hackers-will-manipulate-data-not-just-steal-it/.

4.   Cited in Ian Allison, 2016, "Security firm Guardtime courting governments and banks with industrial-grade blockchain," *International Business Times*, January 4, www.ibtimes.co.uk/security-firm-guardtime-courting-governments-banks-keyless-blockchain-1535835.

5. Trustwave, 2015, "2015 Trustwave Global Security Report," www2. trustwave.com/GSR2015.html?utm_source=redirect&utm_ medium=web&utm_campaign=GSR2015.

6. Verizon, 2015, *2015 Data Breach Investigations Report*, 6, www. verizonenterprise.com/DBIR/.

7. SANS Institute, 2014, "DDoS Attacks Advancing and Enduring: A SANS Survey," *SANS Institute*, 1, www.sans.org/reading-room/ whitepapers/analyst/ddos-attacks-advancing-enduring-survey-34700.

8. Quoted in Oliver Laughland, 2015, "FBI director stands by claim that North Korea was source of Sony cyber-attack," *The Guardian*, January 7, www.theguardian.com/world/2015/jan/07/fbi-director-north-korea-source-sony-cyber-attack-james-comey.

9. Nicole Hong, 2015, "Charges Announced in J.P. Morgan Hacking Case," *The Wall Street Journal*, November 10, www.wsj.com/articles/prosecutors-announce-charges-in-connection-with-j-p-morgan-hack-1447169646.

10. Ted Koppel, 2015, *Lights Out: A Cyberattack, A Nation Unprepared, Surviving the Aftermath*, New York, NY: Crown Publishers.

11. Ted Koppel, 2015, "Ted Koppel: The Internet could be a weapon of mass destruction," [originally published in *The Washington Post*] *National Post*, November 4, http://news.nationalpost.com/full-comment/ted-koppel-the-internet-could-be-a-weapon-of-mass-destruction.

12. Ibid.

13. Cited in Jeremy Bender, 2015, "'They'd love to do damage': The FBI says ISIS wants to go after one of America's biggest vulnerabilities," *Business Insider*, October 19, www.businessinsider.com/isis-and-hacking-us-power-grid-2015-10.

14. Koppel, "Ted Koppel."

15. David E. Sanger and Eric Schmitt, 2015, "US alarmed that Russian ships are lurking near critical undersea cables," *The New York Times*, October 25, www.nytimes.com/2015/10/26/world/europe/russian-presence-near-undersea-cables-concerns-us.html?_r=0.

16. Ibid.

17. Karl Frederick Rauscher and Andrev Korotkov, 2011, "Working Towards Rules for Governing Cyber Conflict Rendering the Geneva and Hague Conventions in Cyberspace," New York, NY: East-West Center; Bruce W. McConnell and Greg Austin, 2014, "A Measure of Restraint in Cyberspace: Reducing Risk to Civilian Nuclear Assets." New York, NY: East-West Center, 2014.

18. R. Vinith, 2015, "How a VPN Protects Freedom of Speech and Fights Censorship," VPN Creative, November 13, https://vpncreative. net/2015/11/13/vpn-protects-freedom-fights-censorship/.

19. Cited in Troy Wolverton, 2009, "Google's 'chief Internet evangelist' Cerf sees bigger, faster Web," *The Mercury News*, May 2, www.mercurynews. com/breakingnews/ci_11637128.

20. Cited in Jack Schofield, 2008, "It's every man for himself,'" *The Guardian*, October 1, www.theguardian.com/technology/2008/oct/02/interviews. internet.

21. Richard Chirgwin, 2015, "US still hoarding zero day app vulnerabilities, say EFF campaigners," *The Register*, March 31, www.theregister. co.uk/2015/03/31/us_still_hoarding_0days_says_eff/.

22. Charlie Miller, 2007, "The Legitimate Vulnerability Market: Inside the Secretive World of 0-day Exploit Sales," *Independent Security Evaluators*, www.econinfosec.org/archive/weis2007/papers/29.pdf.

23. Andy Greenberg, 2012, "Shopping For Zero-Days: A Price List For Hackers' Secret Software Exploits," *Forbes*, www.forbes.com/sites/ andygreenberg/2012/03/23/shopping-for-zero-days-an-price-list-for-hackers-secret-software-exploits/#3a1b1e776033.

24. Kim Zetter, 2014, *Countdown to Zero Day: Stuxnet and the Launch of the World's First Digital Weapon*, New York, NY: Crown Publishing.

25. Sam Jones, 2015, "Cyber crime: states use hackers to do digital dirty work," *Financial Times*, September 4.

26. Joseph S. Nye, Jr., 2011, "Nuclear Lessons for Cyber Security," *Strategic Studies Quarterly* (Winter): 18–38, www.au.af.mil/au/ssq/2011/winter/ nye.pdf.

27. David C. Gompert and Martin Libicki, 2014, "Cyber Warfare and Sino-American Crisis Stability," *Survival* 56 (4): 19.

28. Peter. W. Singer and Allan Friedman, 2014, *Cybersecurity and Cyberwar: What Everyone Needs to Know*, New York, NY: Oxford University Press.

29. Eric Jardine, forthcoming, "A Continuum of Internet-Based Crime: How the Effectiveness of Cybersecurity Policies Varies across Cybercrime Types," in *Research Handbook on Digital Transformations*, edited by F. Xavier Olleros and Majlinda Zhegu, Northampton, MA: Edward Elgar.

30. Michael J. Assante, 2016, "Confirmation of a Coordinated Attack on the Ukrainian Power Grid," *SANS Industrial Control Systems Security* (blog), January 9, https://ics.sans.org/blog/2016/01/09/confirmation-of-a-coordinated-attack-on-the-ukrainian-power-grid.

31. John Arquilla, 2012, "Cyberwar Is Already Upon Us: But can it be controlled?" *Foreign Policy*, February 27, http://foreignpolicy.com/2012/02/27/cyberwar-is-already-upon-us/; Herbert S. Lin, 2010, "Offensive Cyber Operations and the Use of Force," *Journal of National Security Law & Policy* 4 (1): 63–86, http://jnslp.com/wpcontent/uploads/2010/08/06_Lin.pdf; Thomas Rid, 2012, "Think Again: Cyberwar," *Foreign Policy*, February 27, http://foreignpolicy.com/2012/02/27/think-again-cyberwar/.

32. United Nations General Assembly, 2015, "Group of Governmental Experts on Developments in the Field of Information and Telecommunications in the Context of International Security." Seventieth session, Item 93 of the provisional agenda: Developments in the field of information and telecommunications in the context of international security. UNGA A/70/174. www.un.org/ga/search/view_doc.asp?symbol=A/70/174.

33. Ibid.

34. The White House, 2015, "President Xi Jinping's State Visit to the United States," Office of the Press Secretary fact sheet, September 25, www.whitehouse.gov/the-press-office/2015/09/25/fact-sheet-president-xi-jinpings-state-visit-united-states.

35. Jack Goldsmith, 2011, "Cybersecurity Treaties: A Skeptical View," in *Future Challenges in National Security and Law*, edited by Peter Berko, Hoover Institution, February, http://media.hoover.org/sites/default/files/documents/FutureChallenges_Goldsmith.pdf.

36. Cited in Ken Dilanian, 2015, "Cybersecurity firm: Chinese hacking on US companies persists," MSN.com, October 19, www.msn.com/en-us/money/topstories/cybersecurity-firm-chinese-hacking-on-us-companies-persists/ar-AAfB8HR.

37. Michael Kanellos, 2004, "South Korea's cat-and-mouse with piracy," CNET, May 18, www.cnet.com/news/south-koreas-cat-and-mouse-with-piracy/.

38. Michael B. G. Froman, 2014, *2014 Special 301 Report*, Office of the United States Trade Representative, April, https://ustr.gov/sites/default/files/USTR%202014%20Special%20301%20Report%20to%20Congress%20FINAL.pdf.

39. Intellectual Property Office, 2015, *International Comparison of Approaches to Online Copyright Infringement: Final Report*, United Kingdom

Intellectual Property Office, Newport, UK: Intellectual Property Office, www.gov.uk/government/uploads/system/uploads/attachment_data/file/404429/International_Comparison_of_Approaches_to_Online_Copyright_Infringement.pdf.

40. Froman, *2014 Special 301 Report*.

41. Cited in Kanellos, "South Korea's cat-and-mouse with piracy."

42. Intellectual Property Office, *International Comparison of Approaches...*

43. Ibid.

44. Andréa Novais, 2013, "Protecting Intellectual Property in Brazil," *The Brazil Business*, March 26, http://thebrazilbusiness.com/article/protecting-intellectual-property-in-brazil.

45. Ibid.

46. Donald M. Spero, 1990, "Patent Protection or Piracy — A CEO Views Japan," *Harvard Business Review*, September-October, https://hbr.org/1990/09/patent-protection-or-piracy-a-ceo-views-japan.

47. Ibid.

48. Hisamitsu Arai, 2007, "Country Focus: IP Revolution — How Japan Formulated a National IP Strategy," *WIPO Magazine*, June, www.wipo.int/wipo_magazine/en/2007/03/article_0007.html.

49. Ibid.

50. Ibid.

51. Ibid.

52. Emmanuel Hassan, Ohid Yaqub and Stephanie Diepeveen, 2010, *Intellectual Property and Developing Countries: A review of the literature*, RAND Technical Report, Santa Monica, CA: RAND, 8, 21-22, www.rand.org/content/dam/rand/pubs/technical_reports/2010/RAND_TR804.pdf.

53. Ibid.

54. Marietje Schaake, 2015, "Digital diplomacy: trade and human rights in China's internet." Commentary. European Council on Foreign Relations, July 13, www.ecfr.eu/article/commentary_digital_diplomacy_trade_and_human_rights_in_chinas_internet_revo.

55. Ibid.

56. Ibid.

57. Quoted in Xinhua News Agency, 2015, "China unveils Internet Plus action plan to fuel growth," English.gov.cn, July 4, http://english.gov.cn/policies/latest_releases/2015/07/04/content_281475140165588.htm.

58. Ibid.

59. Anouk van der Steen, 2015, "High tech diplomacy in an Internet Plus strategy for China," Rijksdienst voor Ondernemend Nederland [Netherlands Enterpise Agency], September 29, www.rvo.nl/sites/default/files/2015/09/HighTechDiplomacy%20China.pdf.

60. Jon R. Lindsay, 2015, "The Impact of China on Cybersecurity," *International Security* 39 (3): 9-11, www.mitpressjournals.org/doi/abs/10.1162/ISEC_a_00189#.VubZj8r7i_s. Reprinted by permission of MIT Press Journals, © 2015 by the President and Fellows of Harvard College and the Massachusetts Institute of Technology.

Eight: Internet Haves and Have-Nots

1. Spencer Ackerman, 2012, "Cash, and Time, Runs Out for Afghanistan's Wi-Fi City," *Wired*, May 14, www.wired.com/2012/05/jlink/.

2. Ibid.; Nathan Hodge, 2009, "Surge of Nerds Rebuilds Afghanistan," *Wired*, January 30, www.wired.com/2009/01/stability-opera/.

3. Ackerman, "Cash, and Time, Runs Out for Afghanistan's Wi-Fi City."

4. Cited in Ibid.

5. Cited in ibid.

6. Ibid.

7. Ibid.; Hodge, "Surge of Nerds Rebuilds Afghanistan."

8. Cited in Ackerman, "Cash, and Time, Runs Out for Afghanistan's Wi-Fi City."

9. World Bank, n.d., "Data — Indicators," http://data.worldbank.org/indicator.

10. Theodore Modis, 2005, "The End of the Internet Rush," *Technological Forecasting & Social Change* 72: 938–43, www.growth-dynamics.com/articles/Internet_Rush.pdf.

11. Robert Metcalfe, 2013, "Metcalfe's Law after 40 Years of Ethernet," *IEEE Computer* 46 (12): 26–31.

12. McKinsey & Company, 2014, "Offline and falling behind: Barriers to Internet adoption," September, www.mckinsey.com/industries/high-tech/our-insights/offline-and-falling-behind-barriers-to-internet-adoption.

13. W3Techs, 2015. "Usage of content languages for websites," http://w3techs.com/technologies/overview/content_language/all.

14. Godfred Frempong, 2012, "Understanding what is happening to ICT in Ghana: a supply- and demand-side analysis of the ICT sector." Evidence for ICT Policy Action Policy Paper No. 4. Cape Town, South Africa: Research ICT Africa, 35. http://researchictafrica.net/publications/Evidence_for_ICT_Policy_Action/Policy_Paper_4_-_Understanding_what_is_happening_in_ICT_in_Ghana.pdf.

15. McKinsey & Company, "Offline and falling behind."

16. Susannah Fox and Lee Rainie, 2014, "Part 1: How the internet has woven itself into American life," in *The Web at 25 in the United States*, Washington, DC: Pew Research Center, www.pewinternet.org/2014/02/27/part-1-how-the-internet-has-woven-itself-into-american-life/?beta=true&utm_expid=53098246-2.Lly4CFSVQG2lphsg-KopIg.1&utm_referrer=https%3A%2F%2Fwww.google.ca%2F.

17. Frempong, "Understanding what is happening to ICT in Ghana," 35.

18. Alexia Gonzalez-Fanfalone, Sam Paltridge and Rudolf van der Berg, 2014, "Time to terminate termination charges?" *OECD Insights* (blog), June 13, http://oecdinsights.org/2014/06/13/time-to-terminate-termination-charges/.

19. Internet in India, 2013, "Internet in India 2013," Mumbai, India: Internet and Mobile Association of India and IMRB International, 5, www.imrbint.com/downloads/Report-BB55685%20IAMAI%20ICUBE_2013-Urban+Rural-C1.pdf.

20. China Internet Network Information Center, 2014, "33rd Statistical Report on Internet Development in China," January 21, www1.cnnic.cn/IDR/ReportDownloads/201404/U020140417607531610855.pdf.

21. McKinsey & Company, 2013, "iConsumers: Life Online," January, 43, https://tmt.mckinsey.com/content/publications.

22. Iain Marlow, 2010, "High-speed Internet for rural areas pegged at $7-billion," *The Globe and Mail*, October 27, www.theglobeandmail.com/technology/high-speed-internet-for-rural-areas-pegged-at-7-billion/article4257289/.

23. Hernán Galperin, forthcoming 2016, *How to Connect the Other Half? Evidence and Policy Insight from Household Surveys in Latin America*, GCIG Paper Series No. 34, Waterloo, ON: CIGI, 15.

24. Ibid., 10.

25. McKinsey & Company, "Offline and falling behind," 46.

26. Ibid.

27. McKinsey & Company, "Offline and falling behind"; Galperin, *How to Connect the Other Half?*

28. McKinsey & Company, "Offline and falling behind."

29. M. Rabin and Joel L. Schrag, 1999, "First Impressions Matters: A Model of Confirmatory Bias," *The Quarterly Journal of Economics* 114 (1): 37–82.

30. G. Lindgaard, G. Fernandes, C. Dudek and J. Brown, 2006, "Attention Web Designers: You have 50 Milliseconds to Make a Good First Impression!" *Behaviour & Information Technology* 25 (2): 115–26.

31. N. Tractinsky, A. S. Katz and D. Ikar, 2000, "What is beautiful is usable," *Interacting with Computers* 13 (2): 127–45.

32. Mark Zuckerberg, 2013, "Is Connectivity a Human Right?" Facebook.

33. Denelle Dixon-Thayer, 2015, "Mozilla View on Zero-Rating," *Open Policy & Advocacy* (blog), May 5, https://blog.mozilla.org/netpolicy/2015/05/05/mozilla-view-on-zero-rating/.

34. Jon Russell, 2015, "Facebook Opens Internet.Org To All Developers In Response To Net Neutrality Concerns," TechCrunch, May 4, http://techcrunch.com/2015/05/04/facebooks-internet-org-project-is-now-a-platform/.

35. Cited in S. Ramani, 2015, "Zero Rating' will enhance Net access: Zuckerberg," *The Hindu*, October 29, www.thehindu.com/todays-paper/zero-rating-will-enhance-net-access-zuckerberg/article7815746.ece.

36. Russell, "Facebook Opens Internet.Org To All Developers...."

37. Jonathan Zittrain, 2008, *The Future of the Internet and How to Stop It*, New Haven, CT: Yale University Press.

38. A. Langley, N. Modadugu and W. Chang, 2010, "Overclocking SSL," *Imperial Violet*, June 25, www.imperialviolet.org/2010/06/25/overclocking-ssl.html.

39. Cited in J. Reynolds and J. Postel, 1987, "The Request for Comments Reference Guide," www.rfc-editor.org/rfc/rfc1000.txt.

40. Cited in Janet Abbate, 2000, *Inventing the Internet*, Cambridge, MA: MIT Press, 73.

41. Samantha Bradshaw and Laura DeNardis, n.d., "The Politicization of the Domain Name System," unpublished manuscript.

42. Paul Twomey, 2015, Presentation on the Plenary Panel 2: The Future of Multi-stakeholder Internet Governance, Conference on Internet Governance & Cyber-security, Columbia Academy, Columbia University, New York, May 14-15.

43. M. Faloutsos, P. Faloutsos and C. Faloutsos, 1999, "On Power-Law Relationships of the Internet Topology," *Research Showcase @CMU*, in Proceedings of the Conference on Applications, Technologies, Architectures, and Protocols for Computer Communication, SIGCOMM'99, 251–62, Harvard University Science Center, Cambridge, MA, September 3. http://repository.cmu.edu/cgi/viewcontent.cgi?article=1584&context=compsci; A.-L. Barabási, R. Albert, H. Jeong and G. Bianconi, 2000, "Power-Law Distribution of the World Wide Web," *Science* 287 (March): 2115a, http://citeseerx.ist.psu.edu/viewdoc/download?doi=10.1.1.409.2187&rep=rep1&type=pdf.

44. Matthew Champion, 2015, "People using Facebook don't realise they're on the internet," *The Independent*, http://i100.independent.co.uk/article/people-using-facebook-dont-realise-theyre-on-the-internet--xJA_uIE42e.

45. V. Woollaston, 2015, "Do YOU think 'Facebook is the internet'? Two thirds of users do — and millions don't know they're on the web when they log in," *Daily Mail*, February 11, www.dailymail.co.uk/sciencetech/article-2948923/Do-think-Facebook-internet-Two-thirds-users-millions-don-t-know-web-log-accounts.html.

46. M. Barthel, E. Shearer, J. Gottfried and A. Mitchell, 2015, "The Evolving Role of News on Twitter and Facebook," Pew Research Center, July 14, www.journalism.org/2015/07/14/the-evolving-role-of-news-on-twitter-and-facebook/.

47. Jonathan Zittrain, "Facebook Could Decide an Election Without Anyone Ever Finding Out," https://newrepublic.com/article/117878/information-fiduciary-solution-facebook-digital-gerrymandering. From *The New Republic*, June 1, © 2014 *The New Republic*. All rights reserved. Used by permission and protected by the Copyright Laws of the United States. The printing, copying, redistribution or retransmission of this Content without express written permission is prohibited.

48. Adam D. I. Kramer, Jamie E. Guillory and Jeffrey T. Hancock, 2014, "Experimental Evidence of Massive-Scale Emotional Contagion Through Social Networks," *PNAS* 111 (24), www.pnas.org/content/111/24/8788.full.

49. Cited in Vindu Goel, 2014, "Facebook Tinkers with Users' Emotions in News Feed Experiment, Stirring Outcry," *The New York Times*, www.nytimes.com/2014/06/30/technology/facebook-tinkers-with-users-emotions-in-news-feed-experiment-stirring-outcry.html?_r=0.

50. Recounted in E. Nour, 2015, "Meet the Egyptian Repairman who outranked Google and became an internet sensation!" [italics added], Medium.com, May 28, https://medium.com/@eyadnour/meet-the-egyptian-technician-who-is-currently-ranked-at-1-for-google-and-he-doesn-t-even-know-6cf1040efeab#.yw6anewt4.

51. Frank Pasquale, 2015, *The Black Box Society: The Secret Algorithms That Control Money and Information*, Cambridge, MA: Harvard University Press.

52. Cited in ibid., 67.

53. J. Powles, 2014, "What we can salvage from 'right to be forgotten' ruling," *Wired*, May 15, www.wired.co.uk/news/archive/2014-05/15/google-vs-spain.

54. M. Wright, 2013, "Google shows China the white flag of surrender," *The Telegraph*, January 7, http://blogs.telegraph.co.uk/technology/micwright/100008624/google-shows-china-the-white-flag-of-surrender/.

55. *Consumer Reports*, 2015, "A Million Eyes," *Consumer Reports* 80 (5): 24–30.

56. Ibid., 26.

57. Charlie Osbourne, 2016, "Shodan: The IoT search engine for watching sleeping kids and bedroom antics," ZDNet, www.zdnet.com/article/shodan-the-iot-search-engine-which-shows-us-sleeping-kids-and-how-we-throw-away-our-privacy/?tag=nl.e539&s_cid=e539&ttag=e539&ftag=TRE17cfd61.

58. Josh Dehaas, 2015, "'Eerie' music, man's voice creeps into nursery after baby monitor hacked," CTV News, July 23, www.ctvnews.ca/canada/eerie-music-man-s-voice-creeps-into-nursery-after-baby-monitor-hacked-1.2483170.

59. Recollection of Eric Jardine from the panel on Stabilizing Internet Infrastructure.

60. *Consumer Reports*, "A Million Eyes," 24.

61. David Dean, Sebastian DiGrande, Dominic Field, Andreas Lundmark, James O'Day, John Pineda and Paul Zwillenberg, 2012, "The Internet Economy in the G-20: The $4.2 Trillion Growth Opportunity," The Connected World Series, March, Boston, MA: Boston Consulting Group, www.bcg.com/documents/file100409.pdf.

62. Carl Bildt, 2015, "One Net, One Future," Project Syndicate, October 26, www.project-syndicate.org/commentary/cyberattacks-digital-security-by-carl-bildt-2015-10.

63. James Manyika, Michael Chui, Patrick Bisson, Jonathan Woetzel, Richard Dobbs, Jacques Bughin and Dan Aharon, 2015, *The Internet of Things: Mapping the Value Beyond the Hype*, McKinsey & Company, June, www.mckinsey.com/business-functions/business-technology/our-insights/the-internet-of-things-the-value-of-digitizing-the-physical-world.

Nine: A Web of Trust: Toward a Safe, Secure, Reliable and Open Internet

1. Carl Sagan, 1995, *The Demon-Haunted World: Science as a Candle in the Dark*, New York, NY: Random House.
2. Thomas L. Friedman, 2005, "It's a Flat World, After All," *The New York Times Magazine*, April 3, www.nytimes.com/2005/04/03/magazine/its-a-flat-world-after-all.html?_r=0.
3. Robert Lemos, 2014, "The Year of Encryption," *MIT Technology Review*, March 18, www.technologyreview.com/news/525551/the-year-of-encryption/.
4. Ibid.
5. Ibid.
6. Josh Constine, 2016, "ISIS Has Its Own Encrypted Chat App," TechCrunch, January 16. http://techcrunch.com/2016/01/16/isis-app/.
7. Ken Westin, 2015, "Encryption Wouldn't Have Stopped Anthem's Data Breach," *MIT Technology Review*, February 10, www.technologyreview.com/view/535111/encryption-wouldnt-have-stopped-anthems-data-breach/.
8. Tom Simonite, 2015, "White House and Department of Homeland Security Want a Way Around Encryption," *MIT Technology Review*, April 22, www.technologyreview.com/news/536951/white-house-and-department-of-homeland-security-want-a-way-around-encryption/.
9. Pierre Thomas, 2015, "Feds Challenged by Encrypted Devices of San Bernardino Attackers," ABC News, December 9, http://abcnews.go.com/US/feds-challenged-encrypted-devices-san-bernardino-attackers/story?id=35680875.
10. David E. Sanger and Nicole Perlroth, 2015, "Encrypted Messaging Apps Face New Scrutiny Over Possible Role in Paris Attacks," *The New York Times*, November 16, www.nytimes.com/2015/11/17/world/europe/encrypted-messaging-apps-face-new-scrutiny-over-possible-role-in-paris-attacks.html?_r=0.

11. Quoted in Brian Krebs, 2015, "Paris Attacks Stoke Encryption Debate," *Krebs on Security* (blog), November 15, http://krebsonsecurity.com/2015/11/paris-terror-attacks-stoke-encryption-debate/.

12. Cited in Paul Ducklin, 2016, "Cryptographic backdoors? France says, 'Non!'" Naked Security, January 18, https://nakedsecurity.sophos.com/2016/01/18/cryptographic-backdoors-france-says-non/.

13. Cited in John Zorabedian, 2016, "Netherlands opposes backdoors, but encryption still under assault," Naked Security, January 6, https://nakedsecurity.sophos.com/2016/01/06/netherlands-opposes-backdoors-but-encryption-still-under-assault/.

14. Simonite, "White House and Department of Homeland Security Want a Way Around Encryption."

15. Tom Simonite, 2015, "The Seemingly Unfixable Crack in the Internet's Backbone," *MIT Technology Review*, August 6, www.technologyreview.com/s/540056/the-seemingly-unfixable-crack-in-the-internets-backbone/.

16. Samantha Bradshaw, n.d., "Rethinking Trust in Internet Governance," unpublished manuscript.

17. Asia Pacific Network Information Centre, 2016, "Use of DNSSEC Validation for World (XA)," http://stats.labs.apnic.net/dnssec/XA?c=XA&x=1&g=1&r=1&w=7&g=0.

18. UK Government Office for Science, 2016, *Distributed Ledger Technology: Beyond Blockchain*, January 19, www.gov.uk/government/publications/distributed-ledger-technology-blackett-review.

19. Nicole Bullock and Renee Schultes, 2016, "Australia Bourse in Blockchain Move," *Financial Times*, January 23-24, A11.

20. Lorenzo-Franceschi Bicchierai, 2015, "It's Nearly 2016. Why Aren't Banking Apps More Secure?" *Motherboard*, November 18, http://motherboard.vice.com/read/its-nearly-2016-why-arent-banking-apps-more-secure.

21. Joseph Cox, 2015, "Over a Quarter of the Encrypted Web Is About to Be Broken," *Motherboard*, December 22, http://motherboard.vice.com/read/over-a-quarter-of-the-encrypted-web-is-about-to-be-broken.

22. FINRA, 2015, "Report on Cybersecurity Practices," A Report From the Financial Industry Regulatory Authority, 37, www.finra.org/sites/default/files/p602363%20Report%20on%20Cybersecurity%20Practices_0.pdf.

23. Benjamin Dean, 2015, "Why companies have little incentive to invest in cybersecurity," *The Conversation*, March 4, http://theconversation.com/why-companies-have-little-incentive-to-invest-in-cybersecurity-37570.

24. Windows, 2015, "Security in Windows 10," https://blogs.windows.com/windowsexperience/2015/07/24/security-in-windows-10/.

25. Gordon Gottsegen, 2015, "The Windows 10 Security Settings You Need to Know," *Wired*, August 5, www.wired.com/2015/08/windows-10-security-settings-need-know/.

26. Vint Cerf, 2012, "The Internet's Future Depends on Maintaining Its Free Spirit," *MIT Technology Review*, December 4, www.technologyreview.com/s/508201/the-internets-future-depends-on-maintaining-its-free-spirit/.

27. Ibid.

28. Ibid.

29. Michael Chertoff and Paul Rosenzweig, 2015, *A Primer on Globally Harmonizing Internet Jurisdiction and Regulations*, GCIG Paper Series No. 10, Waterloo, ON: CIGI, https://ourinternet-files.s3.amazonaws.com/publications/gcig_paper_no10_0.pdf.

30. GCIG, 2015, *Toward a Social Compact for Digital Privacy and Security: Statement by the Global Commission on Internet Governance*, Special Report, April 15, Waterloo, ON: CIGI, 7. www.cigionline.org/publications/toward-social-compact-digital-privacy-and-security.

31. Ibid.

32. UN, 2011, "Report of the Special Representative of the Secretary-General on the issue of human rights and transnational corporations and other business enterprises, John Ruggie." 2011. Human Rights Council, Seventeenth session, Agenda item 3. A/HRC/17/31. "Promotion and protection of all human rights, civil, political, economic, social and cultural rights, including the right to development." March 21. http://business-humanrights.org/sites/default/files/media/documents/ruggie/ruggie-guiding-principles-21-mar-2011.pdf

33. GCIG, *Toward a Social Compact for Digital Privacy and Security*.

34. Ibid., 9.

35. bid., 2.

36. Michael Chertoff and Paul Rosenzweig, 2015, *A Primer on Globally Harmonizing Internet Jurisdiction and Regulations*, GCIG Paper Series No. 10, Waterloo, ON: CIGI, 2. https://ourinternet-files.s3.amazonaws.com/publications/gcig_paper_no10_0.pdf.

37.   Bertrand de La Chapelle and Paul Fehlinger, 2016, *Jurisdiction on the Internet: From Legal Arms Race to Transnational Cooperation*, GCIG Paper No. 28, Waterloo, ON: CIGI.

38.   NETmundial, 2014, "NETmundial Multistakeholder Statement," Global Multistakeholder Meeting on the Future of Internet Governance, São Paolo, Brazil, April 23-24, http://netmundial.br/ netmundial-multistakeholder-statement/.

39.   Joseph S. Nye Jr., 2015, *The Regime Complex for Managing Global Cyber Activities*, GCIG Paper No. 1, Waterloo, ON: CIGI.

40.   Ibid., 5.

41.   Nick Ashton-Hart, 2015, *Solving the International Internet Policy Coordination Problem*, GCIG Paper Series No. 12, Waterloo, ON: CIGI.

42.   Joseph Schumpeter, (1942) 1994, *Capitalism, Socialism and Democracy*, London, UK: Routledge.

Appendix

The CIGI-Ipsos Surveys

The two cross-national surveys that were undertaken as a part of the background research presented in this book were commissioned by CIGI and administered by the polling firm Ipsos. For each survey, Ipsos provided a detailed note on the sample size, countries sampled and the sampling error. The notes for both the 2014 and the 2016 CIGI-Ipsos surveys are presented below to provide the inquisitive reader with some insights as to how the results were found. More on the surveys can be found at www.cigionline.org/internet-survey.

2014 CIGI-Ipsos Survey

The 2014 survey was conducted by Ipsos on behalf of the Centre for International Governance Innovation ("CIGI") between October 7, 2014, and November 12, 2014. The survey was conducted in 24 countries/territories — Australia, Brazil, Canada, China, Egypt, France, Germany, Great Britain, Hong Kong, India, Indonesia, Italy, Japan, Kenya, Mexico, Nigeria, Pakistan, Poland, South Africa, South Korea, Sweden, Tunisia, Turkey and the United States — and involved 23,376 Internet users. Twenty of the countries utilized the Ipsos Internet panel system while the other four (Kenya, Nigeria, Pakistan and Tunisia) were conducted by Ipsos Computer-aided Telephone

Interviewing (CATI) facilities in each of those countries. In the United States and Canada, respondents were aged 18-64, and 16-64 in all other countries. Approximately 1,000+ individuals were surveyed in each country and are weighted to match the online population in each country surveyed. The precision of Ipsos online polls are calculated using a credibility interval. In this case, a poll of 1,000 is accurate to +/–3.5 percentage points. For those surveys conducted by CATI, the accuracy is a margin of error of +/–3.1.

2016 CIGI-Ipsos Survey

The 2016 survey was fielded by Ipsos on behalf of the Centre for International Governance Innovation ("CIGI") between November 20, 2015, and January 7, 2016. The survey was conducted in 24 countries and territories — Australia, Brazil, Canada, China, Egypt, France, Germany, Great Britain, Hong Kong, India, Indonesia, Italy, Japan, Kenya, Mexico, Nigeria, Pakistan, Poland, South Africa, South Korea, Sweden, Tunisia, Turkey and the United States — and involved 24,143 Internet users. Twenty of the countries utilized the Ipsos Internet panel system while the other four (Kenya, Nigeria, Pakistan and Tunisia) were conducted by Ipsos Computer-aided Telephone Interviewing (CATI) facilities in each of those countries. In the United States and Canada respondents were aged 18–64, and 16–64 in all other countries. Approximately 1,000+ individuals were surveyed in each country and are weighted to match the online population in each country surveyed. The precision of Ipsos online polls is calculated using a credibility interval. In this case, a poll of 1,000 is accurate to +/–3.5 percentage points. For those surveys conducted by CATI, the margin of error accuracy is +/–3.1. All sample surveys and polls may be subject to other sources of error, including, but not limited to coverage error, and measurement error.

Index

About the Authors

Fen Osler Hampson is a distinguished fellow and the director of the Global Security & Politics Program at CIGI. He is also co-director of the Global Commission on Internet Governance, a joint project with CIGI and Chatham House. He is chancellor's professor at Carleton University and a former Jennings Randolph Fellow at the United States Institute of Peace.

Follow Fen on Twitter: @fenhampson

Eric Jardine is assistant professor of political science at Virginia Polytechnic Institute and State University, in Blacksburg, Virginia. From 2014 to 2016, he was a research fellow in the Global Security & Politics Program at the Centre for International Governance Innovation, Waterloo, Ontario, where he worked on cyber security and Internet governance issues. He holds a Ph.D. in international affairs from The Norman Paterson School of International Affairs at Carleton University.

Follow Eric on Twitter: @ehljardine